Intimacy in postmodern times

MANCHESTER
1824

Manchester University Press

Intimacy in postmodern times

A friendship with Zygmunt Bauman

Peter Beilharz

Manchester University Press

Published by Manchester University Press
Altrincham Street, Manchester M1 7JA
www.manchesteruniversitypress.co.uk

British Library Cataloguing-in-Publication Data
A catalogue record for this book is available from the British Library

ISBN 978 1 5261 3215 4 hardback

First published 2020

The publisher has no responsibility for the persistence or accuracy of URLs for any external or third-party internet websites referred to in this book, and does not guarantee that any content on such websites is, or will remain, accurate or appropriate.

Typeset by Newgen Publishing UK
Printed in Great Britain
by TJ International Ltd, Padstow, Cornwall

For Keith Tester, 1960–2019, Hedl Beilharz, 1924–2019, Janina Bauman, 1926–2009, Zygmunt Bauman, 1925–2017

Contents

Illustrations

Preface

How did this happen, a book on Bauman and me? There was a need for separation, after he died, more than in the fact of it. I needed to get all this out of my head. Writing it out seemed like the obvious resolution. So how did it happen? This book was drafted, thought and worked up at home in Melbourne and at Curtin University in Western Australia, where I worked as Professor of Culture and Society from 2015 to 2017. Curtin research professors get to choose their self-appellation. Mine was a nod to Raymond Williams' *Culture and Society*, but it was also *sotto voce* a reference to a book by the same title by Zygmunt Bauman, published in 1966 in Warsaw and never to be translated into English. Bauman was my shadow, and I his, always at this distance of time and place, and yet with some intensity of the intimacy of postmodern times.

Curtin was a brilliant place to work, at the end of my career in the Australian university system. Curtin had what the critical theorist Gernot Boehme calls 'atmosphere'. For me, it was a great place to be, and to think. Steve Mickler had introduced me to my new colleagues as a kind of professor at large, whose role might be to help connect up dots and people, to conduct intensives and events on such topics as presented themselves, to add critical theory supplement. Among the first events I organized were sessions on the work of Zygmunt Bauman. Then there was a penultimate seminar, after Bauman had died, and the final encounter, sharing the draft of this book in this perfect setting, where the premium was put on writing and writing creative nonfiction. Tim Dolin, a major intellectual force at

Curtin, pushed me, asking: 'What *is* this book?' It was a good question. This book is a memoir, rather than the creative nonfiction that is so rich at Curtin, but being able to worry the boundaries in this setting was energizing for me. I had spent most of my life hitherto writing as a sociologist, though in a culture at La Trobe University in Melbourne that was among the most open in the world. We practised sociology in the general, rather than the professional, narrow or special sense. There was much less discussion at La Trobe as to what properly constituted sociology, and much more about what was interesting, important, challenging or exciting. There was much interest in tradition, modernity and creation, but also in just getting on with the challenges of seeking to make sense of our worlds, our everyday lives and those of our students. There was little boundary work, and no serious police activity that I recall. This was a special place.

As I explain below, the death of Zygmunt Bauman hit me and others hard. This was an almost unbearable loss, except that, as with Sam Beckett, we knew we would still go on. We had been friends for a long time, Bauman and me, to the extent that he had a kind of perennial presence in my life – always there, even in silence. He still is. For, contrary to the image of the man of many books and even more words, he was also one who enjoyed silence. Puff, puff, puff.

But I needed to write my way out of this fug, after he died. Progress – even movement – was slow, in the thinking, and then in the writing, which eventually took a year longer than expected. This all took such time as my purposes were varied, confused, therapeutic as well as given to explanation and self-clarification or the settling of accounts. Two people in particular helped me to sort this: Caroline Wintersgill, my editor at Manchester University Press, who had edited *Labour's Utopias* for me in 1991; and Sian Supski, my wife and intellectual collaborator. Working with Manchester was the perfect loop; Bauman had published his first book in English with the Press in 1972. The difficulties of writing were nevertheless considerable, after thousands of words spilling out in the first few days. Thinking about love and death, friendship and loss, was exhausting. It was made possible by friendship, then and now.

Preface

This is a memoir, a story of love, death and friendship – mainly friendship. Friendship is the main dynamic I want to work with; yet 'work' is also an operative word here, as this kind of friendship has to do with work, with intellectual pursuit, or the life of the mind. Friendship, for intellectuals, is, I suppose, inseparable from our work, from the problems we seek to make sense of, from the tasks that we set ourselves. Yet there are many individuals we work with who we would never dream of as friends, either because there are simply limits to be set, or else outright hostilities and jealousies that are also deeply embedded in the life of the mind – or, at least, its institutions, which until recently we of the postwar generation have thought of as special: the universities. Friendship, in these settings, often goes sideways, is expressed laterally to and with our peers or immediate colleagues, those we train with, those with whom we share the coming-of-age ritual that we associate with the writing of the dissertation. And then, we step out into wider worlds, when we make friends with those who are already ready, on the way to becoming more whole than we may be.

Sometimes we may also form friendships with our superiors, those who teach us. Again, not all our mentors become our friends, and there are likely always residuals of the formative relations of supervision in the later possible relations of equal standing. Mentoring, or the transmission and development of intellectual culture, works through and can generate friendship, even though the university environment these days may be less than fully conducive to this kind of process. After Michel Foucault, or with Max Weber, we might say that all intellectual relations are also relations of power. But there are in addition situations in which the partners to a friendship choose to suspend these relations of asymmetrical reciprocity. Friendships include these, relations in which the shared recognition of unequal or different understanding is put aside for choice: we choose each other, as friends, even though there is no single moment of consent or contract. Like lovers, friends do not need to be identical. Like love, friendship happens, remains ineffable. And yet, we might say, it is everything, or almost everything. Perhaps the point is that it makes so much even possible, thinkable.

Cooperation is not the same as friendship, but the latter takes place only where the former first may flourish. This is possible only where the partners are able to share, rather than seek to possess to the exclusion of all others, especially those immediately around us. There is a fundamental tension here, as intellectuals, and especially contemporary academics, are compelled to follow the rules of the self-maximizing individual. Cooperation, the mutual sharing of ideas, is the necessary precondition of civilization in general and intellectual culture in particular.

All serious intellectual endeavour in the human sciences and liberal arts works through these personal lifelines of shared culture. We nevertheless also inhabit a fantasy culture that awaits the arrival of the romantic genius, the 'Big Brain'. We are told to wait for the 'Next Big Thing', and there is a procession of gurus we are duly recommended to follow. Yet, if we watch how we actually work, it is plain that we most often develop through high levels of co-dependency and cooperation rather than solitary creation *ex nihilo*. The most gifted of thinkers in social theory are the sum of their parts, the combination of elements of previous wisdom reconfigured in some new and original way. Marx, in this way of thinking, is the result, as well as a beginning, of intellectual innovation. He, and we, are the sum of our parts. Almost everything we can find in Marx's work precedes or else runs alongside his work. Great thinkers emerge from their culture, their sum total of experience, influences, intuitions, texts and contexts, and their innovations return into those cultures with the passing of time and the lives of individual thinkers. Ditto with Bauman, more than any recent social thinker the sum of a smorgasbord of parts.

Social theory is a pre-eminently social activity, yet we still often behave as though it belongs to individual entrepreneurs. The image jars, for, after all, decent entrepreneurs are also those who are good at putting people, ideas and resources together. Innovation remains enigmatic. It results from the engagement and friction between existing ideas, practices and colleagues, in processes in which the new emerges. Then something magical happens, as in Jimi Hendrix in *The Wind Cries Mary*, or

Karl Marx in *Das Kapital*. Innovation is also global, or cosmopolitan or imperial. Conventionally, in the West, it is thought to have European origins, though it should now be clear that 'European' also necessarily means 'imperial' and 'colonial', and that, whatever Europe is, it is also a result. Creation issues from cultural traffic.

This book is a memoir, a thinkpiece. It is also an assemblage, the result of its own parts. After his death, I came to realize that I needed to make peace with Bauman, and to close my relationship with him and his work, inasmuch as this might be possible. I realized that I had two key historical sources in my newly archived personal papers. There were itineraries of my travels to the United States and United Kingdom over 30 active years; and there was a lifetime's correspondence with Bauman and others. There were a few windows of insight in particular small texts that I wrote for him and that he wrote for me, which are interleaved into the pages that follow as further possible moments of insight into our friendship and our work in sociology. These sources do not always fit neatly together, nor do they deliver a clean teleological narrative from our first encounter to his final exit. But they provided me with what Bauman routinely called 'stimulants': materials to think with, and consequently to help me move on from this disabling moment of prolonged mourning for my friend and teacher. I needed, of course, to celebrate and move on, as well as to mourn.

This book has three parts. The first, 'Itineraries and archives', retraces the path of my life in travel, work and friendship with Bauman and others as it unfolded across the three decades that I knew him. The second, 'Ways of going on', engages with my own work and Bauman's, looking to connect up the direct and indirect influences and coordinates in our respective projects as they developed across these decades. The third, 'Talking the days', follows up with investigations into work as friendship and friendship as work, and surveys the last ten years of Bauman's own writings, which may have come in the under radar for other readers as well as for me, as the sheer volume of his work continued to explode in his later years. By this later moment, making sense of the 'Bauman phenomenon' had become complicated by celebrity and by the hostility that can accompany this in intellectual life, where there is never somehow quite enough kudos to go around. Bauman became a target as well as a celebrity. For me, it was simpler. He was a source of inspiration, and a friend. He played the role of the messenger. At an abstract level, his was often the bad news. On the personal level, there was invariably affirmation and a deep commitment to the tasks of carrying on in the face of this adversity. There was love, and there was work to be done.

Beginning

I was born in 1953 in Melbourne, almost 30 years after Zygmunt Bauman was born in Poznan. He was to become one of the most influential sociologists of our times. I was to become his interpreter, among others. We were to be friends for almost 30 years, until his death in 2017. What was it that brought us together? That is a long story, or a shortish book. This is the book that you are holding.

Why this book? Why another book? Bauman wrote a very great deal. I have also written some across those years. This is the first time I have written a book like this. It is written out of a need for self-clarification, and a need for some distance on that which we shared without ever having had to explain it at all. Friendship may be one of the most important parts of our lives, but in the classical terms of sociology it is a 'taken for granted'. Either that, or else sociologists give scrutiny to friendship between others, but not between themselves. The intellectual culture we inhabit is collective, collegial and cooperative, yet we still behave like possessive individualists, as though some own or hold the exclusive patents to ideas. Most of what we know comes from somewhere else.

Bauman liked to refer to the image of the hammer: we do not know or care what it is, it does not concern us until it breaks. And so, too, it is with friendship. Most often, we do not know what it is till it is gone. How, then, might this content be accessed, or recovered? Obviously there is therapy, and memory. There are different materials, or data, archives, objects, texts, stories, jokes, anecdotes. But there needs also, at least on an occasion such as this, to be a process. In the model of psychoanalysis the medium is talking. I engaged with therapy, but there had to be more, some kind of firmer expression, an *Ausdruck* or objectification of all this stuff of life.

Writing is a process of learning. Learning can also be a process of writing. Writing is central, for me, to seeking to understand. Writing this memoir has been an experience without precedent in my career or in my life. It was a need, but of a different kind from the usual. I was in the transition to retirement, which for me, unlike Bauman, also meant stepping back. I was no longer a working professional. I no longer had to maintain a presence in a university scene that now made increasingly little sense to me, and in which I was effectively invisible, past tense, a dinosaur. It became a kind of possession of a different kind, this need to write out Bauman in this book, which had to be fulfilled in order to move on. It invaded my dream life in a quite novel way, where I would write whole and clear sentences in my sleep, not just have the usual half-baked ideas that might be forgotten, engaging subconsciously with Bauman, but actually crafting whole and relatively elegant sentences in my sleep. This had to end. I had to be done. I needed to write this out. I needed to say goodbye.

But how? The idea of narrating our relationship was easy come by. Working out how to do it was rather more difficult, especially when it came to writing about myself. This is not proper or common sociological conduct, this writing of the self, even if sociologists are not all bad at life writing, or at acknowledging the centrality of the self or the subject in abstract register. The status of the subject in sociology is ambiguous. The claims of social scientificity and objectivity still shadow us. These days, of course, there is also a surplus of the self, as in the ubiquitous selfie. Christopher Lasch was well ahead of his time; we were indeed entering the culture of narcissism into the 1970s, and are now awash in it.[1] Generationally, Bauman was from another place than this. He did not want to talk about himself at all. Probably I tried for a decade to get him

---

1 See C. Lasch, *The Culture of Narcissism: American Life in an Age of Diminishing Expectations* (New York: Norton, 1979).

to talk about himself before drawing the obvious conclusions, and just giving up, playing along.

Writing was one thing. What was it about writing, or working in sociology as a field? Why the need to work in sociology? Why should you, dear reader, read a book about sociology and sociologists, in this case Bauman and me? Sociology as an academic discipline has fully become part of the furniture of the university, arguably, only in the United States, where its institutionalization and legitimization process began with various precedents in 1895 at the University of Chicago as well as in the southern states, where sociology became both applied and critical, both reforming and more discernibly philosophical or Continental in inflection. Anglo sociology came later, formally speaking, as an academic discipline, even though its broad ambitions were apparent early, even before the London School of Economics (LSE). Sociology is often still regarded as a latecomer, in contrast to the liberal arts, with their classical claims and lineages. Philosophers and historians have sometimes regarded it with contempt, dirty-handed, upstart; *redbrick*. These prejudices are likely less apparent in Australia than in England, but they nevertheless make their presence felt here, or there, as well.

Bauman and I shared a deep ambivalence towards the practice or the profession of sociology, though we have both also in our own ways acted as its public advocates. As with socialism, we each refused to let go of the idea, but remained dismayed at what was done in its name. In principle, it was what Bauman would have called a 'promise', or perhaps a 'project'. Everything fell into its purview, all of everyday life, its pleasures and sufferings, its hopes and its nightmares. And yet, by the postwar period, and then afterwards, sociology often seemed obsessed with borders and boundaries, with measurement and numbers, and with a kind of professionalism whose nature and limits sociology had earlier set out to debunk. As Bauman would come to put it, sociologists would aspire to the status of legislators, rather than interpreters. They would hitch their hopes to the prospects of social regulation and reform, and remain oblivious to their own interests in these processes. This is what my early colleague Rob Watts would call 'social ventriloquism', the will to speak too easily on behalf of others, regardless. Bauman early on called for the promise of critical sociology, which would take a step back from this way of thinking, or at least seek to place it as one intellectual concern among others. Remedial, or professional, sociology, in this register, would often carry its own interests unannounced, as in the experience of Fabianism or the Chicago School – *Weltverbesserer*, do-gooders claiming unproblematically to represent those who were unable to represent themselves. Sociology in his alternative way of thinking was, as Ágnes Heller put it, aligned to those three great questions of Paul Gauguin: 'Who are we?' 'Where have we come from?' 'Where are we going?' (No. 4: 'Who is this "we"?' Etc.) This was, as he famously was given to repeat, a discipline based on the disposition to ask questions rather than to seek too quickly to answer them; and the idea of answers, here, was best understood to be a mass prerogative, rather than belonging exclusively to those who claimed to know.

These matters would remain to dog Bauman's later career, when he would be accused of just making it up, as though sociology were no more scientific than literature, conversation or letters. He came, indeed, to want to argue that literature was a necessary companion to sociology understood in this more conventional sense. Sociologists across the globe came to develop an ambivalent relationship towards Bauman. They were delighted that his status helped to legitimize sociology publicly, and horrified that he could behave in such a loose manner, by the criteria of social science – choosing, for example, to value the writing of Jorge Luis Borges over metrics. They could be easily rattled, it seemed, by conduct that included irony. They might want to see evidence, or facts. There might be security checks. They might be less interested in questions than in the numbers. 'Where is your database, sir?'

Mainstream sociology values transparency, and the Anglo or analytic model of clarity. *A* is not *B*; say what you mean, and mean what you say. Bauman, in contrast, came to speak out of this setting, given as he was to crossing over sociology and philosophy, to asking how we should live and not only how we live today. He was not Anglo, but continental, as he was suspicious of clarity when it did violence to contradiction. I am

4

not sure if he ever put this sensibility so plainly, but it might read something like this. If, as a writer you want to communicate to an audience, speak against suffering and for the hope that more of us on the planet might flourish, then perhaps literature is a better carrier of your views than social science, or, at least, as worthy. Social science, in this way of thinking, might remain closer to statistics and to its root term and institution: the state. Literature might reach further out into civil society, into the lives of those who also want to change the world. This might be one reason why *The Communist Manifesto* is a more powerful, or influential, document than *Das Kapital*. It might be one reason why we think of Kafka as readily as Marx, or why Huxley and Orwell are permanent markers of the concerns of modern life. It might help to explain why the fiction writing of J. M. Coetzee or Ivan Vladislavić or Marlene van Niekerk tells us at least as much about South Africa as its social science does. It might begin to explain how one of the most powerful books on the condition of Indigenous peoples in Australia is a family memoir, in Steve Kinnane's *Shadow Lines*, or why *Exit West* from Mohsin Hamid might speak more directly to the global refugee problem than another solid, statistical NGO report. For Hamid, for example, as for Georg Simmel and Bauman, and to follow one image, there are doors – not all of them open to all of us, some, rather, leading from one disaster to the next. This is an open line of suggestion: we can each volunteer our own exemplars of such writing and its effects. Plainly, for Bauman, literature offered at the very least a stimulant, a supplement, a suggestion of other ways to think, and write and provoke. Oranges were not the only fruit.

Sociology, in this way of thinking, might cross over with literature, history and the other fields of intellectual endeavour. It might also be a house with many doors. Writing might be open to consideration as a wider field of expression, communication and persuasion. Sociology might be given to contradiction and, often, to irony, for to contradict forces us to think again, and irony opens the possibility that most of us in fact routinely say something and mean something else; and this is what makes us interesting. Language is not transparent, and neither are we. Irrationality is at least as fundamental to our lives as is the hope of rationality. Interpretation remains a major challenge. Thinking is slippery. *A* can also be *B*. So, for example, the same single individual could be both a victim and a perpetrator. Watch it!

Such was Bauman's challenge. It spoke to me. It was, I suppose, a continental way of advocating the project of sociology. It was consistent with what I knew of Western Marxism and critical theory. It helped to open new doors for me, to east and central European Marxism, and what followed.

This memoir is a story of one relationship with Bauman. Many others had significant encounters with Bauman. He was a generous man, who responded equally to requests from afar and emails from Leeds undergraduates who could hop on the bus with an interest. Bauman was always interested in the Antipodes, though I am not sure that this was why he was interested in me. I came a little later to Bauman, though this was also Bauman before Bauman, well before the liquid modern, which we can date from around 2000. My intellectual formation had taken off 30 years earlier, in year 12, with that special teacher, then in teachers' college, then, most dramatically, with some of the finest minds I would encounter, this time at Monash University, where I was taught by Alastair Davidson, Zawar Hanfi and Harry Redner and many others. The culture that they could manoeuvre was what George Markus called 'an immense storehouse of possibilities'. Johann Arnason, then Ágnes Heller, arrived at La Trobe in the mid- to late 1970s. La Trobe was a powerhouse of its own. The fact that I came to work there was beyond belief, another step in a trail of good fortune.

Melbourne was buzzing when it came to critical theory. These were folk who seemed to know everything, or, at least, who were curious about everything, and would pass you on. For a number of reasons, then, it never really occurred to me seriously to study overseas. There was some enthusiasm in our circle for the work of Ernesto Laclau and the idea of studying at Essex. I had already met Laclau, via Davidson in Paris in 1979, and was in correspondence with him. I had a strong sense of what I still had to learn from Davidson, so I stayed put. Davidson was, after all, the 'Gramsci man', and taught us structuralism and much else besides.

Oxbridge had little intellectual appeal to me, as a Marxist interested in both theory and history, and an Australian of humble origins to boot. Too many negative signifiers. My tangential contacts with Oxbridge culture suggested that folk such as me could be construed only as both ignorant and, worse, unteachable; made of the wrong stuff. My origins and horizons were modest; but here, in Melbourne, I also had this cornucopia of critical theory. You could take it in, and you could add your bit. It was a little like the music scene: we had great players, who you could see and hear, but also you could talk to them, hang out – and we did. They also became our friends. There was cultural traffic, but there was also proximity, and atmosphere, energy and intensity. The life of universities, then, was energizing.

There were other sources and influences for me, many of whom could be contacted by mail. The writing of letters was somehow democratic. Our addressees, leading thinkers such as Cornelius Castoriadis, knew that we wrote to them because they inspired us. They also wrote back, and were happy to meet up if you should be passing by. I began to travel regularly, into the 1980s and 1990s, to Paris, to London, to Amsterdam, later to Leeds, to the United States and to many other lands. In retrospect, it has been put to me that this was a kind of networking. This was not part of our thinking at the time. 'Network' was not yet a keyword, and keywords were not terms you entered into a search engine but vital components in a vocabulary. *This is not a network*. Via the journal *Thesis Eleven*, which we founded in Melbourne in 1980, in memory of a friend who had died young, we set out both to export our own views and to import those of others, though, again, these terms make sense only after the fact. What were we thinking? Our sources were critical theory and Western Marxism, the philosophical trends tempered by a strong sense of place in the Antipodes and of the British Empire. Already we understood intuitively that culture, whether Marxism or rock music, worked through traffic. These cultures moved internationally, and needed to be placed historically. The slogan of 'Transnationalism' came late: in the beginning there was always the world system, already. To be Antipodean was to be born imperial. Is there nothing outside empire?

These were personal choices, to connect, to seek out others smarter than us locally and globally. They were not engaged in for self-promotion. We were told often enough that projects such as *Thesis Eleven* were a waste of time, a folly, a liability, and that Marxism was an embarrassment. Perhaps folly is not such a bad idea, in small doses. Universities, back then, contained careerists enough, but there were also many more hangers-on and enthusiasts, oddballs who knew stuff and were happy to share. Starting a journal made as much sense as writing letters across the seas. Why not?

The reliance on correspondence was a well-established historical practice, now lost in the world of tweets. Who writes letters anymore? Sea changes were under way; everything that was solid looked now to be melting. There were other significant changes across this period, into the 1980s. In Australia, as elsewhere, the universities were transformed into managerial and commercial machines. Perhaps the biggest generational shift for Australian intellectuals involved the passing of the age of expatriate culture, exemplified by Robert Hughes, Barry Humphries, Germaine Greer and Clive James, among many others.[2] They left, to stay. The social acceleration of modernity was well under way in the 1980s. Its carrier, now, was the jumbo jet, the Boeing 747. Cheap mass air transit meant that, with a bit of luck, you could travel to Europe or the United States over the summer break, even in the winter break if you were teaching. You could write a letter to someone such as Zygmunt Bauman and show up on his overgrown doorstep soon thereafter, if the stars aligned.

How did I find Bauman, and how did we make that first contact? In these pre-internet days of the early 1990s, locating the details of persons of interest was not always easy. David Roberts, the Monash Germanist, came to my rescue. He had told me of the *International Who's Who*, a catalogue held in the library that listed details including phone numbers. I called Leeds from London in July 1992 and asked if I might visit. 'Yes, of course,' came the thick Polish accent in response. 'You have come from

2 See I. Britain, *Once an Australian* (Melbourne: Oxford University Press, 1997).

Australia? You must come and stay.' I resisted the hospitality; I did not want to impose upon the Baumans, sight unseen. I took the train from Kings Cross, and I took a taxi to Lawnswood Gardens, and the pair took me to lunch at Weetwood Hall, the hotel associated with the University of Leeds, just down the road, which was later to become my frequent abode. Lunch was stodge, then – bangers and mash – but it was tasty. There was beer, warm. The atmosphere was formal. There was a vibe. What was I interested in? Bauman did not really like my answer, that I was interested in him and his work. I had already decided on a plan, in advance, which I floated with him then. Remember that at this point Bauman was relatively unknown; there was little that had been written on his work, no single monograph on the extent of his achievement to this moment. This was Bauman before Bauman. He was not yet a celebrity; the bigger bang was only to arrive around 2000, with the idea of 'liquid modernity'. I proposed to write an essay, as a kind of reconnaissance or survey exercise for a later possible book, which would expand each section of the essay into a chapter for the book. This was a strategy I had used beforehand, for *Labour's Utopias* (1992), and was to use again later, for example in developing the project of *Imagining the Antipodes* (1997). It was a kind of mapping strategy, quantity surveying in the life of the mind, a way to project-develop or to think out loud, dropping a line to begin.

How had we come to know each other, at this early point? I had been following his work for years, most notably *Socialism – The Active Utopia* (1976), and then especially *Memories of Class* (1982). Having been taught Hans-Georg Gadamer and Paul Ricoeur by Zawar Hanfi, I also devoured his book on *Hermeneutics and the Social Sciences* (1978). I read *Modernity and the Holocaust* in 1989, but came best to understand its importance under the influence of the Budapest School in Australia. Ágnes Heller and Ferenc Fehér had arrived in Melbourne in 1978, and stayed until 1986, when they left for the New School in New York. They were a serious influence on us and our culture, and we became close friends, initially as their students, later as co-workers. With my postgraduate friend Julian Triado I had acted as editor of their combined work with George Markus, *Dictatorship over Needs,* published in 1983. As a Marxist I had long been intrigued by the question of the nature of the Soviet Union for the left. It was a monstrous regime; so what did this have to with the socialist ideal? To assert that it was not socialist was one thing, even if it was a gesture of limited impact. There was a long and noble lineage of such critique, which went back to Luxemburg and Kautsky. But if it was not socialist, what, then, was it? The easiest, lazy answer was that it was some kind of capitalism. If it was not that, it would have to be some kind of *sui generis* totalitarianism, some new form of modern barbarism that accentuated some of the characteristics of modernity while truncating or negating others. Fehér, Heller and Markus wanted to argue that Soviet-type societies were indeed both modern and *sui generis.*

Editing a work is an especially rewarding way to achieve or to advance understanding. It affords an especial kind of hermeneutics, or understanding via close textual engagement. Julian and I pored our way over the text, and various others, line by line. We corrected; they engaged, accepted, or else 'uncorrected'. There was an ongoing conversation about ideas and translation. Then I read Bauman's review of *Dictatorship over Needs,* published in *Telos* in 1984, and the two great totalitarian projects finally began to fall into place in my head as failed and paranoid attempts at hypermodernity. Bauman's work on the Holocaust began to come into focus, as was intended, as a provocation to think again about modernity and its immanent logics and possibilities, and about human capacity, positive and negative.

There were other connections, local and global. I was later to discover that this same David Roberts had been a significant influence on Ágnes Heller and Ferenc Fehér, not least with reference to the aesthetics of modernism. The Hungarians arrived in Melbourne on one-way exit visas when I was 23, more immediately concerned with capitalism than modernity or modernism. David also had a leading interest in modernism and the avant-garde, and its eventual exhaustion. Even in Australia there had been avant-gardes, and discussion of the postmodern into the 1940s at the hand of Bernard Smith, our most important and pioneering art historian.[3] There was cultural traffic between centres and peripheries, and it flowed both ways, even if unevenly. Sometimes we in the Antipodes might even lead in innovation. There were cultural riches in the 'Big World', but also closer to hand. There was, in short, a wealth of wisdom and culture that was on tap in Melbourne, and Sydney, and elsewhere nearby. But there was also the 'Big World'. Once I had learned some of the vernacular, it was also time to step out. Yet I had no strong need to leave, to seek that rupture that earlier Australians had felt so powerfully, and I found that I would always return. I was an Antipodean, an Australian of German heritage, with a strong sense of curiosity about the 'Big World' as well as the place I found myself in. More, I was growing into a sense of wonder about the traffic between these places, near and afar, where there was always connect.

It all begins for me in Croydon, at the foot of the Dandenongs, in the outer suburbs of Melbourne, a long way from Lawnswood Gardens in Leeds. Leeds, like Manchester, was what Asa Briggs called a Victorian city. One of the last chapters of his book, published in 1963, was indeed about Melbourne. Croydon had none of this imperial grandeur, though its name was also suggestive of the projection of imperial naming. But it was a good place to begin, growing up in these 1960s. I had no idea my road would later take me to Yorkshire. As a student it took me more than four hours to commute daily to Monash, which at that moment seemed like distance enough. Little wonder I became so well read. I read Hegel and Marx on the bus and train, later, unsuccessfully, Althusser in those years between 1972 and 1975. Bauman was to come later, first as author at a distance, then as co-worker, then as friend. Nose in a book led the way to the face of the other.

3 B. Smith, *Place, Taste and Tradition: A Study of Australian Art since 1788* (Sydney: Ure Smith, 1945), 245.

Part I

Itineraries and archives

Chapter 1

First decade

I began to travel to Leeds to work with Zygmunt Bauman in 1992. At that time, of course, neither of us knew that we would work together or become friends for all those years. My annual visits to the United Kingdom came, literally, to follow on annual visits to the United States, where I joined in the annual proceedings of the American Sociological Association (ASA). Other Australians also think like this: once you travel out, given the distances and costs, both financial and personal, it is usually worth travelling on, with a round-the-world air ticket or whatever else. I was attracted to what was continental in American sociology, and had a strong sense of curiosity about the United States and Europe. So the weeks away each year seemed continuous, even though the cultures and geographies I encountered were diverse. Transatlantic was an interesting canopy, alongside Pacific and Indian Oceans for me. I would fly into LAX from Melbourne, join in the ASA and visit some other cities – always an eye opener, for there was no such thing quite as coherent as 'America', and some of its bits were also elsewhere, beyond the borders. Then I would fly out from the East Coast to London or Manchester and travel on to Leeds. This would involve changes in climate and culture, but the conversation with my friends at ASA and then in Leeds was continuous. The world of critical theory, like everything else, was subject to uneven development, yet it also all seemed to fit to me.

There is also, of course, this longer story. What did I take into my friendship with Zygmunt Bauman? What was surprising was how much we already had in common, when we finally met up. We immediately entered the same conversation, notwithstanding the radical differences between us in terms of the existing experience of time and place that we each carried.

There was always life for me before Bauman. I met Bauman before Bauman; but there was also a Beilharz before Bauman. There were always books and ideas in my life, not in my family home but accessible nearby. So long as I can remember, from my late teens on I have been drawn to the library and to the archive, though the older I get the physically harder the long day of institutional confinement becomes. The library I first met in primary school. The Croydon Public Library was full of treats, including a nicely illustrated quarto volume on sex, which my mother made me return pronto. There was also an elevated shelf called 'Know Ledge', which I took in my innocence to be other materials beyond classification. Perhaps some knowledge was beyond classification, as Bauman would later come to argue. Libraries were, in any case, exotic and challenging places, full of intrigue and endless fascination. Public libraries can still have this kind of energy; I am less sure about university libraries, which these days look to me like what we used then to call coffee lounges, places to snooze or canoodle.

Then there was the archive. Probably I first met the idea of the archive in 1971, year 12 of high school, when our Australian history teacher, the labour historian N. W. Saffin, would share with us the primary materials he was using in Melbourne's La Trobe Library. I was 17; he was in his 50s. Saffin's big project was to write his five-volume history of the Victorian working class in our home state in Australia, named, as was much else in this empire, after Queen Victoria. His masterwork was not to be completed; on his own death, I placed it in the archives of the University of Melbourne. Yet it was an inspired teaching device, this use of the archive, which was to return to me later. He taught by archival example. While the caricature image of gold mining in the colony, for example, was single operatives with single tents and individual spades, he would unfold maps and floorplans in class to show how company mining worked. It was an industrial mode of production. The way of thinking pointed to Marx. Under his influence, and as a sign of the times, I became interested in socialism and the labour movement and their ideas. After college I began an impossible project on the history of Australian labour and Trotskyism – impossible because, as I later remarked to the novelist Kate Grenville, it was a history of holes (her father had lived in one of these holes).

My research, my doctoral dissertation and my first book finally took on Trotskyism as a way of thinking, a language or what we would these days call an imaginary.[1] I worked under and then alongside the extraordinary historian and theorist Alastair Davidson, whose significance I appraise elsewhere, in another book, *Alastair Davidson: Gramsci in Australia* (2020), and in my own companion collection of essays, *Circling Marx: Essays 1980–2020* (2020). Alastair taught me to pay attention to text, but also to archive. He understood a great deal about communism, but we discovered more together. Trotskyism remained, inevitably, a theoretical but also an archival challenge, whether the focus was on the organization of the movement or on its ideas. So I mined new archives, for my doctoral dissertation at the Houghton Library at Harvard for Leon Trotsky, the Dunayevskaya papers at Wayne State in Michigan and everything else I could find locally or have posted from further afield, this still being a time of letters and packages. I read the entire English-language international Trotskyist literature on microfilm and microfiche and a swathe of doctoral dissertations across the field. Alastair taught me a working principle now rendered redundant by the contemporary explosion of knowledge; he taught me that you should read everything. This was what might confer the right to speak. I became a collector. As my interests spread throughout the fields of socialism, my archives also expanded. Books! Pamphlets! Papers! Photocopies! Stuff everywhere.

For my second book, *Labour's Utopias*, I discovered the extraordinary collections of the International Institute of Social History (IISH) in Amsterdam. Amsterdam became a regular port of call for me. I also worked on G. D. H. Cole's papers at Nuffield, and on the Passfield papers at the LSE. Although by this stage I had been much influenced

---

1 See P. Beilharz, *Trotsky, Trotskyism and the Transition to Socialism* (London, Croom Helm: 1987).

by historians, from Alastair Davidson to Stuart Macintyre, Ian Britain and Alan MacBriar, I had also come to the conclusion – perhaps under the influence of debates about the canon in Marxist circles – that in this kind of research the unpublished works had a secondary status to the published, at least for public thinkers of this kind –Trotsky, the Webbs, the Coles, Kautsky or Bernstein (I would never give up Marx's *Grundrisse*, unpublished or not). I had established a working strategy for myself. First, to read all the published work, and to privilege it as the public face of the discourse, in the realm of public life; then, second, to read the unpublished papers in light of the patterns of thinking that had already become apparent to me. As much as I liked archives, I did not want to be an archive rat, a scholar who did the 16 metres of papers required for a dissertation, leaving the next length for the next labourer to follow. I wanted also to see the light of day, to sit in the Oosterpark after my day at the Amsterdam Institute, or in the Museum Tavern after a day in the British Library, wondering what Marx would have said, complaining about his carbuncles, or what he had to drink, waiting for dinner or the revolution.

But there were always treats, and you could surreptitiously run your finger over the signature of Weber or Keynes in the archives, or, in Amsterdam, check out the originals of *The German Ideology*. There were wonderful tips from people called librarians, who had extreme associative capacities, and were always keen for you to connect. And sometimes, as later in my research, you would blush or even cry at what had come to pass between these flesh and blood actors in the archives, in their love and guilt and pride and sorrow. For there is often intimacy in the archives, even after they have been edited by different hands, censored and classified and catalogued and filed away in those uniform and serried ranks of file boxes.

By this stage my sustained archival activity had likely peaked. I had taken over from Ágnes Heller, the leading student of Georg Lukács, teaching sociology at La Trobe University in Melbourne from 1988, and remained there until the tectonic plates shifted in 2014. The lineage seemed preposterous: Lukács – Heller – me?? But I had been taught already to enter open doors, and I always encouraged my students and friends to do likewise. For the first time now, at La Trobe, I had access to research funds.

This is a vital part of my Bauman story, as I began now to travel annually, first for archives, then – as mentioned above – to the annual proceedings of the ASA. This, of course, was with more archives thrown in: those at the Hoover Institute, at Stanford, and much further work at the Houghton Library, in Cambridge, Massachusetts, later again. At the same time, I found myself designated a theorist, partly by choice or curiosity, partly because it was my teaching brief, a term of my employment – this even though I was begat by historians. From Ágnes, for example, I inherited her course on socialist ideas. This meant a step away from the archives, and in the direction of the library. But I also became an advocate of archives within sociology, publishing postcards on my enthusiasms in local journals such as *Labour History*, and arguing publicly and privately for the project of historical sociology. In my short experience, archives had become sources of immense possibility, though they were almost certainly underworked and often, for that reason, likely to become politically vulnerable in new times. Why not just throw the shit out? Or, at best, why not just digitize it? Such were the public controversies about to open, on the future of libraries and the death of the book, as I laboured in those archives.

Meanwhile, I was teaching a lot (teaching first year as well as second/third and running the fourth year honours programme at La Trobe), writing a lot, supervising up to a dozen postgraduates at a time, learning to write journalism and adopting its best tricks, writing for the dailies and journals, and writing … books, adding to the pile. And I had since 1980 been editing a journal called *Thesis Eleven*, another fine and steep learning curve, which may, as I now calculate, have taken up fully a decade of my life across 40 years of real time. Much energy was spent in the critique of 'New' Labor in Australia, which had arrived in 1983. The postmodern had also arrived: I wrote books out of books on *Postmodern Socialism* (1994) and on Zygmunt Bauman (2000), and I returned to the archives to write books on the great Antipodean art historian Bernard Smith and, later on, the mother of Australian sociology, Jean Martin.[2]

2 See P. Beilharz, T. Hogan and S. Shaver, *The Martin Presence: Jean Martin and the Making of the Social Sciences in Australia* (Sydney: New South, 2015).

The vast majority of this work was researched and written at La Trobe University between 1988 and 2014. La Trobe when I arrived was paradise. Big; too big? Thirty-eight lecturers and above when I began, it was liberal and tolerant, rich and diverse, taking in sociology and anthropology and looking to work the crossovers between them wherever possible. Much of this time was privileged, though when decline later set in it was serious, and the restructures that followed were brutal – as they are. There was staff attrition and non-replacement, and an increase in teaching loads at Bundoora and in the regions – a qualitative increase in non-basic work, defined here as that in addition to teaching, research and writing. There came to be hostility towards sociology as we practised it. This is, of course, a picture of a now lost world, already beyond recognition to those who have come to university life more recently. Ergo its privilege. But, as I shall indicate in these pages, there was no shortage of busyness. We were working like fury, teaching, writing, researching, organizing, editing journals such as *Thesis Eleven* – the latter, in effect, all voluntary or weekend labour (or Sunday labour, as our *subbotniks* were already laboured for the university): 'Weekend? What's a weekend?'

Into the second decade of the new century our kind of work in critical theory or critical sociology had been redefined by our superiors as non-core business, surplus to requirement. Universities had been reconfigured as business enterprises. The writing on the wall said quit or be sacked. At this point, closer to my sixties, I was exhausted. Along this path I had become a professor, which surprised my family as much as it did me. I had set out to become a high school teacher, like Saffin. I wanted to spread the word, or the light – or, at least, the enthusiasm. In those last years at La Trobe it seemed clear: I could dig in, and be the last professor, or possibly be sacked. So I left, with a disabling sense of unfinished business, taking voluntary redundancy. (If you check the internet, you can find Bauman talking about the word and its referent: 'Re–dun–dan–cy!') Yet this was, to repeat, again, a privileged life. The last time I saw George Ritzer, at my final ASA meeting in Denver, 2012, he asked me the right question. How many good years did you have at La Trobe? I did the maths, and said: 'Fifteen.' Well, there you go!

Yet what I could accept, bitterly, about my own career exit I could not accept at an institutional level. Across the path of a generation there was something dramatic going on here, something like the structural and cultural transformation of the university. Across three decades the life of the university was transformed beyond recognition. The image of the liberal arts education was subsumed into that of vocationalization: institutions promising unreal offers of meal tickets to young folk, who paid big money for the prospect. There were more and more managers, and more and more teaching and learning units, fewer and fewer teachers. There was the hegemonic monster of PowerPoint. There was more speed, less or no student reading, a turn away from the library as a place of books. As Marx famously put it in *Das Kapital*, there was more quantity and less quality, more and more commodification and rationalization. Rankings and metrics, endless self-promotion; this is what the lazy or frustrated describe as the neoliberal university, though it may, rather, actually be a symptom of the speed of late modern times. All this presents us with a serious intellectual challenge, if we are to avoid nostalgia, perfectly defined by David Lowenthal as memory with the pain cut out.[3] It is an issue to which I shall return, as the transformation of the university coincides directly with what Bauman wanted to call 'liquid modernity'.

But, by this point, the personal message was clear: it was time for me to go. I had unfinished business in teaching and research, and still depended on their synergies. I still had a vampyric need of students, who always kept me on my toes, kept me thinking – as they still do, though now at Sichuan University, where I am currently professor of critical theory, and there is some need still for my type of skill set, or what we used to call 'intellectual culture'. At La Trobe, as sociology declined, resources also evaporated. I could no longer afford to travel to the ASA proceedings. Travel support had seriously diminished, and then it disappeared, and I was depleting personal funds here in a way that I could no longer justify. This was a loss, because the ASA had become an annual source of

---

3 D. Lowenthal, *The Past Is a Foreign Country* (Cambridge: Cambridge University Press, 1985).

replenishment and renewal of friendship for me. In those better years I could do business with friends from both sides of the Atlantic, talent-spot for *Thesis Eleven*, and at my own expense I would visit places and cities I had never dreamed of experiencing. I had developed a plan to visit at least two smaller cites after each ASA meeting, which invariably occurred in bigger cities because of the number of attendees – up to 6,000 souls – and the ASA's commitment to using unionized hotels. This was a routine that was both personally fruitful and institutionally productive. It fed directly into my own teaching and productivity. There was much to learn in the big cities – LA, New York, Chicago – but, as Ihab Hassan insisted to me, the mid-size cities – such as his own, Milwaukee – were also indicative of another America.

But now the gig was up. It was time to leave La Trobe and my vocation. The point had arrived at which I would no longer call myself a sociologist, though sociology in general was always a decent default position if somebody asked what I did – more like a question of where you had come from. Other doors opened elsewhere, in terms of disciplines and places, in cultural studies at Curtin University in Western Australia, at the Stellenbosch Institute of Advanced Study in South Africa and in critical theory at Sichuan University in Chengdu with Fu Qilin. None of this was on the horizon when I left La Trobe in 2014. These were complete surprises to me. After La Trobe I thought it was over.

I was no longer a working sociologist after I left La Trobe, and no longer knew who I was, except in the past tense. In my last years there I was no longer able to initiate new research. I went part-time at La Trobe for years, looking to buy some research time, or at least some recovery time. I was constantly exhausted, and distracted by what other people insisted were urgencies or institutional imperatives. Each working day now began with a full in tray, and complaints for what could be construed as administrative tardiness. We achieved a great deal, grew *Thesis Eleven* through new generations, organized all kinds of events and visits, both home and away, across Australia and its regions, New Zealand, the Philippines, Singapore, Thailand, India, South Africa, Mozambique, China, the United States, Canada, Denmark and the United Kingdom. Our purpose was to promote cultural traffic and always to connect, to struggle against the follies of isolation that seemed to strike so many individual scholars, our friends who imagined that loneliness was a constitutive part of the scholarly condition. We generated major collaborative projects, such as the teaching text named for Bernard Smith: *Place, Time and Division*.[4] We had always wanted to insist on the centrality of geography and history to the practice of sociology. We were committed, as Bernard Smith would have put it, to sociology in the general rather than the special or professional sense. Probably this made us strategically vulnerable in an increasingly utilitarian culture, in which what mattered more was the claim to monopoly over a specialist field and its allegedly unique skill set.

There was much work to do, and much to be done. The institutional or academic conduct of sociology in Australia was at this point barely a generation old. But other actors had decided that our time was up. There was no discussion, no process, just the writing on the wall. It was time to go.

So I had to empty my room – 're–dun–dant' – and to disperse my books, thousands of them. Unlike Walter Benjamin, I was not unpacking my library but dispersing it. I had been collecting for more than 50 years, a habit encouraged at school by Saffin. His suburban home in Kent Avenue in Croydon was literally full of books, to the extent that there was structural damage to floors and ceilings. The stumps of his weatherboard house were sinking under the weight of print history. My parents had very few books: Arthur Mee's children's encyclopedias, later Funk and Wagnall, *Reader's Digest*. Our walls of fibro cement in Bayswater Road were undamaged, intact.

My own book habit was initiated by Saffin. He gave me Tacitus. What was he thinking? Later he gave me Bellamy's *Looking Backward*; I was attracted to the idea of utopia: that was more like it. I began collecting, and have never stopped. Most of my books were in my office, floor to ceiling, but at La Trobe in brick veneer. Redbrick! Or brown. The roof leaked, periodically, and books went awry, thickened and clotted.

4 P. Beilharz and T. Hogan, *Sociology: Place, Time and Division* (Melbourne: Oxford University Press, 2006).

They grew spores, returned to nature. Some were subjected to a regime of industrial steam-cleaning, but it was all too late.

Disposing of my books on leaving was a wrench. This was an emotionally challenging experience for a boy such as me. I have lived a fortunate life. A product of the postwar boom, I had no experience of the scale of suffering encountered by my parents or by my later friends, their generational peers, Zygmunt and Janina Bauman. I was too young to be sent to fight in the Vietnam War. I had learned how to live frugally from my parents, but had never wanted. Yet I had become redundant, and I now discovered, on leaving my room, not only that I had to get rid of books but also that I possessed an archive. I was disappearing under a mountain of paper, which now had to go. My professorial suite was stacked with books, but was also dominated by a battery of grey metal filing cabinets. The original, 1970s design of my room included a massive walk-in cupboard, as well as a period feature: a wet cupboard – space for bottles and glasses. Only rarely, however, did we drink. There was too much work to be done.

I had kept everything: the early artwork of my children, all my notes on all my projects, lecture notes, papers that others had given me for safe keeping, letters, itineraries, minutes, files for *Thesis Eleven* before it had accumulated a bureaucracy of its own. For, when we started the journal, in innocence in 1980, we also began of necessity to generate a bureaucracy: more archives and files. Now there was too much paper. Why not just throw the shit out?

All those years, when I was just stuffing paper into those filing cabinets after each different activity, I had unwittingly generated my own archive. Fortunately for me, the National Library of Australia (NLA) was interested in taking these files on. As I was throwing out my books I was also editing and cataloging my papers. It was an interesting exercise. Overwhelming, and the stuff of nostalgia, with Lowenthal or without. As I was closing my boxes I was closing my career. Leaving my university after such a time, with a sense of unfinished business, I also had some sense of shame, of humiliation, as though all this work and cultivation had been scarred, devalued, closed up in those boxes, interred in that skip.

So, what should I do with all these materials, which were now some kind of waste? Would anybody ever use the stuff?

Then he died.

It was not unexpected, but it always is, all the same. Zygmunt Bauman died in his Leeds home on 9 January 2017. He was 91. I had been unable

1 The pipette from South Africa.

properly to say goodbye to him. We had been friends for nearly 30 years. He was thousands of miles away from me, but we had worked together, corresponded, and I had visited Lawnswood Gardens annually for, I suppose, at least 20 of those years. I had written a lot about his work. I did not see him as a leader, or me as a follower. I saw him as a sage, a wise man who had experienced so much more than I, and me as his interpreter, among others. His presence, for me, was not that of a guru but a smarter, worldly-wise, more experienced colleague and teacher, and friend. As he often said to me, we seemed to think in similar ways, but we also had our differences. These had to do with time, with what was distinct to our two lifeworlds, but also with place. He was East European, and both terms count. I was Antipodean, one foot in Europe or America, one in Australia: new world, for me; older European world, for him. We spoke of many things, but we never talked about rock music. I had to laugh when one of his interlocutors in his last books of conversations dropped a reference to Led Zeppelin. Who? I can imagine Bauman heading for Wikipedia, only to emerge unedified. Something to do with solid modernity?

So he was gone, rock or not, and I felt lost. January, summer in Australia. When I was younger, in the 1990s, I wrote my way through the summer break. If I was lucky I might get a book done. Books such as *Postmodern Socialism* and *Transforming Labor* (both 1994) I blitzed across those six weeks, after researching and teaching the material across the academic year. Being Antipodean was a challenge, as well as an imaginary advantage. Every piece I read or wrote about my own place was at the expense of what I learned about other places, and the other way round. There was a constant risk of invisibility in and ignorance of both places. The more I learned about other places, the more I realized how little I knew about my own. This is, I think, a common predicament, but one little acknowledged. Hegel writes somewhere about the dangers of thinking you know what you inhabit, what you grow up with, the culture that you simply take for granted. This was why Bauman enthused about the idea of defamiliarizing the familiar. So I had a need to know, and I had a need to write. I had published my first international scholarly paper on communism in Australia in a Gramscian inflection with the Hoover Institute at 22, and began public writing and reviewing just thereafter.[5] Soon I was publishing in spaces such as *Telos* and *History Workshop*, later *Socialist Register*. I even pitched at *New Left Review*, but that was youthful folly; the cheek of sending them a critique of the god-father, Isaac Deutscher. I was young, and stretching. I needed to address both these worlds, near and afar, scholarly and public. Long before I had cause to contemplate the notion, I was working like an antipodean, one foot elsewhere.

Now, after La Trobe, with Bauman gone, and that white man in the White House, I felt lost. I wrote some obituaries, and I shared with Joe Gelonesi some good talk on Bauman on ABC Radio's *Philzone* in Sydney. I came to the conclusion that I would have to write my way out of this. This book is the result of that process.

As I began to think more practically about the challenge I was to set myself, I remembered: there are these things called documents, these places called archives. I had also generated an archive. Actually, I had a serious database. So Sian and I travelled to Canberra, an occasional stop on Bauman's own itinerary out of Warsaw via Israel in the 1970s, and I guess I was the first scholar to look into the Beilharz Archives: NLA MS10188; 5.85 metres; 39 boxes. A life – almost.

Now I had three sources. I had Bauman's own work, including the work of his last years, which I had not done justice to, as I had felt myself drowning under more pressing duties; and he was still accelerating, into that last decade. I had what I had written, which was a lot. And I had my records in the archives; letters; emails; itineraries; plans and project development; engagements with publishers and colleagues; stimulants of memories, which themselves could be sharp or more hazy or vague, or else mistaken. Living across real time, you forget, transpose, misplace. But I had a record. I had an archive to work with and through. When did we first meet? How did it all begin? Were there, in retrospect, different

---

5 My first published piece was 'Australia', in the *Yearbook on International Communist Affairs* (Stanford, CA: Hoover Institution Press, 1976).

phases of development in our work together? This kind of curiosity had never occurred to me before; he was just there. We had been friends and colleagues for such a long time that I could not say for sure. We were just there. For almost as long as I could remember, there had been a 'we'.

What was in these archives? My first point of orientation was in my own travel itineraries, which tracked, among other things, my visits to Leeds. This would give me the baseline of a chronology. This, in turn, was the stuff of a memory test. It seemed as though we had known each other forever. Yet I also now had noticed that, when I assembled the entries for my edited collection *Social Theory: A Guide to Central Thinkers*, published in 1992 from the results of a theory stream I had coordinated for the Australian Sociological Association in 1989 (and still, remarkably, in print), he was not there. I had read and already been influenced by his work, but the bombshell work, *Modernity and the Holocaust*, had yet to explode into my life. In 1992, or at least in 1989, I had not yet placed Bauman in the centre of my life or work.

I had been taught Marx and Sigmund Freud and Weber, Western Marxism, structuralism and critical theory, but I had never been taught sociology. Perhaps this was a backhanded advantage. At this time I was more aware of my deficits. There was a lot to teach myself when I began work in sociology, from Durkheim and Simmel to the Chicago School, and so on. Still, the history of sociology in Australia was full of strays, and there were a few other things I already knew as well. My antennae seemed fine. The presence of Bauman was there, but peripheral. There was a great deal to learn.

My intellectual horizons were expanding, and my newfound capacity to travel in the 1990s took me out, just as the visitors to the Antipodes brought wonderful legacies in with them. Cultural traffic was such an enabling process. New ideas were forever arriving on our shores, and we in turn sent out our more lonely messages in bottles. Over that generation it is possible to imagine that the flows of culture, south to north, might even have become a little more reciprocal. Yet the points of contact needed to be personal. Good ideas had carriers, who could be as interesting as their ideas were. Ideas were also embodied, connected to persons.

How did these doors and currents open? Through scrutiny of the itineraries and travel applications in my papers I was able to work out exactly
when I was where. There are some gaps in the record. I had disposed
of my diaries in the panic of finally closing my office door – that last
moment when there is no return. The advice received was that the NLA
was interested in narrative diaries, not daybooks. This was an action
I came to regret, but some of the shit just had to go. These were not exactly
Austen's letters, or Carlyle's draft of *The French Revolution*, anyway. There
was simply nowhere to keep all the detritus of my life. It went into the
industrial waste skip that was delivered to my office as a symbolically
laden part of the restructuring process. So much waste, as Bauman would
have observed. Redundancy ends in the skip. Pulp nonfiction!

So where was I? How had all this come to be? How did Bauman and
I come together? Research travel funds first became available to me at
La Trobe for the working year 1989. I had spent 1987 working with
Stuart Macintyre and Ian Britain at the University of Melbourne History
School on a postdoctoral grant facilitated by the marvellously maverick
anthropologist Greg Dening. This was the project that was to become
Labour's Utopias, the book that was to help bridge Bauman and me. 1988
I started at La Trobe, spent the year getting my courses up and finishing
work on the published sources on my subjects, Bolshevism, the Soviets,
Fabianism, the British, and German social democracy. In September
1989 I visited the International Institute for Social History in Amsterdam,
staying with class analyst Mino Carchedi, and travelled onto Nuffield for
the papers of G. D. H. Cole. Oxford spired; its magic opened up to me the
massive cavern of Blackwell's bookshop, the faux mediaeval beauty and
frog ponds of Nuffield, the splendour of the Sheldonian Theatre and its
antique musical treats. I worked on the archives of the LSE in London on
the papers of Beatrice and Sidney Webb and R. H. Tawney, some of whose
papers on usury evidently shared the chicken shack that he had inhabited
after the war, so adorned were they. I stayed with Michele Barrett, who
was to become my friend and London host for many years. Michele was
generous and engaging, a fine scholar whose interests included Marxism,
feminism and literature. Over the years she introduced me to many of her

friends, including Catherine and Stuart Hall. One year I saw Stuart on the occasion of his birthday party at Michele's. When I told Bauman I would be seeing Hall, his eyes lit up: 'Ah! Stuart Hall! You must take him my best greetings and kiss him once on each cheek.'

When Stuart and I met in the hallway I passed on these greetings from Leeds, and the news about the kisses – both. Stuart Hall looked at me with that charming smile, raised a finger and said: 'Later!' We had met before, in Melbourne in 1983 for the first Marx centenary, and we had already carried his views in *Thesis Eleven*. Like Bauman he was a Gramscian essayist, though his prose was always more crystalline. As Hall's memoirs show, he also felt ever the outsider.[6] Both Bauman and Hall were in a sense naturalized, claimed locally, and in this way misplaced and misunderstood. Neither Hall nor Bauman was an Englishman. I knew Catherine less, but had always admired her work. I may have blotted my card when, at a paper she gave at La Trobe, there was a request for three minutes' silence for the passing of Edward Thompson. It just slipped out; I heard myself say, in a small but audible voice, 'Thirty seconds for Louis Althusser?' These people were not precious in the way that some of our colleagues could be. Probably there is always something precious about gatherings of a disciplinary kind, whether sociologists or historians. Academics are tribal animals. Gatherings of friends were always more open. I became fond of these folk, as of Michele's son, Duncan, with whom she later wrote an amazing book on *Star Trek*, a fine model of alternative collaboration. I also got to know Paul Hirst, a veritable dynamo, a rare Englishman who knew about folk from the Antipodes, such as Bernard Smith and Inga Clendinnen. Paul was an enthusiast, a booster. He reviewed *Labour's Utopias* positively for Routledge, and always had a reading list for me, whether on guild socialism, architecture or globalization. We met annually for years, over big lunches that fuelled him but slowed me down. He was my kind of sociologist – one for whom disciplinary borders mattered less than the problems that face us and

---

6 See S. Hall and B. Schwartz, *Familiar Stranger: A Life between Two Islands* (London: Allen Lane, 2017).

the traditions available to us to help make this project of understanding work. Then he, too, was gone.

In 1990 I did not travel abroad, but worked further on *Labour's Utopias*. In 1991 my application for travel support was unsuccessful, but I gained support for research assistance, for which I employed a young Trevor Hogan to research the ideological history of the Australian Labor Party. I worked in different local archives, including those of H. V. Evatt at Flinders in Adelaide. Evatt was an intellectual giant, a big personality, and liked to show people so. He was Labor's new liberal, an intellectual of ravenous appetite, significant ambitions and many strange mannerisms. Evatt's archives contained some surprises, including his spectacles and false teeth. This cumulative research resulted in *Transforming Labor*, published in 1994, whose logic was that the story of radical labour was over, as the social movement called labour had disappeared into the state. It was a parallel argument to Bauman's of a decade earlier, in *Memories of Class* (1983).

The year 1992 took me to Aalborg in Denmark for the conference of Ezra and Jacob Talmor, publishers of the journal *The European Legacy*, on the history of European ideas. These were crazy, high-energy, interdisciplinary events, where arguments would sometimes break down under the image of Babel: too many languages, few of them much shared, but great goodwill and good friendships to be made. This was the wonder of Babel; if someone made a passing comment about Czech or Lithuanian socialism, the native speaker present would immediately intervene in their mother tongue in order to straighten things out. Other like events were to follow, for example in Graz. I travelled on to Amsterdam, to London again for the LSE Library, to Oxford for Nuffield and to visit the Ashmolean, where I gloved up alongside a sullen young punk to inspect the Ruskin files. We admired the watercolours together in silence: modern, traditional and postmodern all at once. I took a train to Cambridge to visit the archaeologist Peter Gathercole, with whom I shared an interest in the work of Vere Gordon Childe. This was the moment when I decided that I had to write about Bernard Smith. And, as memory serves, I took a day trip to Leeds.

As related above, we began – Janina, Zygmunt and I – at Weetwood Hall for lunch after a drink at Lawnswood Gardens. There was a great deal of talking and smoking – mainly smoking. It was a good encounter, but like any other such it could have led nowhere. There had been some prior indirect contact, in the manner of those interested in and committed to the life of the mind. There had already been correspondence, letters and work on our journal, *Thesis Eleven*.

Prior to this first meeting in 1992 a line had gone out between Bauman and me via *Thesis Eleven*. There was a pretext. Having become, by the conditions of my employment, a sociologist in 1988, I participated in the annual Australian Sociology conference at the Australian National University (ANU) in Canberra in that year. Hitherto, my people had been in history or politics; my doctoral dissertation was in politics, which gave other purists heartburn. When it comes to disciplinary policing, essentialism still rules. At the invitation of Barry Hindess, another disciplinary transgressor, I now gave a paper on *Legislators and Interpreters*, which had appeared in 1987, and was one of the first works in sociology to take on the postmodern as a challenge to intellectuals and to the sociology of intellectuals. I had reviewed the book for the local sociology journal, and had taken the liberty of posting Bauman a photocopy in an airmail envelope, presuming that he otherwise would not see it. This was a message in a bottle, sent from south to north. Eventually it arrived, washed up around Whitby – Captain Cook in reverse. Our relationship began, and ended, in words.

My first foray was earnest, if not precocious. What was the fuss about? This is what I wrote.

Zygmunt Bauman is one of the most consistently interesting and provocative analysts of our time. This much was already evident in books such as *Socialism: The Active Utopia* (1976), *Hermeneutics and Social Sciences* (1978), and most recently and least forgettably, *Memories of Class* (1983). *Legislators and Interpreters* is no exception. It represents, in some senses, a series of responses to some of these earlier views. In addressing debates about modernity, post-modernity and post-modernism Bauman takes up again questions about the impulse of socialism and its great arch, the

Enlightenment. In dealing with the sociology of intellectuals, Bauman effectively returns to the theories of hermeneutics – for intellectuals neither can nor ought any longer aspire to the role of legislators; they can now perhaps only be interpreters. And in pushing further questions about control and discipline, Bauman extends the kinds of interests and themes in factory civilization which were so brilliantly essayed in his previous book.

If this consistency of project is more reminiscent of the critical impulses of the Enlightenment tradition, however, Bauman now and here also writes in the shadow of post-modern relativism. On the one hand, his work retains a sense of integrity and systematicity; on the other it now roams, ruminates, wanders across the wreckage of modern social theory, prodding some objects, kicking others, finding illumination in odd unexpected places and casting off sundry unredeemed hopes of Marxism and critical theory. Bauman indeed deliberately leads us through the junk heaps of modern industrial civilization in order to view these problems. Social theory, as well as social practice, has come a long way from the ordered cosmos of Versailles and the social scientist fantasies of Saint-Simon. With Bauman we look backward, to these modern origins, as well as forward, but from the specific vantage point of post-modern culture within Thatcher's Britain.

And yet, predictably, necessarily (?) Bauman's relationship to the Enlightenment remains ambivalent. The vast expanse of his book is directed against the punitive effects of the enlightenment gaze, and the subterranean message is against Habermasian rationalism. Bauman plots out the coeval rise of modern state power and the discourse of modernity. The subsequent divorce of state power and intellectual strategies of control leave us, today, in the post-modern condition. The discourse of modernity is constructed in terms of order, control, planning, certitude, truth; this discourse arises in tandem with the means of surveillance now associated, thanks to Foucault, with the enlightening image of Bentham's panopticon. While historians and some sociologists have made the panopticon-idea a new centre in explaining modernity, Bauman's primary interest, at least in the earlier part of the book, is the discourse which accompanies it. The discourse of *les philosophes* meant that to acquire excellence, men must be taught. They need teachers, those who know. Those who know then expect also that it is they who should legislate. To put it another way, the newly emerging social engineers needed tools of power, but they also needed a grand design for a better society and terms of discourse appropriate to their own self-promotion as would-be legislators.

As Bauman argues, the new kind of power which arose out of this configuration had two striking qualities: it was a *pastoral* power, and a *proselytising* power. It was a power which turned intellectuals from gamekeepers into gardeners. Life could no longer be simply tolerated; it had to be organized in order to maintain the proper distinction between reason and the passions, setting apart authority and the swinish multitude. For Bauman this means that the educative aspirations of the Enlightenment were strictly circumscribed; the hope for the rabble was not to educate but merely to control them. Thus Robespierre characterized the model school as one in which everything would be visible, everybody would be under observation, no detail would escape the rules and the Jacobins, of course, would be the teachers. Bauman concludes that the substance of enlightened radicalism was the drive to legislate, organize and regulate, rather than to disseminate knowledge. The historical image of Rousseau has already been allowed to elbow Kant out of this picture; Diderot, D'Alembert, Voltaire and Holbach instead are summoned in order to prove what contempt the Enlightenment had for *'les betes feroces, furieux, imbeciles'*. This contempt for the popular was then to be directed outwards, as well as down: the civilising project, Bauman argues, was necessarily an attempt to stamp out all relativity, hence all plurality of ways of life. The gardeners of the West set out to tame the savages both at home and abroad, in darkest England and Africa alike.

Napoleon was right, then, to view the ideologists as competitors for state power. Ideology, usefully rechristened sociology by Comte, takes on the virtually Faustian task of remoulding the world. But by the twentieth century the vision of the project can no longer be elevated over the piles of corpses, and now post-modernism, an aesthetic principle, expands finally into social theory. Yet the idea of postmodernity is not at all identical with that of post-industrialism, as Bauman usefully explains. Post-industrialism remains within the logic of modernity – progress ever onward, upward, futures controllable if societies are smart enough. The post-modernist discourse, in comparison, looks on the immediate past as a closed episode. The rules of the past dissolve; instead we inhale pluralism at least, relativism at most, until the absence of clearly defined rules of the game renders all innovation impossible. The avant-garde dries up, in art and politics alike; once protest is accepted, it becomes part of the scene. Intellectual communities henceforth talk among themselves, with the more intrepid souls attempting to translate or interpret between groups. Commodified critical culture comes to be understood less as a mass market abomination than as a system of diverse taste-systems which needs not to be rejected but rather to be adequately tapped. Amidst this complexity and difference, there is simply no call for intellectuals who would be legislators. Jacobinism is redundant.

Yet this complexity and difference is mediated through markets and this means, especially into the eighties, that some people have no access to post-modern culture (or rather, they have access only to the bits that are inexpensive). What we face now is not a dual labour market but a dual society, and here Bauman revives Disraeli's 'two nations' motif in order to explain the divide. The postKeynesian economic regime needs consumers, still, but it does not need to subvent mass consumption any longer. The new poor do not matter as consumers. As Bauman puts it, the work ethic has an ever diminishing relevance to the reproduction of capital, whose profits now depend more on the manipulation of markets than on the exploitation of the labour force. The poor have a different systemic function today: they are held up (or down) as the living embodiments of the only alternative to the consumer market which that market itself acknowledges. They are *'les betes feroces, furieux, imbeciles'* in new guise. The receding Beveridge-image of welfarism confirms the sense that the economic system need no longer plan to increase effective demand; it needs the poor to stay poor, as an adequate example, and so post-modern culture remains at the behest of those who can pay, for film festivals, for theatre, ... for books.

Now somehow, despite the persuasive and gloomy nature of his case, Bauman nevertheless manages to come to some optimistic conclusions, to the extent that one awaits the expelled if not executed [Jürgen] Habermas to at least reappear by the back door, as Bauman speaks positively of the project of 'discursive redemption'. The issue, for Bauman, is that the potential of modernity is still, despite all, untapped, so that modernity's promise needs yet to be redeemed. This redemption would involve the separation of the values of autonomy, self-perfection and authenticity from the renderings presently forced upon them by the market. The appropriately public forms of discourse can thus open the way, again, for the conditions of emancipation which are offered by the project of modernity. This is Bauman's 'modernist' conclusion. It is juxtaposed to a 'post-modern' conclusion, where interpretation amounts to quite an adequate task with which to keep intellectuals busy. This is a refusal (of) strategy, an anti-strategy which Bauman here associates with [Richard] Rorty. And Bauman seems to stand with a foot in each field, one foot in the decaying junkyard of British manufacturing, leaning on Jeremy Seabrook; the other with Rorty, in the momentary ease of the academy: for this is the strength of his insight, modern/postmodern, socialist/hermeneutic.

The only reasonable criticism I think which can be made of this condition is to ask, is it the only possible construction of our contemporary situation? To ask this question is also to beg another: that of Bauman's reading of the Enlightenment project. The values to which Bauman returns are, to some extent at least, Enlightenment values: autonomy, in the case of Kant, and self-perfection, reminding us of Schiller. Authenticity may be a little more problematical, though there are certainly grown-up children of the Enlightenment such as Heller who would likely place equal value on it. Yet Bauman has already, earlier, read these values out of the Enlightenment, and thus flattened it of its noble impulses. To think along these lines is to ask the question, are intellectuals today hopelessly bound to internal discourse with their peers? And the answer, perhaps more evidently in a society such as our own, is no. Intellectuals who engage only in internal dialogue surely among other things choose to do so. They also teach, speak, argue, write outside of and beyond professional forums. They think, and argue, and judge, and if they do not cultivate these attitudes in others then this, again, is a choice. Zygmunt Bauman has spent a life thinking, writing, arguing and judging. This important book shows this yet again. We can share with Bauman the horror of intellectuals viewing themselves as world-historic legislators, and yet insist that they can do more than merely interpret within scholarly communities. For the conduct of social theory in the age of noise will surely become more important, not less. *Contra* Robespierre, there are other ways to teach, and other ways to live.[7]

Not a bad review; handy, perhaps, as a first calling card. Perhaps I was sharper when I was fresh and young. I set off to the central photocopier at La Trobe, stuck the results in the mailbag without any particular expectations. I got a letter back, much to my surprise, in Bauman's spiderlike scrawl: 4 July 1988. Thirty years ago; a promising beginning, though neither of us were to know this at the time. There was no communion between us yet.

---

7 P. Beilharz, 'Review of Bauman, *Legislators and Interpreters*', *Australian and New Zealand Journal of Sociology* 24/3 (1988).

He wrote:

Dear Peter Beilharz,
I am very touched – and excited by your wonderful review of my
work: have I indeed written all these wise and profound things? There is
no greater reward for a writer than to see sage people sharing his own
opinions. Thank you, thank you very much! [...]
With very best wishes
Yours ever
Z

He usually signed 'Z'; I guess that was distinct enough. We used to call him
'Ziggy', after Bowie, or Freud, but never to his face, where it was always
'Zygmunt'; never 'Professor'. My enthusiasm for his work was complicated
by his own intellectual generosity and pluralism. My interest in Bauman
at the Canberra event was compromised by a momentary enthusiasm for
Rorty, whose ideas I had met chez Bauman. As Bauman was given to say,
his was a house with many doors, or of many rooms, and each had a procession of interesting interlocutors. I had to read Rorty, and others, before
I could return to Bauman. Bauman's work was a source of frustration and
distraction as well as focus and insight. These roads led outwards, and away,
as well as back home. This was, I suspect, one reason for the limited appeal
of the early work of Bauman in English. To take it on, you would already
have to know a lot, or else be prepared to spend time chasing philosophers
and rabbits across the Yorkshire Dales in order to begin to make sense of
what he was up to. His argumentative mode then was typically associative,
crabwalking sideways rather than mapping and following the linear. You
had to work at it. It did not come, as he liked to say, in bite-size pieces. He
was no advocate of easy intellectual consumption.

In the meantime other patterns of traffic opened between Lawnswood
Gardens and Bundoora, the outer suburban campus of La Trobe. We
also began to collaborate on *Thesis Eleven*. Bauman began by reviewing
an Australian book on the postmodern. David Roberts asked him to
review the Monash General Literature volume on *Postmodern Conditions*,
published in 1988. Roberts in turn reviewed *Legislators and Interpreters*

in our pages in 1989. Bauman's own review appeared in *Thesis Eleven* in 1990, some years after we had signed Bauman up as an editorial advisor, in 1987. Clearly, our mutual antennae were up. Bauman's review is a serious engagement, a full five journal pages long. It indicates his own ambivalence about the postmodern, combining unease, about the postmodern impulse that leads to mutual indifference, and enthusiasm, for the pluralizing of art forms and arguments that then went under this category. Critical theory began from the sense of agency, and the commitment to the value of emancipation. Are intellectuals today even sufficiently capable of addressing such challenges? Such was the scope of Bauman's review at this point. He understood from early on that the postmodern controversy was unavoidable, even if its especial significance was as a second-order take on the legacy and importance of both modernity and modernism.

Thesis Eleven came to be a platform for both of us, for our endeavours and those of many others. At this stage, in the first of its now four decades, the journal was most clearly marked by our origins in Western Marxism and critical theory, by our interests in Australia and by the projects of alternative thinkers such as the Budapest School and Socialisme ou Barbarie. This involved expanding the Marxist optic from that of the critique of capitalism to that of modernity and modernism, and, in turn, the postmodern. Modernity came to be a key concern for us as we realized its capacity to pluralize, to take into consideration other modernities, such as those of fascism and Stalinism, and others again, from the Philippines to South Africa and, later, China. The work of Bauman seemed to have a home here, though perhaps more under our first defining category, critical theory, than our second, historical sociology. Certainly, Bauman had an interest in the other.

Much later he would review a book of my own, *Imagining the Antipodes*, for *Thesis Eleven*. This was a good omen: unlike many others better established in our field, he did not expect only to be reviewed, not to do the humble yet vital work of the book reviewer himself. Intellectual work, in this way of thinking, was always plural and conversational; there were always precedents, other doors that opened onto understanding. He began publishing essays with *Thesis Eleven* in 1989, first up on 'Sociological Responses to Postmodernity'. As he wanted to insist, the postmodern was the phenomenon to be explained rather than the privileged means available to explain it. (Thereby hangs a tail, or a tease for the book that you are holding: how should I seek to untangle the 'Bauman phenomenon', if not by means of thinking with Bauman?) Many of these essays I had to shoehorn out of him, later by email, earlier by solicitation when I visited. As I became a regular visitor to Lawnswood Gardens he would share the latest book manuscript with me, giving me a sheaf of paper as I went upstairs to bed, and then sending me off on my way home laden with offprints and proofs and essays in the making. I would then solicit this or that from him for our journal by letter or email. He was not a hustler. I was astonished by later claims that Bauman was a careerist or academic climber. All I knew from him was generosity, curiosity, friendship and the occasional piece of mischief. His sense of modesty could be cutting, self-effacing.

In 1993 I discovered the United States, and, like all such discoveries, this was personal. Craig Calhoun had interviewed for a chair in sociology at La Trobe in 1992. We barbecued in our suburban backyard, got on like a house on fire – and almost set the house on fire: eucalyptus, the highly flammable local that makes us so vulnerable to the spread of bushfires. He brought empty bag space, hoping to take home copies of *Thesis Eleven*. We shared a strong commitment to critical theory and historical sociology, and began to plan what we might be able to teach together at La Trobe. It all failed to come to pass, but we became strong friends. Craig, ever the booster, insisted that I come to the United States, and saw that I was invited to join in my first ASA meeting in Miami. I travelled to Miami and then to New York, visiting with Ágnes Heller's son, Yuri, in the upper West Side; and then I flew to San Francisco, staying with Martin Jay, my PhD examiner in the Berkeley Hills and working at the Hoover Archives in Palo Alto. Miami was a crazy place to begin. There had been a spate of carjackings of German tourists. I did not drive, but I did look like a German – or so I was told. Unlike Detroit, later, there was at least no stray gunfire at night. There were seven homicides in Detroit the week I finally got there, rather later. In all my time growing up in

Croydon I remember one murder, gangland, at the Ringwood Skating Rink. These were different worlds.

I settled on a new travel plan. From 1994 I began to take a round-the-world trip, beginning early August in the United States for the ASA, then coming home via Leeds. Often Bauman would pick me up from the railway station, warning me in advance that I would recognize him as the shabbily dressed man. He never was; anorak and pipe. But he was fond of words such as 'shabby', and he was often self-deprecating. I remember one occasion when he came ambling down the staircase at Lawnswood Gardens in a dinner suit with a frilly 1970s dress shirt. He was trying it out, in order to see if it still fitted for some big coming event. It did. He was lean. He was a good recycler. We laughed. He was able to laugh at himself.

He was also able to laugh at me, and to tease me incessantly. He was worried that I would become lost to the Americans. He felt disdain for the ASA, for professionalization and for the profession of sociology, as he did indifference for its British equivalent, the BSA. He had early established his public contempt for American sociology, which he called 'Durksonian', a hybrid structural functionalism begot of Émile Durkheim and Talcott Parsons. Yet he also frequently used other, alternative American sociologists as his interlocutors. After all, the United States was full of foreigners, migrants and refugees like himself, who had turned left rather than right across the Atlantic. His own sensibilities were European, East and Central European, Ostmodern more than postmodern. He was older than me, more fully formed, more worldly-wise, and he had a different sense of self-sufficiency. He had struggled to establish his own academic identity in the 1960s, but had done so very successfully by this moment in his life, in the 1990s. I was a generation younger. I was still finding my way, vacuuming up ideas. I remained happy to go into those open doors, wherever they were. There seemed to be more doors for me in the United States than in the United Kingdom. When I began to visit the United Kingdom there were still strong senses of hostility – or, if you like, invisibility – to do with class, habitus, to do with the colonies or the Antipodes. Nick Cave and Kylie had yet to arrive, as part of that process of global reflux. There were relatively few, such as Michele Barrett or Paul Hirst (or Zygmunt Bauman), who then would take me seriously.

In 1994 the ASA proceedings were held in LA. This was, indeed, something of a circus along the lines that vexed Bauman. It was held, hilariously, in the Bonaventure, the John Portman hotel of three massive, imposing shiny mirror cylinders that had become a postmodern design icon, essayed variously in the work of Fred Jameson and Ed Soja. I found myself in Hotel California. Like other postmodern palaces, its main claim to fame was that it was unworkable – or, more literally, that you could never find a way out, especially if you were a novice from Australia, and jetlagged to boot. I had an amusing encounter at the ASA with Mike Davis, who was promoting *Cities of Quartz* (1990) at an author-meets-critics session, one of the brightest features of the convention culture. There were sparks, as when Harvey Molotch opened by bagging the bad news guys, aka critical theorists. Where was the good news? Well, in the city of LA it was fractured, as in other American cities. I wanted to meet Davis, to shake his hand, as I was teaching out of the book at La Trobe and was among his admirers. My name badge had *Thesis Eleven* as my affiliation. His offsider said to me, 'What's *Thesis Eleven*?' Davis responded: 'You don't know? *Thesis Eleven* is the leading journal of critical theory in the world!' When I relayed this story to my fellow editors, in Melbourne, one wiseacre responded further: 'You should have got him to write it down!' But it slipped away, like the best of smiles.

At this ASA I introduced myself to another scholar who became a lifelong long-distance friend. His name was Jeffrey Alexander. He also knew *Thesis Eleven*, which, as the editors used to joke back then, was a kind of oversized calling card. I spent decades carrying sample copies around the globe for show and tell. The most amusing result came at one Canadian ASA, when my backpack came out of the Pearson Airport carousel torn open at the zip, with my underwear on display and the sample copies missing. This I took to be a backhanded compliment. At least someone was reading *Thesis Eleven*, or playing football with those bubblewrap packages.

From LA I drove south to La Jolla with Calhoun in a red Mustang Convertible, the only rental car available at LAX Hertz for the theory section conference to follow, and made other friends, such as Chris Rojek, Steve Turner, Lyn Spillman and Steven Seidman. Then I began to travel home via Leeds, London and the IISH, stopping en route in Boston to meet with the publishers of *Thesis Eleven* at MIT Press. I could get so much done in three weeks away that I would be busy following up for a year.

In 1995 the ASA meeting was held in Washington, DC. This was an auspicious event. I brokered the shift of *Thesis Eleven* to Sage with publishers Steven Barr and Chris Rojek in a Dupont Circle bar. Working with MIT Press had been a major step up for us. Janet Fisher and her staff were fantastic. The quality of their production work gave us a little more time to work on our intellectual project, for, as with much else in life, we had begun a journal without any very clearly defined purpose, and even less well established capacity. We were making it up as we went along; perhaps that is what praxis also means. MIT Press had a serious presence and a fine design aesthetic. Sage had a global social sciences presence, so this was another step up, or perhaps out. On study leave, I visited Chapel Hill with Calhoun, working on the history of American sociology in the Green Library. I had been to the Phillips Gallery in DC to see the Klee, which then turned up on the cover of his fine book *Critical Social Theory* in 1995. We had beer and pizza and listened to *Disraeli Gears* up very loud on those big old box coffin speakers. This was a serious friendship, consolidated later by many visits to Craig's New York University digs in Mercer Street, and later again at Borough Market in London when he ran the LSE. Craig was welcomed to the LSE as 'the Cheerful American'; interpret as you will. I would have called him a possibilist. I travelled to Ann Arbor to give a paper on my work on postmodern socialism, and then to Sussex, to research the archives of Leonard and Virginia Woolf, visit Rodmell and Monk's House for a never to be completed book on radical companions (the Webbs, the Woolves, the Coles, the Pember Reeves, and the Antipodean Palmers, Vance and Nettie; more teamwork, again). I was interested in what Ágnes Heller called the emotional division of labour between the sexes, and in the relation between private and public intellectual life.

I was also interested in intellectual collaboration, and how couples such as these worked, alone and together. Of course, I also had this curiosity about the Baumans. They had not written together, but the influence of Janina's memoir of surviving the Warsaw Ghetto on Zygmunt's Holocaust book was well known. I had long been convinced that teamwork was a key dimension of intellectual activity. Most writers do not believe in it so much as in that notion of the romantic genius that is peculiarly their own, or, at least, in immaculate conception. I felt more like a sponge, always ready to take on from those around me, not least those who did different things from me, such as art. This may be one aspect of being Antipodean, the sense that there is a big world outside the one you find yourself in – this both in terms of personal geography and in terms of field, or discipline. I visited Kate Challis, Bernard Smith's granddaughter, and the artist Gary Cutting at Sid Nolan's house at Hampstead, and finished with my annual pilgrimage to Leeds. As with the work of *Thesis Eleven*, there was no set agenda for these encounters. The moment I walked through the door at Lawnswood Gardens the conversation would begin, punctuated by food, wine, walk, sleep, trips out. Of course, I would be looking to interrogate him about his work, but he would more often want to talk of other things, and to have me lead. You could never really ask Bauman, as academics are dully obliged to do, 'What are you working on?' He was working on many things all at the same time. There was one small point of conversation, among others larger that were to connect us. I had begun in this period to visit the Research School of Social Sciences at the ANU in Canberra on a regular basis, working on the archives of radical and reforming thinkers at the National Library of Australia. Full circle; one of several. Bauman always wanted to know about Canberra. It seems to have been the place in Australia that left the most lasting impression on them both.

For me, there were always other worlds to discover. 1996 took me to Mexico City, at the invitation of Pablo Gonzalez Casanova at the National Autonomous University of Mexico. I spoke on globalizing the Antipodes and shared events with Daniel Singer and Randolph David. New worlds were opening. I was invited to visit Chiapas by the Subcommandante

Marcos, an opportunity I was unable to take up. I flew to El Norte to stay with Don Levine in Chicago, where I also met with Marshall Sahlins. Dipesh Chakrabarty, a vital postcolonial connection to Australia, was out of town. The ASA meeting was held in New York. I roomed with my old friend Bill Martin, and we launched *Thesis Eleven* as a Sage journal with a party at the Hilton Towers, overlooking Central Park. I flew home via LA, visiting with Jeff Alexander in that other, Californian Venice. He took me on a tour of the canals, and the early Gehry surf beach house – timber before titanium – and we talked about life and postmodern socialism.

In 1997 I was invited to deliver lectures on Antipodean modernity in Brazil, in São Paulo, a city of a kind I had never seen before – almost as much concrete as a contemporary Chinese city. There were many fine minds here, not least those of alternative thinkers such as Vandana Shiva and Boaventura de Sousa Santos. I was advised on enquiry that my lectures should last for three hours, which seemed excessive until I worked out that the audience kept disappearing for coffee and cigarettes. This was a circulation, of elites and ideas and others. The lectures were revolving affairs. I visited Buenos Aires, stunned, per the good advice of Ephraim Nimni. The place was more beautiful than Paris, and had a different, edgy kind of vibe. I had bought an Argentinian, or Chinese, suit for my final gig, an event sponsored by the Harvard chair of Australian studies at Cambridge, Massachusetts. I spent several days in Boston, and renewed my friendship with the great past Labor prime minister Gough Whitlam, who was charmingly avuncular to me. Only as events came to a close was I slipped, under the table, a business card that congratulated me: I was to be offered the chair for the cycle 1999–2000. I couldn't believe my luck. When the poet Chris Wallace Crabbe called me back home to inform me, I had to ask him to tell me twice. He told me twice on the phone, and then wrote me the finest love letter: a poem, whose closing lines often return: 'Goodbye, Peter, see you soon/I'm off to the cricket this afternoon.' He is a good shepherd.

Occasionally the planners of the ASA convention would direct their 6,000 annual participants north, across the border to Canada. 1997 also took me to Toronto, where I met with the German sociologist Claus Offe, and even momentarily took on his identity when he lent me his name badge in order to gain access via security. I enjoyed being Claus Offe for a day, but I doubt if much of the brainpower of his kind of critical theory rubbed off. I walked some, escaped the venue and met up with Leo Panitch, editor of *Socialist Register*, where I had published on the Australian left a decade earlier per Ralph Miliband. My other big opening in 1997 was across the Tasman. For some time I had been convinced that the Antipodes should be manoeuvred together, intellectually – that to understand Australia you needed to understand Aotearoa/New Zealand, and vice versa. Historically, this was one big labour market and field for cultural traffic and social reform.[8] The social laboratory that had drawn streams of social democratic visitors from the north a century earlier was a shared enterprise. Given the Big Brother complex, however, it now proved difficult to find willing collaborators across the ditch. There had in the meantime arrived a parting of the ways, and toxic new nationalisms, which drove Australia and New Zealand apart. At this point I was asked to review the sociology programme at Auckland University by Ian Carter. This opened a new chapter of personal discovery for me, along with the dawning sense that, although these stories needed to be told together, they were also different. The patterns of local modernism were distinct, including a strong sense of Taranaki Gothic together with Kiwi Bauhaus, and at least as bicultural as multicultural. My Antipodes were indeed distinct.

In 1998 the ASA proceedings took place in San Francisco, a distance from New Zealand yet continuous in horizon as a volcanic harbour city of the Pacific. Not so much was left, in any case, from the 'Summer of Love'; the doors of perception were long since closed, but City Lights still shone. I travelled to Tokyo to join in an event on the subaltern with Tessa Morris Suzuki, and with postcolonial thinkers such as Dipesh Chakrabarty, Naoki Sakai, Sanjay Seth and Raj Pandey. It was a profound experience, as in São Paulo and Mexico City, a combination of exhilaration and alienation: Shinjuku, the main drag – another modernity altogether. I had been

---

8 See P. Beilharz, *Thinking the Antipodes: Australian Essays* (Clayton: Monash University Press, 2014).

to Tokyo before, but still found the culture at the same time intriguing and impenetrable. In 1998 I also organized a *Thesis Eleven* section for the International Sociological Association (ISA) congress in Montreal, working together with Alexander, Calhoun, Hans Joas, Johann Arnason and Alain Touraine on the topic 'uncertain democracy'. We seemed to be ahead of the game. It was, as the Australian Jake Najman said to me afterwards, a triumph, and it pointed on to the ISA meeting in Brisbane, where we would all of us meet again. But not Bauman, who eschewed this institutional scene, and was able to, as he was already a celebrity, and was always a loner. The only professional organization I ever heard him enthuse about was the European Sociological Association, which was smaller and closer to his own sense of belonging – a promise, rather than an institution or a regime.

What had I learned, after this decade? Its aura may in retrospect seem to be one of frenzy, endless busyness, with opportunities to grow and learn, to work and collaborate, to build friendships both with Bauman and others, especially on both sides of the Atlantic from the distance of the Antipodes. These processes came together, associated freely in my mind, to the extent that I can no longer easily analytically separate them. I had not gone out looking for friends, yet travel, the other, these worlds big and small, all fused together for me. There was energy and possibilities to burn – or, at least, it seemed so then. There were what felt like constantly expanding horizons, encountered together with the senses of continuity that came from a strong sense of coming from Marxism and its kindred traditions as critical theory. Yet this was also, of course, just some other version of beginning.

Chapter 2

Second decade

The decade opened with promise, as well as Y2K angst. I took up the Harvard chair in the middle of 1999, and we saw in the millennium in Cambridge. This was a cusp, from 1999 into 2000: interesting times. The Harvard chair of Australian studies has a magical aura for Australian scholars, even if it is essentially a majestic teaching gig. I taught three courses, one more than the standard two, and spent a great deal of time either in the Widener Library or else sick. Likely overwork finally caught up with me. Something in me let go, or broke down. Every other week I was in the Harvard Medical Centre. Although my levels of busyness remained, the pressures were different away from home, in this academic paradise, where the culture of trust was still intact. Ivy League; another world. There was no monitoring or performance measurement; you were left to do your work. There was no sniping or bullying that I saw. Everybody was too busy working. So I did my work, and a great deal besides. We explored, wide and far. Our children, Nikolai and Rhea, went to school, and Dor, my first wife, was the minder and scout. They were challenging but happy days.

There was much activity at Harvard, which also acted as a hub for journeys out, away from the riches of that bubble on the Charles River. I was invited to Ottawa, to be hosted by Kim Nossal and my student Fuyuki Kurasawa. It was cold. Cars were plugged into car park heating devices overnight so they did not freeze up. Not in Australia. I flew to Kentucky for the first conference of the International Consortium of

Social Theory, where Mark Poster was the star, and went with my family to Arkansas for Henderson State University's big event on Australia and New Zealand. We drove via Little Rock. Ross Terrill brought us to Austin, blues on every corner, and Desley Deacon and John Higley took us to dance at Hot Springs (we were unable to find Robert Johnson, though we did stay in Al Capone's hotel). I gave a paper at the ASA meeting in 2000, in Washington, DC, on Bauman's modernity. Nobody came. Libby Schweber became a good Harvard friend. She was the only sociologist I came upon around Cambridge who cared about Bauman enough to teach his work there. Maybe Bauman's indifference was reciprocated. Libby invited me to give a paper to the Social Studies Colloquium at Harvard. That was better attended; even her pop came along. I found most interest with older, or younger, folks. There were super-smart young folk who could turn the box labelled 'Sociology' upside down in order to see what might fall out. They were smart; the elders were curious. Schweber Senior also wanted to talk about Mr Bauman, though as I recall he was himself a scientist. I regret this, as I failed to learn more about Mr Schweber. He insisted on taking me out to lobster dinner so we could talk Bauman. It was all grist to the mill. What, after all, was the fuss about Bauman? What was it that made him a person of interest?

Together with Trevor Hogan I went to visit with Frank and Fritzie Manuel, master scholars of utopia.[1] Claudio Veliz, my past professor from La Trobe, took me into the culture of the Professors Program at Boston University, one of those wonderful places where students are challenged laterally by exposure to the sharpest minds of the best teachers first up. Moral (long gone from many universities): use your senior staff at first year!! I developed friendships with Dan Bell, Bernard Bailyn, Orlando Patterson, Patrice Higonnet, Nathan Glazer and others, all of whom wanted to talk about Bauman, for my book, *Zygmunt Bauman: Dialectic of Modernity*, arrived in time for Christmas, and my *Bauman Reader* arrived soon afterwards, making it as a Harvard Bookstore Bestseller

---

1 See F. Manuel and F. Manuel, *Utopian Thought in the Western World* (Oxford: Blackwell, 1979).

(I think the data was cooked; this was a blip, though the *Reader* did get around). In these books my purpose was to help profile the diversity of Bauman's work, and the work that had already been forgotten, from the beginning of his career in Leeds. In Cambridge, as elsewhere in my

2 Bauman at the lectern.

experience, interest in Bauman was first of all in the Holocaust, then in the postmodern. Likely there was a broader academic impatience with Bauman, who was difficult to apply, or to operationalize. Where was the toolkit? I was hoping also to expand the canvas, and to keep the themes of culture and socialism present, to argue for the diversity of themes and interests in his work. For a big machine such as American sociology, it was, necessarily, a matter of business as usual.

Harvard was an astonishing experience, in every regard. I taught about socialism and sociology, about public intellectuals and about Australian modernity. For one class on socialism I took my students to the Houghton, where we together gloved up to look at Bellamy, Trotsky and other archival treats. Saffin would have been smiling. Archives! The final paper for my Australia course was fun. I took along the draft of Stuart Macintyre's concise history of Australia, which we used with his consent as a text. The final paper involved the requirement that students write the missing conclusion. I then bundled them up, and sent them to Stuart in return for his gift to us. I remained uncertain as to what kind of effect this kind of teaching had. Most of my students at Harvard were happy to presume that Australia was just like the United States, only smaller and a bit slower. Not a bad start to understanding, but there remains a bit more to it.

There were many other lessons to be learned, for me. Rich as the departmental or disciplinary culture of Harvard could be, I found myself attracted to the centres that bridged across them. I joined in events of the European Studies Centre and the W. E. B. DuBois Centre, and observed the energy that could come of voluntary association rather than the appointment of individuals to professional academic units that they then feel impelled to defend. Iain McCalman at the ANU had already suggested to me that the *Thesis Eleven* journal was the ideal platform for a centre. So another result from my Harvard sojourn was the establishment of the Thesis Eleven Centre at La Trobe, in 2002. Its achievements were extraordinary, at home and away. For some 20 years, from 1980 to 2001, the journal had acted, as Antonio Gramsci had insisted, as a platform for intellectual organization. From 2002 the Centre had some university budget, and by now a fine web of friends and colleagues spread around the world. As the journal had developed an import/export strategy for ideas, so the Centre brought thinkers in and out of Australia. We came to understand that the limits of academic networking included the politics of the revolving door. Routinely academic visitors would be expected to deliver their two hours and then be ignored, left in their hotel rooms before returning to the airport. This was to waste resources, capacity and humanity. There was so much to be learned.

This is not the place to assess the project or the proper achievement of *Thesis Eleven*. George Steinmetz surveyed the first 25 years of the journal for our 100th issue in 2001.[2] I outlined some of its human achievements in conversation with Craig Calhoun in 2017, available on our webpage, thesiseleven.com. We put a premium on this task, also to connect, to matchmake, to connect up younger with established folks, and so on. Much of this worked on the level of friendship, or resulted in friendships. It made of *Thesis Eleven* a little public sphere, an independent zone working first within the university system and then alongside and in collaboration with it, but free of its more toxic symptoms, and outside the more bizarre developments that came to characterize the university system across these times.

We developed a routine of sharing our visitors with interesting locales of different kinds, sharing our city and getting them out of town, to see nature, music, art, geography, geology, food cultures. All this was based on high levels of trust and friendship. If you took on visitors in this way they would also work with postgraduates, share ideas and interests, dance and laugh as well as walk and talk. Walking would become a primary medium of this engagement. And they would walk back. All this activity worked on the simple premise that the common culture needed to be exercised through the cultivation of ideas and the friendships that made them possible. Process was at least as important as content. Left to itself, academic culture is typically anomic, given to policing, to symbolic violence and self-promotion. It is a perfect field for what Bauman and his peers, Beck and Giddens, were later to problematize as individualization.

2 See G. Steinmetz, 'Thirty Years of Thesis Eleven', *Thesis Eleven*, 100 (2001).

Team and culture building happen only when individuals are able to opt into different kinds of cooperation. This involves a willingness to come out of your foxhole. But this takes a great deal of effort, given that the professional culture into which academics are trained and inserted is saturated with narcissism and resentment, and that, increasingly, academics are too afraid, too jealous and too busy to be able easily to cooperate.

So I learned a lot at Harvard, directly and osmotically. Equally profound was the travel experience we were afforded to and from Harvard. We returned the long way home locally, by Amtrak and Greyhound, an experience in itself, given that these once popular means of travel had by now become the transport conveyances of the poor and infirm. Our travels took in New Orleans, DC, New York and Charlottesville, where I threw a kidney stone, the cost of which would have sent us into irreversible debt were it not for Harvard's health insurance. I now understood why my younger American academic acquaintances would never ask about salary, but more often would ask if you had insurance. I always had a task trying to explain that, in Australia, we had standard pay rates and a union, as well as a national system of health insurance. We continued on through Baltimore, which despite its pomo harbour dress-up, felt like a place under siege, Vegas and LA. The family vox pop vote was New Orleans five, Vegas zero, though staying in the ass of the Sphinx hotel on the strip generated some family mirth, as did participation in the contest of 'All you can eat'. There were scuffles among the punters waiting on line, which seemed quite absurd amidst this excess of *bain marie'd* abundance. This was life straight out of the Simpsons. There was so much food that people were anxious about missing out. Abundance resulted in anxiety. This was utopia in reverse.

Even more challenging, perhaps, was the trip out to Harvard in order to begin in the first place. This was the first serious opportunity my family had had to travel together. My parents had been obliged to travel, in the 1940s, but that is another story. So we began where they had begun in the 1920s, in Germany. Although my parents were German, I had to this point spent my life in denial, and in the Antipodes. My first port of call, on my first trip out, when I was 26, was Paris, centre of Marxist theoretical culture. Fond as I was of Marx and critical theory, I could not come at Germany at all. Even though I had family and tradition with me, Germany meant only one thing, or at least One Big Thing: Nazism. The problem was still there on first encounters. As we visited these charming little villages I could still hallucinate the ghosts in brown shirts and the swastika flags flapping in the squares. Maybe I had watched too many movies, for there is so much in the visual field of Hitler, later, so much less of Stalin or Mao. In any case, although people like me harboured fantasies about what Bauman had called the active utopia of socialism, we also carried the fear of the active dystopia: fascism. The first book I bought in my first year of college, even before Marx, was an anthology on fascism. I understood its importance, but not how it worked, let alone my own responsibility for it – or not. These, like my German relatives, however, were my people, or the people of my people. I do not recall any particular sense of tipping point, but there, in my forty-sixth year, we were. I wanted my family to see Leeds and Lawnswood Gardens, to meet these people who had come to mean so much to me, and it somehow now seemed right to seize the time with my German past. Perhaps, unlike Bauman, I still needed to blame these people, my people, the Germans, for the tragedies of the twentieth century. Perhaps I was still working with excessively simple distinctions between victims and perpetrators, A and B. In any case, it became apparent enough to me on first contact that they also had their share of historic suffering, and that I needed to work at reducing the immense moral condescension of posterity.

My folks are in the south-west. So, full of absolute hospitality, they bounced the Australians on tour around Stuttgart, Gmund, Ulm and the surrounds, Deckenpfronn and Lorch, and we took ourselves to Frankfurt, Munich and Berlin by train. I began to achieve a different sense of the damage that had also been wrought upon the local people. Deckenpfronn, for example, had, we were told, been firebombed in those last, crazy, supersenseless days of the war. These were, of course, stories I knew about from reading, W. G. Sebald and so on. To visit the town cemetery was another thing. There was a large-scale floor map, a flattened sculpture of all the homes in the little town, and the names of those who had helplessly perished in flames hiding in cellars and cupboards. You could only look, and mourn. In Berlin, the site of Hitler's own deep ambivalence, Claus Offe hosted us, and vacated his apartment in the Prenzlauer Berg for the four of us. He was my kind of critical theorist, never losing sight of political economy and the state as well as culture, always a step ahead, and also a keen advocate of Bauman, as for Bauman's successful nomination to the Adorno Prize. Berlin was then that uncanny mix of building cranes, dusty Marxist monuments and its other many pasts. There were more ghosts on the street corners, and a contempt for tourists not unlike that which you can encounter in Manhattan. I came to like Germany, or at least to accept that part of my psyche that is connected to it through my parents, and to reassess its triumphs alongside its tragedies.

From Frankfurt we flew to London, to stay with Michele and frogmarch our children through the obligatory tourist experiences of empire. Then we took a train to Leeds.

The Baumans had also insisted that we stay, all four of us. They greeted us, beaming, at the forest that fronted their home in Lawnswood Gardens. Some of the story is told in the memory capsule of my paper 'Bauman's Coat', written for the second volume of Keith Tester and Michael Hviid Jacobsen's forensic on *Bauman beyond Postmodernity* (2007). It reads as follows:

What is the project of Zygmunt Bauman? Many things. As his interpreter, among others, I have sought to characterise it variously as a critique of modernity, as a critique of order, as a Weberian kind of Marxism, an East European critical theory, as a sociology of surplus populations, and so on. I remain attracted to the idea that its outside contours are those of a sociology of excess. Modernity is excess; socialism was excessive, especially in its giganticist, Faustian ambitions, rebuilding the world of nature as well as the social; capitalism is excessive in its gargantuan appetite for labour, for endless growth, for sales, for exploitation in its protean drive to consume, to consume us and the planet as we consume it and especially those less fortunate than us, at home and afar. The critique of excess is a critique of waste, of human waste, of wasted lives.

It suggests the desirability of a measured life, where balance matters, where life is framed by a sense of limits and modesty is a priority.

It suggests an intellectual orientation to the world in which we are interpreters and critics, recyclers rather than gurus or celebrities. It has been a great source of pleasure and inspiration for me personally to be able to discover that in Bauman's case the text message and the everyday example are consonant. Bauman lives a simple life, in Leeds, in the same place with the same companion, Janina, over the decades. In a world he now calls 'liquid modernity', some things persist. Few things persist like their relationship. Wherever he goes, there will she be.

The only apparent excess in this domestic picture, sedate between their travels, punctuated by the frenzy of writing, is the legendary excess of hospitality shown to those who visit Lawnswood Gardens in Leeds. Giganticism occurs in this world only at the dinner table. English breakfast; coffee mid-morning. Scotch at noon, three four mounted courses, red wine, Australian if I can find it on my way in from the railway station. Sleep, restoration, walk, evening meal, delicatessen, or game, something grand for visitors, more booze. The conversation flows at the same rate. Generosity and hospitality abound; curiosity about the stories that the traveller brings, reports on family and passing encounters, good wishes to carry back to others, everyday chatter itself profound, telling, anecdotal, proverbial. Talk goes on for hours, with walk, at table, travelling in the car, in the wingchairs of the sitting room. It moves easily from the most abstract to the most intimate, the most commonplace to the most detailed. Its wisdoms are little, and local, and not only global or cosmopolitan. Oftentimes it is the smallest curiosities that call out the greatest insight. It is as though I enter another world, the world of my others, as their guest and momentary legatee.

Bauman's autobiography and mine are full of shared intellectual resonances, but not life experience. In his eighties, the life experience of my parents is closer to his. But there is more. An anti-Semitism I have never suffered, as a gentile. Exile, repeatedly, from Poland to the Soviet Union; back to Poland, in the army, reconstruction; dismissal, personal reconstruction as a sociologist, dismissal again, exile, Leeds, belated recognition. My path of life, in contrast, has been as smooth as that of my generation, born into the fifties. No scarcity, except relative; no ultimatum, to move on, to be ready to travel by the morrow; rather a series of opening doors, even from modest origins, leading of all places to the privileged land of the professoriate.

Plainly we had one thing in common: gifted and dedicated teachers, those who could both instruct, direct and inspire and yet encourage. If this happens to you, as a student of fortune, there is perhaps a moral obligation, a sense of duty to do the same, to pass it on. But more, Bauman and I (at least on his account) seem somehow to share something of modernity's civilizational legacies via the life of the mind. As a child of the sixties, I had been to utopia in my mind, in the library. And this is where I met the person called Zygmunt Bauman, in the book he called *Socialism: The Active Utopia*. Through the journal *Thesis Eleven* which we had founded in Melbourne in 1980, a line went out between us. Australia had its share of the East European diaspora in critical theory. It was a blessed moment. Bauman had visited us in 1970, and again in 1982; the Budapest School in exile arrived in 1978. There was a sense of something in common, even across these significant gaps in life experience and location. Teachers and students can pick each other, even across cultures, when they are thrown together by accidents of world history.

Bauman's excessive hospitality has something to do with his life experience of scarcity. Deprivation can encourage mean-mindedness, or its opposite. In Bauman's case, I have never known anything other than the most indulgent kind of generosity. But there is more, a sense of connecting, of willingness to connect, that you can see in Zygmunt's eyes, and in Janina's.

When I was able to finish the project that opened my eyes, the book which became *Labour's Utopias*, we asked Bauman to recommend it. At this point I think we may have met once. And so he wrote, for the cover of my book:

> This is a book that should be read, re-read and kept handy for future consultation. Its value will grow over the years, quite the contrary to most current, hastily-written and ill-judged 'obituaries' of socialism. Beilharz has produced a profound, thoroughly researched study of labour utopias … This is a monument to human hope.

> I still draw breath reading this. It's not the book I had written; the quotation is better than the book. It would serve better as a description of his own book *Socialism: The Active Utopia*. Applied to my book, this is an indication

of Bauman's excess. Incredible generosity, and that hermeneutic trick that reads for gain rather than to reject or defeat. More, it reflected our sympathies, Bauman's own fondness for the land of Marx's final exile, its labour culture and its earlier utopian hopes. Leeds was a fitting place for him to remain, even as Europe, East and West, became his travel agenda and audience.

So it became a ritual for me to visit Leeds, annually, where I would be fattened up with food, drink and ideas, but also enjoy the company of just being, sitting in silence, watching films together, drinking in the pub after walking, never feeling that I had to perform even when there were serious things I needed to discuss.

There were comical, and bracing moments, as when the Antipodean visitor travelling for summer was caught short without a coat, as we went out to walk in the hills over Otley. Kitted out in Bauman's coat, the experience was ordinary and sublime at the same time. Small change, a paper clip in the pockets of this coat drawn warm about me; a view, and wind and a story about arrival in these parts, all bracing. It reminded me of another story, of Marshall Sahlins' coat. Sahlins was visiting Canberra in winter for an event in honour of Bernard Smith. This was the place the Baumans had seen in the extremes of summer. At a book launch his overcoat disappeared, favourite pen, notes, other things on board. Before the week's proceedings had expired, it showed up again. The anthropologists thought that perhaps someone had been cold, or short-sighted, and taken it in mistake. My guess was that someone hoped rather to borrow it for the magic to wear off, to steal the aura rather than the cloak itself. As for me, god only knows what's rubbed off. Affection, inspiration, friendship given of accident, of the accidental encounter of life beyond. I needed then to share it around.

When my family visited Leeds, ensemble in 1999, it was like a kind of home-coming, as though we had known and understood each other for much longer. When we asked advice for our further travels in Yorkshire, Bauman came into the room beaming, bringing the now ragged maps with which his family had navigated their new habitat into the days of settlement in the seventies. We left sad to go, full of instructions for Whitby and Wensleydale, the moors and further afar, with a sense of love conveyed for this countryside and its openness, with pre-cut lunches sufficient for a small army, and with a sense of joyous sorrow. As it came time for us to head off, Bauman sat us all in the kitchen, four of us, two of them, and told us that we should sit together thus in silence for five minutes, and then leave in silence. This meant that we would see each other again. I was too moved to ask whence this ritual came, if it was Jewish, Polish, or incidental. Anyway, I was bidden to silence by a man whose wisdom I defer to. We departed with wet eyes, and a sense of great good fortune, that it should have been possible across generations and continents to encounter a friendship such as this, one from which I could learn so much that I will never be able properly to articulate its results or forms. But there are words that do not need to be spoken.[3]

This piece was first published in 2007. It was the only time I can remember Bauman reprimanding me, for publishing this glimpse of his private sphere in a life that was, indeed, so intensely private. Bauman did not want to be a celebrity. He did not want the details of his private life to be shared. He failed the photogenic TV persona test, was hopeless at the ten second grab, and he insisted on his privacy, which I had breached. He stopped me on the stair at Lawnswood Gardens: 'Don't do it again!' he admonished me. Yet I felt compelled to share, for all this immense humanity, and I received messages from others, such as the Norwegian philosopher Arne Johan Vetlesen, who could see the Bauman they knew in what I had written, and were pleased to see this humanity celebrated. If Bauman was to become a celebrity, he was to be an unwilling one. In an academic world where self-promotion is now a standard entrance requirement, this was a rare thing. He was a modest man.

We explored the neighbourhood together with the Baumans: the Adel Church that Janina was so fond of, the local parks and gardens, the local pubs, the cemetery just up the road, the Otley Hills, the Corn Exchange and canals. We drove out, to Huddersfield, to Harrogate, to Harewood, to Whitby, for Bauman understood the historic connection to Australia. We met Dracula on the cliffs there – which scared the hell out of our children – and watched the local seniors turning a charm in the waltz in the old community hall, sandwiches and tea urns beckoning. We went on to the historic armoury museum in Leeds (he would not go in; we did not go in, but ended up, rather, in the car park, discussing willing executioners).

---

3 P. Beilharz, 'Bauman's Coat', in M. Jacobsen, S. Marshman and K. Tester (eds), *Bauman beyond Postmodernity: Critical Appraisals, Conversations and Annotated Bibliography 1989–2005* (Aalborg: Aalborg University Press, 2007).

Bauman drove like a German, wringing breathtaking acceleration from a small Nissan Micra. He explained to us that most road accidents occurred when drivers went too slowly. Solution: accelerate! He also used to insist that he was the living proof that smoking tobacco did not kill. Professional sociologists would have been mortified, rushing for the data. There was always a touch of the contrarian to his ways. A straight face, with a hint of smirk behind. In a world that failed to wear truth on its sleeve, irony was his friend.

My family moved on, to Cambridge, Massachusetts, where copies of *Dialectic of Modernity* arrived as my Christmas gift, and Dor and I read the proofs for *The Bauman Reader* sitting on the stairs of our apartment at Mather Hall, reading out aloud, trusting two sets of eyes rather than one. In November 1999 Chris Rojek invited me to edit a boxed set on the existing work on Bauman for Sage. Bauman's response to this news was predictable: 'You want to put me in a box!' The spectre of mortality was always there; he had survived so much already. I had plans for another book on Bauman, whose working title was something like *Bauman And*, for I remained intrigued by the cast of thousands of thinkers who paraded through his work. I had come to argue that his work was conversational, so that the question of interlocutors became ever more important. The idea was unable to find a publisher, as was a plan for *A Companion to Bauman*. These were, apparently, still early days for the Bauman industry. And the book proposals were coming from Australia, of all places, though perhaps it helped when for a year they came on Harvard letterhead. Rojek was different; he had already worked out that good things might come from the Antipodes, and was actively recruiting authors from Australia and New Zealand. After the flight of left-wing academics from Thatcher's Britain to Australia's New Labor, connections became more open than earlier tradition had allowed.

Back home, I returned to my new professorial office at La Trobe. This was *serious*. The room was due for a remake, for new décor, and there was a budget. With Mary Reilly I worked out a plan that took as its inspiration the painting by Lydia Bauman that we had been able to use for my book cover. I had the poster she gave me framed, in turquoise, which seemed to bring out the colours of her painting of *Flax Fields in France*. Mary, our social sciences admin officer, who also had a soft spot for Gmund, and I together chose the furniture coverings and carpet to match, and I had on the wall the photos that Bauman was later to take of my son and me in Leeds. It was a great room. My colleagues would borrow it if there was a TV crew, as there was for me with John Hipwell and Nick Bolger for the BBC, or for larger meetings. It was big enough for planning sessions and small seminars. Folk would come by to chat or to borrow books or ideas. Now it is subdivided into small boxes in the pursuit of higher product-ivity ratings.

I continued to work on the possibility of bringing the Baumans to Australia; they had been twice before, in 1970 and in 1982. I missed both these events. In 1970 I was still in high school, distracted by girls and rock music, not yet ready to receive Marxism or critical theory. From 1982 I was chained to the teaching wheel at the Phillip Institute of Technology, where the weekly load was 16 hours, teaching across five courses and trying to bring my dissertation to a close, so I missed Bauman's presen-tation at La Trobe, even though it was just 20 minutes up the road. In 1982 Bauman had returned to the ANU as a visitor to the Humanities Research Centre, which offered an astonishingly rich intellectual cul-ture to visitors from near and far. Bauman and Janina spent the months from July to September 1982 in Canberra, his project being recorded as work on 'Objectively grounded interpretation', though his fields were listed in the *ANU Reporter* for 23 July 1982 as sociology of culture and social theory. This was evidently still Bauman before Bauman. We were waiting for polyvalence. Amusingly, however, his stay overlapped with that of Richard Rorty, whose project was to work on Heidegger and prag-matism. We do not know what contact there was between Bauman and Rorty, though the latter became more than a byway for the Pole. What we do know is that Rorty became a local hero for adopting an orphaned baby wombat, christened Rainy (research topic: not Kant and the platypus; Rorty and the wombat. Damascus?). There are no such folk stories concerning Bauman in Canberra, though he did become attached to the place and always spoke fondly of it.

I began to try to secure a Bauman visit to Australia from 1994. Early plans involved fabricating support and garnering funds across Melbourne, Sydney, Adelaide and Canberra. First attempts foundered on budget. In 2002 the La Trobe vice chancellor, Michael Osborne, volunteered the idea of a hop-trip to Australia, which would allow the Baumans to break up their trip and, most importantly, to stop in order to smoke. Long-haul flights were difficult for the Baumans for many reasons, but most especially because they would be prevented from smoking. Bauman's email response to me, 25 July, carries the title 'Bauman's speechlessness'. But it was not to be. Already at this point the Baumans were resisting long-haul flights, preferring to fly within Europe from Leeds via Schiphol, where you could smoke with others in the stigma of a sealed Perspex box. Three hours in the air was the max they set themselves. Melbourne would take closer to a day in the sky, and the trip could leave you lagged for a week.

Even when I first began to visit Leeds, there were constant invitations to travel and speak that poured daily into the wire mailbox on the Lawnswood Gardens front door. The couple would set aside a day, I think, per week to consider and decide the offers. It kept them alive, engaged, and, at least for this earlier period of our contact, dictated Bauman's work schedule. He would write lectures, which would turn into essays and sometimes books, rising at 5:30 to type until noon, with a break for coffee and to cook me what he called 'English breakfast'. He would get a day's work in before noon, and then do other things. From the moment we met he was urging me to retire, as did Bernard Smith. The prospect of retirement included the possibility of writing more freely, and without the encumbrance of looking sideways at your colleagues or upwards at Big Brother. Yet retirement was also a major ritual, the last major life step of the privileged before death. My correspondence file makes it clear that concerns about longevity were active for Bauman from around 1999. Bauman was one of the few sociologists to have written a book about death, *Mortality, Immortality and Other Life Strategies*, in 1992. Once when I asked he told me that this was his best book, his favourite child. Perhaps the status of favourite depended on its being unloved by others. It remains a fine book, and a significant gesture within the field of sociology. Its meaning was also subliminal. He was keen to do anything he could to push death away, but he also understood that it routinely chooses us, rather than the other way around.

Bauman, of course, played games with me, and with himself. When I came to visit regularly he would each year give me the manuscript of the latest book, saying to me: 'Here it is, my last book.' This was not just play. On 6 March 1999 he wrote to me that he was unsure as to whether he would be round long enough to finish *Liquid Modernity*. Mortality was on the map for a long time, even after what Bauman had survived during the war: scurvy, terrible cold, hunger and deprivation – mortal uncertainty on a daily basis. Bauman was always waiting for death.

Barely home from my travels, I skipped the ASA meeting in order to join in the Castoriadis celebratory event on Crete in 2000, giving a paper on 'Bauman and Castoriadis: An Exchange of Sympathies', travelling home via London and Leeds. It may be a conceit, but it is possible that Bauman's late interest in Castoriadis was triggered by such connections or attempts at matchmaking. Bauman's interest in Castoriadis seems to have arrived around 1997. Whether causal or not, this was the year David Curtis had published his *Castoriadis Reader*. I had alerted Bauman to the fact, and asked Castoriadis to send him a copy, which he did. Bauman wrote to me, with thanks: 'What do you want me to do with it?' We were hoping that he might review it in a prominent place, such as the *Times Literary Supplement* (*TLS*), where he had published reviews earlier. Believe it or not, in these times Castoriadis also had trouble securing a reading away from home. Bauman wrote to me on 3 June 1997 that he had missed the magnum opus, *The Imaginary Institution of Society* (1975). Bauman came late to Castoriadis – at least, later than we in Melbourne had, via the translations of the London Solidarity Group in the middle 1970s. Sometimes the English Channel could be broader than the oceans. The *Reader* arrived in Leeds on 27 July 1997. Bauman was later to confess his own love of Castoriadis; but he died prematurely, on 26 December 1997. His presence in Bauman's work was to become a perennial. They were never to meet, despite my attempts at connection. Who knows what might have come of this? I could imagine Bauman and Heller in the same room; I am less sure how Bauman and Castoriadis might have got on, though that Scotch would have helped (for Castoriadis, Chivas).

In Leeds in 2002 Bauman and I engaged in project development work on the box set and we shared a local public event at Leeds Metropolitan, the first time I heard him lecture. He was in fine form; a few notes in a small black pocketbook; 'Ladies and gentlemen' as a circular refrain ... and this was before his hearing had seriously declined. As it later deteriorated further, Bauman developed the charming mannerism of approaching individuals in his audience very closely, so that those with questions or comments might speak directly into his cupped ear. Lately I notice myself doing the same; perhaps it is mimetic. I follow.

I gave a paper at the ISTC event at Sussex on 'Bauman and the Black Book of Communism', a version of which was later to appear as 'The Other Totalitarianism' (2002). The International Social Theory Consortium was a noble attempt to begin again, to bring together the strays who wanted to work outside the big professional organizations such as the ASA and BSA, and to argue until the cows came home. Would Bauman have approved? Probably, though after his time in socialist Poland he was never a joiner. He enjoyed his solitude; and he had the comfort of knowing that those who were interested would come to him, as I did. As Bauman was some-times given to saying to me, it seemed that, at my best, I could read his mind. The meeting in Sussex was an auspicious moment, for it was the moment when I got to know Keith Tester better. Bauman had matchmade us as a couple in Leeds; and I now realize, belatedly, that a good deal of my activity in culture building involves matchmaking, sharing, passing it on. Bauman had brought us together at Lawnswood Gardens, intro-ducing me to Keith as his Antipodean brother. Ours was to become a valued friendship, partly, I suspect, because it was never poisoned by the toxins of competition or jealousy. We had curiosity in common, but nei-ther of us needed monopoly rights on our teacher. In different ways, nei-ther Keith nor I ever felt that we quite belonged in this professionalized world of self-advancement. Keith and I thought in similar ways, but with differing sensibilities and curiosities. Our respective curiosities about the big world were certainly different; he was at home in his province, around

Sussex, and I was inclined to spend more time out. Although we were close, his premature death in 2019 makes me wonder if I ever really knew him at all. I suppose that I did, but only the part he wanted to share with me, which was often mediated by our mutual relationship to the chief, Zygmunt Bauman himself. My relationship with Keith was direct, but there was always the elephant in the room.

I visited Bauman's daughter, Lydia, who was working as the artist in residence at Lincoln Cathedral. I felt a close bond to her for many years. There seemed to be something special between us, some unspoken understanding of a similar kind to that which I had with her father. This is the ineffable, easy air of friendship when you simply somehow know that you belong, are truly welcome.

In 2001 I gave a paper on Bauman at the ASA proceedings in Anaheim, resisting the easier temptations of Disney. Leo Walford from Sage took me out of town to eat serious Mexican. The evening was fine, but when it was time to return to the tourist sector the cabs had disappeared, or else perhaps they never came this far out. The genial restaurant owner sent us home in the back of his brother's flatbed truck, refusing payment. This was life in a B grade movie. I travelled on via Cambridge to stay again with Libby Schweber. I went on to present a paper on Bauman for Harald Welzer, who I had met at Lawnswood Gardens as he was interviewing Bauman, in Essen via Hanover and Hamburg. In Hamburg, through Bauman, I met Uli Bielefeld and the folks of the Hamburg Institute for Critical Theory. (When I asked Bauman who his Germans were, he said I have only hamburgers! He did not feel well exposed in Germany, and referred poignantly to France as his unrequited love affair.) Finally I visited Marx's home town of Trier, where I did some historic field-work, learned about the Rhine and Rome, and gave a paper on 'Australia as an Alternative Modernity'. One of the postgraduates in the seminar understood it perfectly. The days of the social laboratory, of Australia and New Zealand as innovators in the social policy of protection were gone; Australia and New Zealand were still pioneers, but now of New Labour. As this young man put it, in that charmingly formal English of the Germans, Australia was once an alternative modernity, but this was no longer the case. It was a view that Bauman would have endorsed. Around this time, when Bauman asked me what I was working on, I explained that I was writing about the peculiar path of Australian modernity. But no, he said to me, this is the same global story as everywhere else. It remained a difference between us, the means of arriving at conclusions, even if the conclusions were the same or similar. I had been raised by historians, and brought on by comparativists, who were also inductive in approach, and given to notions such as historic specificity or later, path dependence, in which global trends are mediated through local cultures and traditions. Difference always needed to be mediated against similarity.

In 2002 I returned to Harvard to act as William Dean Howells Fellow in American literature 1880–1920, in order to conduct research on the work of Edward Bellamy at the Houghton Archive. I took my first trip to Warsaw via Leeds, visiting with Jacek Lewinson, the nephew of Janina Bauman, then to Prague and to Budapest to visit with Ágnes Heller and her son Yuri and his family. Seeing the Palace of Culture in Warsaw was a revelation into the power and shame of Stalinism. Brutalism took on a new meaning when you stood in front of this edifice. The ASA meeting was in Chicago, where the architecture was monumentalist rather than brutalist, but the city again was profoundly European in its formative urban cast and peoples. And it was *Black Metropolis*, and so much more. Chicago and Boston became my favourite US cities. I worked daily at the Houghton Library for some weeks, leaving our digs early while my teenage daughter slept in and then caught up with the friends she had made in 1999/2000. A year after 9/11 Rhea and I flew together on a small plane to Charlottesville; Logan Airport was empty, as though it was some kind of jinx day. The atmosphere was eerie. The flights were uneventful, the atmosphere calm, and it was good to arrive in Virginia. I gave a paper on Bauman for Krishan Kumar, and we hiked in the Shenandoah Valley with Krishan and his partner, Katya Makarova. My daughter spotted a baby bear up a tree. 'Cute!' she exclaimed. 'Run!' yipped I. We ran, though it occurred to me later that mama bears are also likely good at running. Whatever the case, this was not the outback of Australia, where even the fiercest of animals often run in the opposite direction.

It will be apparent that all this work took me away from my family. There is now no way I can make that good, though I think it is true to say that my children were serious beneficiaries of that year in Harvard and of the wider world I had entered into – not too much for them, but enough of a challenge to help call them out into a world much bigger than the one that I had grown up in at the foot of the Dandenongs. I had to learn to be brave by myself, when I began to travel, and it terrified me. In the beginning I was always waiting for the plane to fall out of the sky, or else to be mugged in these big cities. Travel for my children is so much easier, second nature. So Rhea came with me in 2002, and Nikolai, her elder, joined me to travel in his gap year in 2003. With Nikolai we began in Mexico City, hosted by the philosopher Maria Pia Lara. I gave a paper on 'Bauman and Plan B Modernity', thinking about Bauman and Australian modernity together, for part of being Antipodean was also that I needed to think social theory and Australia together. And we visited the obvious shrines and altars: Trotsky, Kahlo and Rivera, San Angel and Coyoacan. We spent time with amazing folk, such as Nestor Garcia Canclini, whose book *Hybrid Cultures* (1995) I had earlier devoured. The ASA meeting was in Atlanta. Nik acted as waiter at the Yale party, working the room better than I could. We did some music tourism in Manhattan, went drum shopping at Manny's, did Memphis, Stax, the Sun Studios and Graceland. The Gibson Factory had been taken out by a typhoon. We walked Beale Street, and went to the Lorraine Hotel, where Dr King had been murdered in 1968. We wept, and wondered why. Some things do not change.

Next we travelled on to Boston and New Haven. By this time I had many good friends in the ASA, and this came to be its rich texture for me. I could never quite convince Bauman of the importance of this for me. He seemed to think I was too American and insufficiently European. But most of my American friends were European in that special American kind of way that you find, especially in New England. Their frames of cultural reference are as often Continental as Midwestern. And many of my European friends came to the ASA meetings, for, like Claus Offe, they felt at home there.[4] The longer traditions of sociology, such as those in Chicago, were French and German, even Polish. My American friends had that European frame of reference for which Continental philosophy and culture were standard points of orientation. They were born, or else had become transatlantic. More, this was a door that had opened for me. There were enough closed doors already for an outsider such as me. I was bound, ever, to be peripheral on both sides of the Atlantic. 'Oh, you're from Austria?' But no, I came from Australia, and I was always happy to return there.

So Nikolai and I caught up with Calhoun at Atlanta, and Ivan Szelenyi, Peggy Somers, Mabel Berezin, Julia Adams and many others. And, when we were chatting in a corridor at the Hilton between sessions with friends and colleagues of Jeff Alexander, another door opened. 'Where are you headed next?' asked Phil Smith. 'Springfield, Massachusetts,' I replied, and this was not another joke about the Simpsons. Nik and I were going to the Edward Bellamy House, to do some history work there. 'That's up the road apiece,' chimed in Ron Jacobs and Eleanor Townsley. 'Come stay with us; we'll pick you up at the railway station.' So we got to know Mt Holyoke, Olmsted design and all, and Ron and Eleanor and their girls, and Ken Tucker and many others. We had a few days in London, to follow, then took the train to Leeds. We stayed upstairs chez Bauman, met with pioneer Bauman scholars Richard Kilminster and Ian Varcoe, and Bauman took some photographs of us. The proofs appeared at our bedroom door upstairs in the morning, after he had been up late playing with Photoshop. Bauman had been an enthusiastic and gifted black and white photographer. Chris Rojek, his enthusiastic early editor at Routledge, had used one of his images of the Manhattan street as a cover for the paperback edition of *Intimations of Postmodernity*; but, in general, Bauman's

---

4 See C. Offe, *Reflections on America: Tocqueville, Weber and Adorno in the United States* (Cambridge: Polity Press, 2005).

photographic work was known only to colleagues and friends.[5] Bauman was good at dirty realism, including Leeds under Thatcher: hardened souls sleeping rough, the town boarded up and desolate, the ads reflecting the irony of a presumed progress against the images of human suffering. He was also talented in portraying the romance of landscape in Yorkshire. In an earlier moment, when he was on leave in Newfoundland working on *Legislators and Interpreters*, he also constructed a portfolio of photos of the Canadian wilds. There were some fine nudes, and some very strong domestic portraits of everyday life in his Leeds file. Looking at them, and at the images of Bauman on the internet, made me wonder if the man who was not TV-bite-friendly did perhaps know how also to hold himself for a still shot, when he became the subject. He made a good still.

By now he had taken over the larder at Lawnswood Gardens as a dark-room, but the process was expensive and he had eventually stopped, given up. Until Janina, one step ahead, had some years later come to grips with the digital revolution, and new equipment appeared as a gift between the two. The snapper was back.

And here, incidentally, there is another archive for some future scholar to mine. More than one. There will be serious excavation work on the papers of Janina and Zygmunt held at Leeds in the Brotherton Library, and currently undergoing classification. But Bauman also left a photo archive, and, like the recently available photo archives of Bourdieu, and Coetzee, these images will be a rich source of further research and understanding as well as aesthetic appreciation. He was a fine photographer, as well as a sociological impressionist. The relationship between word and image in his own project will keep some other new researchers busy. There was at least one other Bauman, and his legacy was silent, visual and atmospheric. Perhaps, in this other medium, he was the photographer rather than the painter of modern life.

Further into 2003 another door opened, this held ajar by my brilliant colleague Trevor Hogan, into the Ateneo de Manila University in

---

5 See Z. Bauman, *Intimations of Postmodernity* (London: Routledge, 1992) and *Pictures in Words, Words in Pictures* (Leeds: Bauman Institute, 2010).

3 The photographer returns.

Quezon City. Manila was an amazing modernity: native, Spanish, American and Filipino all at once. Our interlocutors were locals who were at the same time more European than us, immersed in Foucault or Ricoeur via the Jesuit offices of Boston Theology College and Louvain. 2004 was another year for discovering Aotearoa, this time via Christchurch, where our graduate Chris Houston connected us up with Philippa Mein-Smith and Peter Hempenstall, who formed the New Zealand–Australia Study Centre in order to collaborate with the Thesis Eleven Centre and to spread the word of its own. Centres seemed to multiply through mimesis. 2004 was also the year of a slowly ticking time bomb; be careful what you pray for. I was awarded two federal Australian Research Council Discovery Program grants. One interstate colleague wrote to congratulate me, saying: 'You must be the envy of your friends.' She had a research chair. I had a teaching chair; La Trobe at this point had no research chairs, and the grants, though substantial, had no provision for teaching relief. This was what Max Weber had called the irrationality of rationality. We had been given money, when what we needed was time. The hamster wheel was accelerating.

In 2004 the ASA meeting was in San Francisco. I travelled on to Chicago, staying with Levine, and to Milwaukee, to visit with Ihab and Sally Hassan, who we had visited earlier for an event in Mildura with the writer David Malouf. Ihab was one of those wise men who always had the capacity to pull me up, make me think twice, or a third time. There was always need for fresh thought. That was the great message of Ihab and his friends, such as Philip Glass. Ihab himself told the story of delivering a lecture on, and in, silence. Think anew, and hold your nerve! For, if you say nothing at all, your audience will at first chuckle, and then shuffle, and then want to kill you for the incredible crime of time wasting. As for me, my life was more pedestrian. Around 2002 I had been involved in curricular reform at La Trobe, introducing a new second-year course, 'Current Issues in Sociology', as a feeder into two third year courses: 'Theory, Culture and Society', a theory course I taught together with John Carroll; and the pre-honours course called 'Practising Social Science', the latter combining sociology and anthropology, as did the fourth year at La Trobe. I also began teaching at Mildura, an impressive irrigation town and cultural centre in the Murray Darling Basin, in the far north-west of my home state, duplicating some of these materials for the regional BA. There were good friends in Mildura, such as our old comrades the cultural and food entrepreneurs Stefano de Pieri and Donata Carrazza, the entrepreneur and philanthropist Ross Lake and the artist Neil Fettling. The newly formed Thesis Eleven Centre immediately became involved in local activities, including the annual Mildura Writers Festival. The teaching was intense and intensive, and the weeks I flew up were crazy, as I would then teach next day at Bundoora, though the local campus in Mildura and its culture still often worked on country time. The challenge for me was, rather, combining this activity with my already existing duties at Bundoora. Teaching at Mildura was a privilege and another education, as our charges were mostly new to this game, and as intellectually demanding as newcomers can be: outside the box, whip-smart but without academic manners. Mildura was a central node in the countryside, a vital part of the food bowl. It was red and dry, and smelled good when you walked: asphalt, dirt, salt, eucalypt, citrus and grapevines. It was a good place to remain grounded; and a world away from Lawnswood Gardens: oak and beech, shadow, moss and damp. These were my antipodes. Mildura was closer to home, even though it was drier than Croydon. These were good places to work the senses.

Some of these developments in my teaching and thinking were connected with my time out at Harvard, where I felt as though I was not being monitored and free to experiment more than at home, where there were increasingly enemies and jealousies with which to shadow-box. There were those at La Trobe who thought of me as a waste of time and space, who saw my every single outside achievement as further proof of my alleged delinquency. There was sometimes a sense that there were only two options: cultural nationalism or cosmopolitanism. I despised nationalism, and wanted be an antipodean, one foot in each world. I brought back from Harvard a willingness to use film and music in a way I had not easily done beforehand. Eventually I worked these media into the assessment, so that they could not be seen as mere decoration by students or by the more dyspeptic of my colleagues.

I was impressed by teaching duos such as Cornell West and Roberto Unger at Harvard, and so suggested to John Carroll that, as the two dissenting professors, stereotyped as left and right, we should teach Marx, Weber and Durkheim together, in the room at the same time. The course was a great success, and leaving it behind when I left La Trobe is one of my larger regrets, though there are also others. I had always been a Marxist, and also believed that difference and disagreement were the life-blood of university culture. As Ihab Hassan said to me, you need to learn to think against yourself. Civil harmony was important, civility mattered,

71

but agonism and argument were also vital. So John and I became friends, in this setting, to the splenetic pleasure of my left-wing opponents, who were much happier working with people they agreed with, safe within the culture of conformism. There are few things as comforting as working with people you agree with. Then there was the external irony, that many outside the university also disagreed with us; but we did not need to speak to them, so they could be ignored, made not to matter. The result is too easily the life of the ideological silo, and its attendant intellectual laziness. Conformism, of course, was a long-term concern for Bauman, whether in universities or elsewhere in everyday life. As Dirk Baecker put it, writing in *Thesis Eleven*, conformism results perhaps less from looking up, anticipating the will of the Leader, as looking sideways, at what your colleagues or peers are doing.[6]

Bauman was my friend, but he was also a friend of John Carroll, among many others. For this, indeed, is how friendship works; it is anything but identikit, one size fits all. What is striking about friendship is, rather, how diverse your friends can be. Bauman admired John's work, not least the critique of humanism, which was interesting because Bauman also remained, despite himself, a humanist. Bauman knew that humanism out of control was capable of creating monsters. This was a risk that I personally preferred to characterize as Faustian, for not all humanisms created monsters. Bauman had also had his structuralist moment, not least in engagement with Claude Lévi-Strauss, to whom he was also constantly to return. John's was a different cultural universe, if with connecting doors, and echoes with teachers such as George Steiner, and earlier inspirations such as Edmund Burke. He launched my Bauman books at the Carlton Readings bookshop in Melbourne in 2002. My own launch notes, in my archives, quote Bauman on Carroll: Bauman had said to me of John on my adjacent visit to Leeds that he admired John because he stuck his neck out: 'When the crowd moves to the left, John Carroll shifts to the right; when the crowd shifts to the right, John Carroll shifts to the left. John Carroll does not like crowds!'

6 D. Baecker, 'The Hitler Swarm', *Thesis Eleven*, 117 (2013).

Bauman met with my student Rob Campain, whose dissertation was on Carroll and Bauman, and he lapped up Adrian Barker's smaller thesis on Tzvetan Todorov and Bauman, offering Adrian a direct line to Todorov; always connect. He always found time, when I filed a request. He acted as examiner for the dissertation of Fuyuki Kurasawa on the ethnological imagination. Vince Marotta wrote a fine dissertation with me on the stranger, also under the influence of Bauman, as well as that of the Chicago School, Park and Simmel. I taught honours courses on Bauman, both before and after the publication of my own monograph in 2000. Later I collaborated on an honours course on the Holocaust and social sciences with Robert Manne, across sociology and politics. Rob did the lion's share of the work, for his approach was autobiographical, and he was steering. His purpose was to revisit the literature on the Holocaust serially, as he had encountered it across the path of his life. He led the course. I covered Bauman and some other recent arrivals, such as Goetz Aly and Omar Bartov. I linked Rob up with Jeff Alexander. Jeff joined us for a class at La Trobe, and there was further collaboration between the two in the project that resulted in the book *Remembering the Holocaust* (2009).

In 2005 the ASA meeting was held in Philadelphia. I drove back to New York with Calhoun – as with Bauman in the car, always a fine time to talk, often more so than when you set out to be serious about it. (Mixed memories of Bauman here: sometimes you could not talk, tearing around those ring roads at breakneck speed: it would be enough of a challenge just to hold on.) We listened to some very early Clapton, laughed and chewed the fat, arriving in Manhattan at dawn. This was not the only time we drove together. We went house shopping together in upstate New York, as I had gone car shopping with Jeff in New Haven, and food shopping, and done work together in the kitchen and grill. Jeff and Craig became some of my dearest long-distance friends. As I used then to say, we had infrequently exercised relationships, but the minute you walked in the door I knew I could bare my soul. They helped me through my darkest of times, and to persist, and begin anew. They were always keenly enthusiastic about my own work, and to hear news of Bauman. They offered me friendship, curiosity, insight and affirmation.

Craig had an intuitive connection to Bauman through the tradition of critical theory. Together with Claus Offe, Craig had endorsed my book, and Peter Wagner and Jeff had endorsed my *Bauman Reader*. Although Jeff was a boy Marxist, and engaged seriously with Marx in his massive four-volume debut, *Theoretical Logic in Sociology* (1982–3), his leading star earlier was Parsons. This was the tradition that Bauman was allergic to, calling it Durksonianism. It is possible that Bauman's mashing of Durkheim and Parsons became a kind of roadblock for him. As he later put it to me, Parsons was veritably the thinker and advocate of solid modernity. Marx, Weber, Freud and Simmel were all central for Bauman; not Durkheim. Mutual respect grew between Bauman and Americans such as Jeff, perhaps encouraged by third parties such as me, resulting among other things in the inclusion of Bauman' s views in the *Durkheim Companion* (2005), which Jeff and Phil Smith edited together. As for me, I had long admired Jeff's work, but had come to sociology late; and Australian sociology was a redbrick culture, emerging with some power and influence in the 1970s, often in tandem with Marxism and feminism. Parsons was never a roadblock for me, as we were already on different roads. The Durkheim I read, under the influence of Johann Arnason, was close in affinity to Gramsci. Of course, Australian sociology had its own Anglo history and local precedents, going back a century, but they were typically in the statistics, demography, colonial policy and race regulation of settler colonialism, and then settler capitalism. Little wonder that Foucault was to have such an academic following in Australia into the 1980s. Its state history looked like a Panopticon, and its victims were often racialized. White Australia, as the graffiti put it, had – has – a black history.

In 2006 I began my travels in London, then to Leeds, where Evan Jones Morris and Andrzej Wojeik were working on a film with Bauman. This came to be a more common occurrence; when I arrived at Lawnswood Gardens there would be folks with recording devices, cameras, lights and fluffy 'Muppet' microphones. I had met Welzer in this way, and now watched as Bauman was filmed in the local park doing his St Francis act with the local ducks, who followed him ensemble for the camera as if on cue. Bauman gave me a microcassette recorder as a gift: 'Do you

like gadgets?' He did. I think I disappointed him, as I did not use it systematically between us. My prejudice, at least since my first encounter
with Castoriadis in Paris in 1980, was that it was better not to allow the
machine its inhibiting presence. You might miss out on some choice cuts,
or even on a prime publication, but things in general moved more freely
in the absence of a tape recorder on the table between you.[7] Yet, as with
Mike Davis earlier, sometimes you wished it was on file, especially for our
Australian colleagues who thought *Thesis Eleven* was a joke, or at best a
distraction from the pressing issues of national culture; they didn't read
it. You had to travel further afar for notice. As Mark Davis later put it to
me about the apparent invisibility of the Bauman Institute, the closer you
got to Leeds the less you heard of the Bauman Institute. The closer you
got to Melbourne, the less you heard of *Thesis Eleven*. Outside, that was
another story, as global data gathered by Sage indicated. *Thesis Eleven*
had achieved a global presence; not bad for an idea from Melbourne.

From Leeds I travelled on to Boston; New Haven, to see Jeff Alexander;
New York; to Santa Fe, for work on our Jean Martin biography project;
Montreal, for the ASA; and then to the north-west Pacific: Seattle – the
Experience Museum, Hendrix meets Gehry; Portland – Powell's Books,
the shop so big they give you a map at the door in case you get lost indoors;
Vancouver, the calm splendour of its 360 degree vista, the sadness of
its abundant homeless. I delivered the keynote for the Sociological
Association of Aotearoa New Zealand in Hamilton, New Zealand, and
travelled down to Dunedin to meet with social historian Erik Olssen.
On a separate visit Trevor Hogan and I worked our way through New
Zealand, presenting our project on thinking these Antipodes together.
In 2007 I discovered Detroit, thanks to George Steinmetz, whose film
Detroit in Ruins I had come upon at the same time as he turned out to
be reading my book on Bernard Smith. This was an antipodean snap.
Detroit was a stunning experience, Motown in ruins though the studio
was intact, modernity in ruins; dead yet resonant, like the Sun Studio
in Memphis. We toured the dead sites – Packard, Fisher, River Rouge,

7 See P. Beilharz, 'Remembering Castoriadis', *Thesis Eleven* (2020).

the Michigan Theatre, Motown itself – and the living: the community art scenes and gardens; the green spaces, where nature had taken back from glass and redbrick; locals in the streets, like those in Mildura who wanted to share with you their bottles and check if you had spare change. The magnificent Art Institute was closed for repairs; I had to return on a subsequent occasion to see the Rivera murals of industry, Fordism and its cosmos of industry, the 'Wow!' experience of a lifetime working in politics and aesthetics and the trafficking of cultures. On the street you could feel the imagery of photographer and artist Charles Sheeler everywhere; only now there were literally no people left on the post-industrial landscape. Organic regrowth, green stuff, urban decay, but very few people in what used to be a buzzing world city in the modern times of Chaplin.

This trip, like many, now began for me in Santa Monica, to break up the flight. The ASA 2007 meeting was in New York, where I gave a – for once – well-attended paper on Peter Carey. I had met Carey earlier, and was much taken by his Antipodean sensibilities, not least in *The Strange Life of Tristan Smith*. While at Harvard I had hoped to bring both Carey and Robert Hughes to Cambridge, but without luck. I was successful in bringing to Harvard the war artist George Gittoes, who Bernard Bailyn saw in the moment as echoing the work of German New Objectivity painter Max Beckman. I visited Jeff, and Ron and Eleanor, after ASA. I am reminded looking at my notes that I often worked as a discussant as well as a presenter at these big events. Being an Antipodean in the American scene was often, as Raewyn Connell once put it to me at an ASA meeting, a matter of being relegated to the sideshows. There were always bigger things going on, not least with the big stars. And it was also, of course, a labour market, a labour exchange, a feature unknown to me in Australia. Most young folks were there for interviews, for job talks. Once at the coffee queue the fellow in front of me read my name badge (a lot of this goes on), sniffed and said, 'Oh, you're from Pennsylvania?' He was connecting me to the local town of La Trobe, up the line from Pittsburgh, and a direct connection to our founder, Charles Joseph La Trobe. 'No,' I answered, 'I am from Australia.' 'Oh, you're here for a job?' I said 'No', again, and again he seemed nonplussed. Perhaps there were too many negatives coming from this upstart. Why else would I come to an ASA meeting? Maybe this is why Bauman didn't get it either. The American Sociological Association was like the Olympics, or maybe like speed dating; but if you could find friends and colleagues in the sections, in my experience, worlds opened up. And they did, as I became friends with Ritzer, from the first publication of *McDonaldization* by Pine Forge in 1999, and so many others: John Hall, Alan Sica, Gary Fine, Peter Kivisto, Andy Abbott, Randy Collins, earlier acquaintances such as Immanuel Wallerstein, Irving Louis Horowitz and Iván Szelényi, and an emerging younger generation of scholars. Then I travelled on to Leeds, and then to Paris and to the Morvan, to visit my teacher and mentor, Alastair Davidson.

In 2008 I was on long service leave, and travelled to the United States and Europe with Dor. We shared with Alastair again, and Kathleen, went to Dijon, on to Rome and to Naples, and to Boston, where we could see our American friends gathered at the ASA proceedings. It was the last time we were to visit Leeds, to stay in Weetwood Hall and visit Lawnswood Gardens together. Bauman was always very sweet to us. He presented us with an inscribed copy of *The Art of Life* (2008). But things were troubled. Our marriage ended late in 2009.

In 2008 *Thesis Eleven* business took us to Delhi and to Ranthambhore, where we enjoyed the company of Charles Taylor as our rapporteur. As mild-mannered as he was engaging, this was the second time I had met him; the earlier occasion had been in Montreal, whence he had to break off a keen discussion about *Thesis Eleven* in order to deal with a leaking home roof. This was my kind of philosopher.

Had I ever seen such architectural beauty as Ranthambhore? On arrival our colleagues walked the walls with dilated pupils, jaws dropped. It was all so beautiful; and yet: who built these Seven Gates of Thebes? We travelled on to Kerala for work with local feminist activists working on the journal *Samyukta*. 2009 took me back to Europe, to Copenhagen, for an event with the Socio-Aesthetics Project. I visited with Jeff in New Haven, and sat in on some of his classes, as I had earlier audited Patrice Higonnet's brilliant classes on Jacobinism at Harvard, where he chose to engage directly with my work. This was a luxury: how often do we get to watch our gifted others teach? I travelled via Toledo by bus to Cleveland, to visit the Rock Museum designed by I. M. Pei: sufficient reason to visit Cleveland in itself. It was a shrine, a glass pyramid hugging Lake Michigan that is a monument to the material but also the spiritual culture of rock music. Its many treasures included Duane Allman's 1959 Les Paul, as per the 1971 Fillmore Album. They even have Les Paul's experimental guitar, the Log. A different kind of Pole there; similar vintage to Bauman, distinct lifeworld: Lester Polsfuss, another innovator, the solid-bodied guitar maker of modernity, the solid axe with the liquid tone. What would those two have talked about?

I had begun to work with Sian Supski, who had another kind of Polish connection, and was to become my new love. The next surprise door was in South Africa, facilitated by my new friend Peter Vale. The work and project of *Thesis Eleven* was profiled at the South African Academy of Sciences meeting in Bloemfontein. I travelled in through Johannesburg and Port Elizabeth, stayed in Grahamstown with Peter, and we visited Cape Town, Bloemfontein and Stellenbosch. We drove across the splendour of the Karoo, and once again the car became a carrier of open-ended learning and laughter, structured this time, however, by the open horizon of the visual. My first taste of South Africa was the proverbial sublime, exciting and terrifying all in one. This was a pattern of modernity, after and together with apartheid, which was impossible, unsustainable and yet full of competing populations looking to make a life apart, and together. South Africa was to become a major focus for curiosity, learning and research. I have still barely scratched the surface.

The second decade of my relationship with Bauman was, I suppose, one of consolidation. Its most intense moments of collaboration and intimacy came together with those books that I wrote or edited on his work and its contexts. Both of our worlds were expanding, and pluralizing; but they were not the same worlds. A repertoire of engagement had settled between us. Neither of us would be able to predict the next decade, except with some sense of finality as to the impending finitude of it all.

Chapter 3

Third decade

Into the third decade of our time on Earth together things were slowing between Bauman and me. Leeds was now a little further away. The shadows of mortality remained nigh. There was too much busyness for both of us. Bauman had been tied to Leeds, as Janina's health declined. I was exhausted just coping. Travel still connected us, and email. In 2010 I visited Germany, doing the rounds of my relatives, returning home via Leeds, where Keith Tester and I visited Bauman together. So we were, in some sense, the sons. And he would often urge us to the table: 'Children! My dears! Lunch is ready! You must eat! Start working!' There was a great deal of ritual clinking of glasses. 'Na zdrowie!' This was a very funny moment, for me, as the mischief was not, for once, at my expense. A common welcome at the door at Lawnswood Gardens, after the embrace with stubble that could draw blood, was something dismissive about whence I had come; 'Where have you been? Oh, he has been in America again!' America was a constant tease. He even accused me, on first visit, of wanting an American shower rather than a bath. Bath was fine, but there was a difference between us, and our biographies. When Bauman was in his teens he had to deal with Hitler and Stalin. There was not much time for grousing around. For my generation, in Australia, there was a distant war going on, in Vietnam, but otherwise America was jazz, blues, rock and Hollywood, as well as race, whitey on the Moon, Dr King and Black Power, and Big Brother in Vietnam. Bauman and I were also worlds apart. He was a child of that turbulent period between the wars. He was East Central European, and he would always remain a Pole and a Jew. The fact is worth remembering, by those who would later view him as a kind of eccentric Englishman, displaced only by his particular rendition of the discipline of sociology.

On this occasion, with Keith as my companion, we followed the usual routine, plying our way through the jungle of the front yard and the jokes about Darwin. My gardener is Darwin, he used to say; whatever survives belongs in the garden. As he used to say, in a different register, my chef is Sainsbury; but this was also misleading, as, following the example of his mother, he was a fine chef. He took the logic of the gamekeeper seriously, in liquid modern suburban life also. He was a gamekeeper, not a gardener.

He was indeed a good provider, as well as gamekeeper. Earlier, visiting with Nikolai, he fed us potted meat, self-pickled hare stewing in the dining room, which also served as the cellar, and pheasant, which was difficult to procure. He took Yorkshire very seriously, and was proud to make it another home on his journey (this choice, at least, among the many in his personal itinerary was voluntary). I chipped a tooth on a remaining shot pellet. These encounters were serious learning experiences. 'Slowly I line the cellar ...,' he would warn me in an email.

Visiting Bauman together with Keith, I for once avoided the comedy half-full bucket balanced on top of the half-open front door. Bauman bustled us together into the wingchairs in the sitting room, and delivered the standard opening question: 'What will you have to drink?' Keith answered, with an upward inflection, '... White wine?' This was not the correct answer, and we both knew it. Scotch, Famous Grouse; or gin and tonic, of substantial measure; perhaps borderline Campari; these were the right answers. The trap had been set. Bauman to Tester: 'White wine? What is that?' Then he disappeared into the kitchen, forbidden territory to the guest, labelled 'Uwaga Pies!' ('Beware of the Dog!'), to reappear with a massive platter of snacks, mainly seafood. Keith had written his doctoral thesis with Bauman on animal rights decades beforehand. They were old friends. He had been a vegetarian forever. Keith looks at me, me at him, me at Bauman; Bauman at Keith. This is an awkward moment.

It is broken by Bauman, with a small smile: 'But, Keith, it is okay; these are fruits!' I ate more than my share, so that the plate would look empty and Keith would be safe. And then there was the usual heaped lunch and wine: red. The three of us, after Janina died in 2009. He sent me a single line to tell me that Janina had died. And he descended into his own private despair for some time. Janina had been in decline over these years, during which I ceased to stay over, and routinely went instead to Weetwood Hall, the nearby university hotel for my annual stay. Keith and I stayed over at Weetwood Hall, and then drove together to his home in Worthing. Again, the car chat was wonderful, as was the tour of his world, in Sussex. He was an incredibly generous and stimulating friend. His death in 2019 deprived me of a serious friend, and of that triangular relationship with Bauman. When it came to later Bauman matters, and to news of encounters and events that came in under the radar, Keith was always my first call. Now that he is gone I wonder if I did him justice; but we certainly shared a great deal, and he never gave me cause to question our friendship.

I was very fond of Janina, who also used to play with me. Our email correspondence makes it clear that she was impressed with my manner; I was polite and considerate. My mother would have been pleased. After a bit, though, it began to annoy her. Too English? I was too polite. So she introduced a swearbox, a pound for each surplus politeness, 'thank you', 'please' or 'sorry'. I teased her back, with a 'danke schoen'. She shot back at me, '50p!' Their own routine also had its mischief. When he had backed the car out of the garage for an excursion, he would hoot the horn, and she would jump just as she got to the passenger door. Every time. They had their routines, and they were not only those of simple affection.

Although I was a tourist, I had also become very fond of Yorkshire. I changed my travel pattern. Earlier I had routinely come through Heathrow, not my favourite airport, and increasingly one that was difficult practically to negotiate. The culture of Heathrow seemed calculated to accelerate anxiety. Instead I would now fly into Manchester, much more civilized a scale, and stay over in a grand railway hotel or take the direct train across the Pennines. I could search Friedrich Engels' other city, visit the John Rylands Library and Chetham's Library, where Marx and Engels had put their heads together, and meet up with new friends such as the labour historian Kevin Morgan.

There were always flowers. I first brought Janina cornflowers from the railway stall, only to discover from her that they were a favourite, so lovely yet also so common, so quotidienne, and a line back to Poland, where, as she told me, they would grow along the road. Often the pink heath was in flower, out of the window on the TransPennine Express, and the countryside was beautiful – so much so that on one occasion my accidental American travel companion, on her first beer for the day at 8 a.m., exhorted the weary locals on the train to lift up their eyes. Bauman would have been pleased. Our fellow travellers ignored her. Americans! For them, the locals, this landscape was merely ordinary, taken for granted.

But Bauman would not always have been pleased. Once when I was checking in to a Manchester hotel I noticed that the name badge of the young man serving me was Polish. I asked, 'Are your people from Poland?' 'Yes,' he said. 'What brings you to Manchester?' 'Oh, I am working with the most important sociologist in the world. He lives in Leeds. He is a Pole, Zygmunt Bauman; do you know that name?' He looked at me blank. Bauman … that is not a Polish name. He is not Polish. I was chilled. Our conversation ended.

Janina had also come to love her adopted nation, which offered her the dream of belonging. She described with tenderness some of her early local encounters, when kindness to the stranger still applied. She said to this man, the stranger in the shop, that she was graceful, substituting 'c' for 't'. He agreed with her: she was, indeed, graceful. She found herself happy shopping in the anonymity of the small supermarket, where you did not have to make a fool of yourself by trying out broken English, risking correction. Janina's writing remains remarkable, perhaps especially *A Dream of Belonging* (1988), which she loved a little less, not least as she had employed the device of renaming some central characters, as in Konrad for Zygmunt. *Winter in the Morning* (1986) will always have a special place. But *A Dream* tells a story still powerful, in its own quotidian, in the new start, in this struggle to make a new life in Leeds. When we spoke about this second book she seemed keen to push it away, to want to move the conversation on. My most recent encounter with the text elicited a gentle protest. It represents everyday life writing at its best. She also wanted, however, to keep me to my own word. So she signed my copy of the book, 'To Peter, waiting for your book, Janina.' She was welcoming me, and putting me on notice to deliver. Should you have no further patience for what I am writing here, turn to Janina Bauman instead. She makes every word count.

There were by now other Baumans also in my life. I had become friends with the twins, especially Lydia. Having worked with the art historian Bernard Smith in the 1990s I had the benefit of a belated and accelerated course of instruction in art. I was happy further to be instructed by Lydia. I found her work and her sense of art history astounding, yet delivered, like her father, with a manner both firm and gentle. There were some good stories from Zygmunt about the pleasures of experiencing your children grow, and outgrow you. Zygmunt is in a Warsaw bookshop, buying some books on art. He hands over his credit card, in this moment when the post-1991 regime is smiling on him. The cashier recognizes the name, and asks, 'Oh, are you related to Lydia?'

In 2010 we celebrated the life and work of Janina at the first Bauman Institute (BI) event in Leeds. Zygmunt and his family were present; he did not speak. Mark Davis and I had brainstormed the idea earlier with Keith Tester outdoors at Weetwood Hall. The celebrity invites included George Ritzer and Saskia Sassen and Griselda Pollock. Keith made an inspired suggestion: why not ask Daniel Libeskind? The leading architect was also a Polish Jew; this was a serious lateral. He came, and he stole the show. He was a brilliant performer, with a superb grasp of the visuals, as you might expect. At the event dinner Keith and I placed our things in a corner location, leaving central space for the big animals. We returned after a drink to discover that our places on the periphery had been occupied. The only spare seats were with Ritzer and Libeskind; people were working around them. We sat with them, and I introduced them to each other; I had known Ritzer for years. They had a wonderful, unexpected reunion; they had both attended the same public high school in the Bronx, the

School of Science, and, though a year or two apart, even remembered the same teachers. It was a magical moment, for us, for them. Its mood was educative, its spirit democratic. Libeskind claimed to know our work on Bauman, which was a little too kind to be quite likely. There was no magic here for Bauman, however, except that maybe Janina was also somehow there among us, a present absence. He succeeded in working the corners.

Bauman was enormously proud of his daughters. Lydia I had some kind of affinity with. Irena I came to know less well. We met several times and visited her new project home and the office of Bauman Lyons. Some sense of Irena's project can be found in the book by Bauman Lyons Architects, *How to Be a Happy Architect* (2008). I remember her explaining that, if you were designing a space for the unemployed, curves would work better than corners; they did not like corners. It would not do to work the connection too much, but the ambience here is continuous with the broader social concerns indicated by her father. Evidently she helped him to think about space and design. For the frame of Irena's work is one in which architecture is practised against the backdrop of constant change, which the practice often plays into by disconnecting rather than connecting. In this field, as in others of social consequence, an eye for continuity and a will to move slowly go a long way.

The twins were my peers, Anna a little older. We met several times over the years, with instant affection and geniality. She was elsewhere, in Haifa, or mobile, in Michigan or London, working as professor of mathematical education in the wake of Basil Bernstein. Anna Sfard makes one of several cameos in Bauman's work in *What Use Is Sociology?* (2013), in which her presence is intellectually authoritative, but the radiant pride is that of her father. Bauman introduces her argument first, with reference to the story 'The metaphor is dead – pass it on!'. For Anna, one of the most important messages of the contemporary research on metaphor is that language, perception and knowledge are inextricably intertwined. He defers to her, but the view is held in common: no thinking outside metaphor. What is sociology a metaphor for?

So Zygmunt and Janina had their three parental utopias, and all that followed. This serves to remind us that Bauman's thinking was mediated

by family, including his grandchildren; and also to remind that his immediate household was one of women. There are feedback loops at each generational point here. It also serves as a memo of the less well known. We do
not yet know much at all about Bauman's time in Israel. But he was politically and intellectually engaged there, though he hated it, while Janina was
more ambivalent and Anna stayed. All, in addition, a weird warp between
Bauman and me, with my own family history reaching back to the time of
the Templers in Palestine, arrivals and departures between 1923 and 1941.

Bauman and I were not done yet. In 2011 I was able to share Zygmunt's
company again, this time out, in Jena. Lutz Niethammer, author of the
best book on *posthistoire*, had invited us to an event organized by the Imre
Kertesz Kolleg of the Schiller University, in the grand romantic town,
on 'Approaches to the Postmodern from Eastern Europe'. This struck me
as a clever idea, as the Paris–Frankfurt axis had been allowed for too
long to dominate Anglo discussion in these fields. Some of my favourite
critical theorists were East European, or, they might have said, East-
Central European. The guests of honour were both my friends: Ágnes
Heller and Zygmunt Bauman. I was taken to be the only person involved
who knew both projects well enough to compare and discuss. This was
a tease. For, although there were serious sympathies, not least in the
interest in turning the idea of modernity in the direction of different
totalitarianisms, there were also significant differences between them.
Bauman had never taken Lukács so seriously. When I quizzed him on
this, he told me that he had entered by the wrong door, the one marked
Destruction of Reason, the book of Lukács that Ágnes also described to me
as the two-volume pamphlet of his Stalinist period. Gramsci – that was
another matter. Gramsci's *Prison Notebooks* were translated into Polish
in 1950. Bauman had written on Gramsci as early as 1964, before either
he or the Sardinian had become naturalized as an Englishman. In 1996
Bauman told me he had read Gramsci in 1960/61, written about him in
1962 and published on him in 1964 (actually, 1963). Within the culture
of Polish communism, and elsewhere, in the Anglo world Gramsci was a
radical thinker. Here the Poles were well ahead of the Anglos, for whom
Gramsci was often to be identified later with cultural studies, as though

Gramsci had come from Birmingham rather than Sardinia. In Hungary, Fehér and Heller told me, they could not take on Gramsci because they could not deal with Machiavelli, with the Prince, whether modern or earlier. 'The Modern Prince' was, for them, a Trojan horse. Gramsci was emotionally unavailable to them, just as Lukács was not a ready resource for Bauman, in Poland. Clearly, the idea of East European critical theory would be in need of further specification and unpacking. There were serious differences here, as well as some broad cultural affinities, not least those following on the Marx renaissance of the 1960s and the longer Continental tradition of thinking sociology and philosophy together.

Being together with Ágnes and Zygmunt in Jena was warming, if uncanny. Bauman's hearing was difficult, and they both just spoke, perhaps past each other; maybe this was unavoidable. I did my best to work out a checklist across their two projects, searching out the correspondences, which came to fruition as a later paper written for Fu Qilin's journal *Comparative Literature: East and West*.[1] I looked to viewing their work under five headings: biography, and generation; themes and concordances; intellectual strategies; relations to Marx; and relations to the modern and postmodern. The challenge forced me to think more frontally than I had previously about the nature of these two projects of two of my favourite thinkers. In Jena I was also to act as respondent to Perry Anderson, who was unable finally to make it because of illness. It was disappointing not to meet with the finest of modern Marxist minds writing *en anglais*, not least because I had disagreed with him since *Considerations on Western Marxism* was published in 1976. But it is Anderson who will be remembered, not me. The quality of his thinking, the breadth of his knowledge and the finesse of his prose style will always see to that. Jena, in any case, was a treat, a window onto the old East, with an economy apparently consisting of the ideas that followed the historic aura of the town, from Hegel to the romantics and the ubiquitous currywurst stands, one on every street corner. That was a long road, from

---

1 P. Beilharz, 'Bauman and Heller: Two Views of Modernity and Culture', *Comparative Literature: East and West* 1/1 (2017).

Hegel to the sausage stands via the DDR. The experience reminded me of one of the reasons I was attracted to sociology in the first place. You can learn so much simply by watching, observing, defamiliarizing the familiar, wondering about these creatures called humans.

Finally, being together with Ágnes and Zygmunt at the same time was both rewarding and challenging. Ágnes had broken her hip and had it replaced, but insisted on hobbling everywhere, across the square, to events and back to dinners and breakfasts. She was unstoppable, always intrepid, and remained so until her death in 2019. Zygmunt was at this point still deep in mourning, and tended to avoid company, though we bumped into each other repeatedly – in the bar, in the lobby, in the lift, at coffee – like a bad movie. Once I caught him smoking alone in the square. We sat together in silence on that bench, amidst the cobblestones, as we had also in earlier, happier times. Whereof one cannot speak.

Jena pulled me up; for mortality was always there. I was also likely still moving too quickly, though not as quickly as Bauman had hitherto. In 2011, on leave, I also did the ASA meeting in Vegas, a city that seemed in ten years to have got much closer to postmodern hell, or at least Babylon. Sex was for sale in your face on the strip where families walked, even at breakfast. I revisited Detroit, with Mathieu Desan; New Haven; Leeds again; and Barcelona, where my distant undergrad Nick Bolger was now making a life and films (the week before me, it was Oprah). He gave me the Robert Hughes tour; Hughes' book on Barcelona had also become something of a guide book. I returned home via Copenhagen, for further meetings with the Socio Aesthetics crew affiliated with *Thesis Eleven*. Back home, we organized a major event with friends from Delhi, Manila, Johannesburg, Yale and the Bauman Institute in Melbourne. We ran a special session remembering Janina and celebrating Zygmunt, and Mark Davis premiered the documentary on and with Bauman, *The Trouble with Being Human These Days* (2013). All this was engineered by the remarkable Christine Ellem. We may not quite have been changing the world, but we were certainly working on our little segment of it.

2012 was to be my last ASA meeting. It had been made plain to us at La Trobe that the future of the university was exclusive of us, or of the kind of work that people such as me did. Our efforts were to be sacrificed in order to facilitate a restructure, or two: 're–dun–dan–cy'; 're–struc–ture'. A rump of hard-working mid-career academics was to remain in sociology, which was remarkable enough. The higher-ups could have closed us down altogether. Looking back to 1992, and those earlier days, I gave a paper on 'Labour's Utopias Revisited' at Denver,[2] discussed by Andy Abbott, and met with old friends such as Calhoun, Alexander, Ritzer, Rojek, Gary Fine, Phil McMichael, Jonathon van Antwerpen. What would happen next? I really had no idea. My university was lost to me, and my vocation as a sociologist was under question. But I followed my nose, or my habit, and travelled on through New York and Boston to Manchester and Leeds via that TransPennine Express and a cab through Otley to Lawnswood Gardens, where the lone sage awaited me as I struggled to negotiate my luggage through the overgrown shrubbery to his door. He greeted me with open arms, as ever, as I told him my own small sad news: that my La Trobe story was over. But, then, he had been urging me to retire since we first met; retirement might afford the chance finally to get some work done. He was, as ever, the optimist for others.

Some doors open, if you are lucky, as others close. 2013 took me south, in contemporary parlance – actually, west and north – to South Africa and to China. A *Thesis Eleven* team visited South Africa in February. Oxford University Press, the publisher of our text *Place, Time and Division*, had been put on alert by Peter Vale; might this Australian precedent help in the assemblage of a South African text such as ours, an independently conceived text that, like *New South African Keywords*, could reach across introductory audiences? It was a great idea. We met with a dozen leading sociology educators from around South Africa for a day at Spier Winery, outside Stellenbosch. Ultimately the encounter was unfruitful, I suppose partly because of the Big Brother factor; there are very interesting challenges in working this crossover, like those in New Zealand, but even more extreme. Transcolonial relations are often fractious. There are also enormous challenges in the teamwork that it

2 P. Beilharz, 'Labour's Utopias Revisited', *Thesis Eleven*, 110 (2013).

takes to conceive and edit a major textbook. I gave my paper on 'Marx, Modernity and Motion' at the University of Johannesburg. We had some fun together, Peter Vale and I. This paper of mine used two voices, one in dissent with the other, querying claims as they were unfolded. I asked Peter to bark out the lines of protest from the back of the hall. No one seemed surprised by this, as though heckling was the norm. Perhaps this was the new democracy at work. We travelled to Bloemfontein for a day seminar, and to Cape Town for a *Thesis Eleven* session at the University of Cape Town on utopias for Deborah Posel. All this in what some would call a dystopia, or at least the most challenging of extreme modernities, formally free of apartheid and yet so deeply entangled in its legacies, material and ideal. China was to follow. I joined in the Beijing Forum, and discovered Beijing and Shanghai for myself. My paper was on the question 'What Makes a Good City?'. And, although, like other outsiders, I was overwhelmed by the scale of these Fantasia-style cities – the population of Australia would fit into Shanghai – I was also keen to be open to them as social experiments. Some of my fellow European attendees seemed to think that ruthless criticism was the best place to start. I had been taught to listen first, and to remember the mote in your own eye.

2014 took us back to Leeds, for a major event on cities with the Bauman Institute. Mark Davis and his friends had achieved a great deal with the BI, partly through talent and persistence, partly through the openness of its approach. The BI understood from the beginning that its job was not to follow the leader so much as to encourage curiosity about the massive tapestry that he had established; this, and to move on. The collegial friendship here was deeply important. Bauman did not join in the event. We made a separate trip to visit Bauman. I was now travelling with Sian Supski. Together with Sian and Trevor we visited Lawnswood Gardens. Bauman was alone, but armed and ready with his own welcoming routine: effusive greetings at the front door after we had breached the eternally overgrown front garden. There was abundance, of nature, of hospitality and good cheer, along with the dialogue of the deaf. Neither Bauman nor Trevor could hear very well; but, as Trevor had explained to me earlier, when we visited the Manuels in Boston, there was a way of playing along that the deaf were adept at. Another lesson in the resilience of knowing how to go on.

2014 was a strange year locally. As I was about to exit my field and the university to which I had given my loyalty for almost three decades, I was invited for the first time in this long career to give a keynote at the annual event of the Australian Sociological Association (TASA). The timing echoed Bauman's own recognition by the BSA; as he had said to me on that occasion, they have finally acknowledged that I exist. The keynote in Adelaide was fine. I spoke on 'Five Modern Utopias', with stimulating and generous discussion from British visitors David Inglis and Sylvia Walby. We returned home after time on Kangaroo Island, where there are more wallabies than sociologists. It seemed right: a different kind of door to exit. I had been deinstitutionalized at last, free as the fauna. Until I received a call from Curtin, in Western Australia; I was offered a research chair, and licensed to develop the Stellenbosch connection.

Sian and I had yet to satisfy our curiosity about South Africa, and returned there for a six-month residence at Stellenbosch, working at the Stellenbosch Institute for Advanced Study (STIAS) in 2015. This was the steepest learning curve I was yet to encounter. I had long been committed to the use of the idea of settler capitalism, and certainly there were some typological parallels in New World experience, not least with reference to the dispossession of indigenous peoples. But this was a black-majority country, which had only recently begun to emerge from the brutality of apartheid. We set out to engage in a project on domestic modernism in South Africa, and shifted our focus to seeking a bridge to this experience through the writing of Ivan Vladislavić, who we had encountered and befriended on our earlier visit to STIAS.[3] There were some more intersections with the thinking of Bauman here, in particular with reference to the role of literature as a window for the social sciences. By this, later stage of his career Bauman had generated some notoriety among the sociological police for his advocacy of literature as a way of seeing and thinking. Our experience was that, although South African social

---

3 See P. Beilharz and S. Supski, 'Finding Ivan Vladislavić', *Thesis Eleven*, 136 (2016).

sciences writing and research were more than usually robust, not least in urban studies, the power of word and image – adding in here, for example, contributions of the artist William Kentridge and the photographer David Goldblatt – was decisive for us as newcomers.

STIAS was also a wonderful test and challenge, as the majority of our colleagues were working in science. The model was like Princeton, where everyone was thrown in together. The ship was steered by the genial physicist Hendrik Geyer. There were stalwarts, such as the writer Athol Fugard, who enjoyed taking the piss out of Australians on a daily basis; and others who helped teach us, such as Saul Dubow, Shireen Hassim, Karin Brown and Vidya Nanjundiah. There was the young physicist Thomas Vidick, who decided to read the fiction of Vladislavić after our presentation on his work. He was working on probability, and wondered what he might learn from this other way of thinking. This is the kind of environment that STIAS offers. There was the charming and scintillating Walter Mignolo, who was talking about decolonization while the Stellenbosch students were looking to set it into motion, and the penetrating insight of Goran Therborn, who was putting together years of Marxist thinking with issues of inequality in life and health chances. There was the chemical engineer Lars Pettersson, who became a close friend. He knew a great deal about the Allman Brothers Band, as well as oil, and later introduced us to the king of Swedish blues, Rolf Wikstrom, in Stockholm. Wikstrom beamed when I told him he played like Peter Green, the sweetest of British blues guitarists.

2015 was the year Bauman turned 90. We wanted to steer clear of the day, leaving that to him and to his family, and so decided to visit him from South Africa soon thereafter. It was a trepidatious journey. Like our South African friends, we found everyday life there even more exhausting than elsewhere. There was a constant state of personal and security alert. More, our visa status had been jumbled on entry, and, although it was easy for us to exit Cape Town, it was not entirely clear that we would be able to re-enter in order to finish our time and business in Stellenbosch. We flew via Manchester, and followed my routine of a railway hotel and the TransPennine Express.

We found him there in Lawnswood Gardens, as usual, and yet there was a difference, a dramatic change of mood. It was a magical moment. As we entered the hallway Bauman introduced us to his second wife, Aleksandra, and basked in her glory. Everything was different. At this point of his life he seemed to be completely in the moment, happy to sit back and offer the occasional joke or smile. He had come alive again. There was life and affirmation again at the jungle and in the dining room. He was back.

To the sitting room: 'What news from South Africa? What will you have to drink?' We tried to explain our encounter with this entangled modernity. It was a serious challenge, as the one lesson we had learned was that there was no short story to tell about South African experience. We brought small gifts: fine South African brandy from Stellenbosch, and a tiny pipe or pipette that we had found at a craft market at Franschhoek. It was, of course, supposed to be a joke, a novelty, for the pipe was his symbol and regalia, even when it was displaced momentarily in his hand by tailor-machine-made cigarettes or the latest prosthesis, the e-cigarette. He liked gadgets, and he was addicted to smoking. How often did he announce, 'Now! It is time for guests to engage in passive smoking!' He immediately took to packing the pipette with tobacco, lighting and drawing on it with evident satisfaction. He pronounced it good, and we laughed. The joke, as usual, was on us.

I had brought another gift, this one not for keeps. This was a heavily annotated copy of *Legislators and Interpreters*, borrowed from the Stellenbosch University Library, to which I shall return. It was the first Bauman text I had reviewed, all those years ago, the result of which is reprinted in the pages above. In the meantime I had written a book about Bauman's work, and written many essays, partly because of the open-ended fascination that comes of the apparently crazy quilt of his publications. Bauman works with, or touches on, so many of the things that seemed also to concern me and my students, colleagues and friends. Consider, for example, only the bumper year of 2016: books of conversations on management, evil, language, and strangers. Across

4 Examining the Stellenbosch copy of *Legislators and Interpreters*.

almost 60 books and numerous papers in English alone, Bauman touches on a wealth of themes, issues and problems. Little wonder that he has been chastised for leaving things out, a charge that itself reeks of the impossible Enlightenment dream for which any decent theory should be universal and comprehensive, and the worst charge is lack rather than presence. So I had continued to write on his work, not only because it was thick and rich but because it dealt with moving objects.

While we were at Stellenbosch I was writing an essay for *Revue Internationale de Philosophie* on maelstrom and modernity, connecting Bauman up not only to Marx and later to Trotsky but also to the iconic work of Marshall Berman: *All That Is Solid Melts into Air* (1982). This had taken me to the library, to reconsider the central historic text called *Liquid Modernity*, published in 2000. Bauman had told me this book was coming slowly, as was the book I was then working on, *Zygmunt Bauman: Dialectic of Modernity*, which also finally emerged in 2000. The central irony here was that my book on Bauman's work ended just as what is arguably the most important book of his second or third phase appeared. For once, I was too early. By the time his book appeared, I was done, for this moment, and moving on to all the other things I had put on hold to finish my work on Bauman.

I had to rediscover *Liquid Modernity*, the book and the motif, in order to begin to think Bauman anew. There are likely several different reasons for this predicament. After many years I probably had some sense of needing to move on from Bauman's work. I imagined that I knew how he thought, and how he would think. Perhaps we had become too familiar. I had already shared Bauman's jokes about liquidity, which he laid on more thickly with the passing of time, to the extent that it became something between a joke and a mantra. He would often utter the term with a smile, or as a tease. So, for example, did Janina tease me when sending solid love in an email, or Zygmunt in inscribing the copy of *Liquid Love* he presented to me: 'To Peter, who knows me better than I do – with *solid* gratitude ...' Two years later, when he inscribed my copy of *Society under Siege* 'To my dearest friend – Peter the Great', his ebullience got the better of him. Janina was always his dearest friend. It was touching, however, to be called 'Sweet Peter' by the man I respected so deeply.

It is always possible that rhetoric also got the better of him. Words! Like Carlyle, he was capable of thundering, in print more than in person. He was both a public figure and a private person. There are many echoes, many voices and interlocutors evident in the thinking of

Zygmunt Bauman. One of the more remote echoes in Bauman's work is the voice of the Victorian sage Thomas Carlyle. Bauman was interested in what Carlyle called signs of the times, and he imagined the symbol of liquidity as one possible way to flag these signs. For Bauman, as for Carlyle a century and a half earlier, there were dramatic changes upon us. What Carlyle named as the revolution of industrialism and its culture was, for Bauman, the post-Fordist dissolution of the old, more solid Western order of things. Bauman claimed to take his inspiration from Marx: all that is solid melts into air. This image pre-dates Marx; it echoes, rather, Shakespeare and *The Tempest*, and evokes the world of Carlyle as much as that of Marx or Bauman. Carlyle had essayed past and present, and looked out for those signs. He had anticipated the mechanical age, what for Bauman in his own time was solid modernity. Carlyle had railed against the cash nexus, and been awarded due recognition for this contribution by Marx and Engels. Even more powerfully, as my student Trevor Hogan showed in his 1995 dissertation, he was the theorist of modernity as revolution.[4] For Carlyle, as for Bauman, revolution was the speeding up of change, as for both 'all that is solid melts', whether in the *Communist Manifesto* or in *Sartor Resartus*. Both Carlyle and Bauman thundered against the signs of their times. Both changed the ways their times engaged with themselves. Both, finally, worked before, or beyond, discipline. Both left a lasting impression, and a wake of controversy.

When it came to liquid modernity, as Bauman began to promote the image, I was more sceptical. Convinced as I was of the necessity of metaphor, without which we could not think at all, I was not entirely persuaded that this was a good or useful image. I could see in advance that it would be set upon by lazy followers, who would take it as an excuse for thinking or continuing to puzzle with the mess that confronted us in post-postmodern times. My previous subject, the Australian art historian Bernard Smith, whom I also loved and respected, had himself also spent the last years of his life campaigning for a category to replace

---

4 T. Hogan, 'Modernity as Revolution: Thomas Carlyle' (doctoral dissertation, La Trobe University, 1995).

the modern. His chosen term for the world of art was the 'Formalesque', which he had also succeeded in getting into *Encyclopedia Britannica*, the idea duly endorsed by Ernst Gombrich. People nevertheless persisted still in talking about 'modern', and 'modernism', despite Bernard's semantic crusade, even as those terms stubbornly held together the contradiction between period style and present attitude. Perhaps here, as elsewhere, we just needed to live with the contradiction. Did it really matter that a word such as 'modern' could be taken to be more than one thing? Myself, in the junior league, I had never had much faith in the imperative to invent new language. I had always imagined that language looks after itself, as it is practised, though I can also see that language is politically plastic, after Orwell. So I had, in effect, put the idea of liquid modernity on hold, and now needed to settle accounts with it.

In retrospect, it may be fair to say that I was at first too allergic to a term that seemed to be too clever or elastic by half. I often thought that the point about liquidity for Bauman was best imagined as mercurial, in his earlier term: that which was slippery, which eluded the clear fixity of A/B thinking, either/or. In a closer sense, the idea of liquid modernity struck me as not only too big but perhaps as too small. For its best light was cast on the end of Fordism and its elusive postwar certainties, full male employment, steady relationships in work and home in the West. These dreams had their imaginary power, but they were only to last a generation, selectively applied in the West. They make sense to members of my generation, in our 60s, but little sense at all to our children, who might hope for calm but are ready for turmoil and constant change. As Bauman was later to quip, these young folk had not only been born modern, but born liquid modern. The condition of liquidity for them was normal; the idea of solid modernity would make no sense. The old ways of thinking, for example about loyalty, have been seriously undermined in this fearful new world.

It is also possible I was just too grumpy with the term. After all, I had long understood that smart people could do interesting things from within limited conceptual frameworks. The followers of Louis Althusser often struck me as exemplars of these ironies: smart people whose energy, insight and industry could generate good results even from within a prison house of compulsory categories, such as repressive state apparatus and ideological state apparatus, or taking an epistemological break. As Engels liked to say, in good German fashion, the proof of the pudding was in its eating.

In this spirit, let me suggest that, whatever categories we might settle on to characterize our new times, the category of liquid modernity was an attempt to transcend the now likely inescapable semantics of modern and postmodern.

I now realize that the exemplary case for the use of a category in the spirit of liquid modernity is in the need to make sense of the institution whose transformation underpins much of this book: the university itself. I do not remember sharing this particular text with Bauman, but in 2013 I wrote a paper on 'Critical Theory and the New University'.[5] I had not looked back at this since then, but turned to it now, in writing this book and thinking about the transformation of our times. The question stares us in the face. How could the universities become transformed beyond recognition in a generation?

In an earlier moment, Habermas, in the 1960s, had sought to address the structural transformation of the public sphere. In Australia and elsewhere we had experienced the cultural and structural transformation of the universities in the 1990s. In the 1970s the universities were, rightly or wrongly, understood as the seedbed of critique. And a generation of us likely overinvested in universities as special places of *Bildung* and critique. This was, in fact, a fair description of cultures such as those of La Trobe Sociology. Then something – or, at least, some things – happened: in Australia, the construction of a Unified National System at the level of bureaucracy and administration; the introduction of competition and rankings between universities; commercialization, and vocationalization; the dramatic expansion of management and PR in contrast to teaching and research; the increasing PowerPoint substitution of information for

5 P. Beilharz, 'Critical Theory and the New University', in *Through a Glass Darkly: The Social Sciences look at the Neoliberal University*, M. Thornton (ed.) (Canberra: ANU Press, 2014).

intelligence: a whole raft of complex changes that we routinely blame on neoliberalism but that warrant much more work of analysis and explanation than that lazy and frustrated gesture allows. For neoliberalism, at best, might also be a question rather than a final answer.

My purpose in 'Critical Theory and the New University' was to offer two associated gestures towards understanding this attack on our earlier lifeworld. The first was to suggest the path dependence of developments across the 39 universities in Australia, for their fates differed radically depending on their wealth, position and status. As the leading historian Stuart Macintyre put it to me in conversation, the core 'Group of Eight' Australian universities would survive into the future, but the other 31 might be reconfigured or closed or consolidated in any imaginable way. Think Lego. What the scene will look like in another generation is beyond present imagination (what will the British system look like a decade after Brexit?). The second was to look at broader social transformation, especially in what Hartmut Rosa calls the processes of social acceleration.[6] The acceleration of time, in particular, seems to transform university life; informationalization replaces contemplation, argument, reading and engagement as we once knew these practices. Or, as Gernot Boehme put it, even mobile phones, for example, have for their part helped to generate a culture of 'nowism'.[7] Universities, which at least to some extent used to run on slow time, are now also needful of instantaneity. 'I sent you an email five minutes ago, and you haven't replied!' The issue is as much cultural as technological, however. So, the figure with whom I think more consistently, here as elsewhere, is Bauman. For the transformation of the universities seems to fit the image of liquidity, all that is solid, etc. This does not attach me in any primordial way to the idea of liquid modernity, but it aligns my way of thinking with its purpose. What this suggests is that the idea of liquid modernity is a good possible place not to end so much as to start a conversation. And this, as I recall, was also the best utility of the earlier idea of the postmodern;

6 H. Rosa, *Social Acceleration: A New Theory of Modernity* (New York: Columbia University Press, 2013).
7 G. Boehme, *Invasive Technification: Critical Essays in the Philosophy of Technology* (London: Bloomsbury, 2012).

not, as Bauman would have put it, as a way of answering our questions so much as of asking them: not as a solution, but as a query.

Bauman had a need to escape the idea that he was a postmodern. He was a twentieth-century modernist, in the sense of Simmel, characterized by David Frisby as a sociological impressionist.[8] Simmel had, 100 years ago, characterized the life of the metropolis as marked by excessive stimuli, such as time, speed and money, which issued in the blasé character. Modernity in this way of thinking could be a strong stimulant, but one that also called out the need for some personal calm and contemplation. Bauman maintained a strong conservative element in his thinking, the kind of scepticism towards progress that also wants, for example, to leave nature alone, or at least to entertain the possibility of limits. Ergo the earlier advocacy of gamekeeping as a global attitude over gardening. Bauman was also taken by innovation. He was also a modern, if perhaps a reluctant modernist, as Hannah Arendt has been called.[9] He was struck by the radical and innovative impulse of the early postmodern, after the hardening of solid modernity and its repertoire, before the onset of the postmodern ennui, which echoed that of the modern ennui. He was not attracted to the blasé character. Nor was he taken by the Futurism of Filippo Marinetti, or Trotsky. He was beware of the Faustian spirit of modernity. Yet he could also see, and feel, tectonic changes in our everyday worlds. The university, to follow this example, was solid after the war, and almost virtual, in the institutional sense, into the new century: solid, in the sense that it invited some form of immersion, then; virtual, now, in the sense that students would no longer need to attend the campus or partake of its cultures. Universities had become non-places.

This was also a difference between us. In a distinct sense to the use of these categories just now, we could also say that Bauman was a traditionalist; my generation was modernist, and given to the project of intellectual modernization; the next more fully postmodern. Yet we also know

8 D. Frisby, *Sociological Impressionism: A Reassessment of Georg Simmel's Social Theory* (London: Heinemann, 1981).
9 S. Benhabib, *The Reluctant Modernism of Hannah Arendt* (New York: Rowman & Littlefield, 1996).

that Bauman, the traditionalist, spoke plainly to the rising generation, not least in the so-called South. Part of the semantic problem is that the markers move with us; we are all moderns now, and indeed postmoderns, endlessly given to reinvention, whatever our other desires for identity or meaning in time and place.

I needed, then, to re-enter the labyrinth of liquid modernity myself. In the Stellenbosch University Library, 15 years after its first publication, I found the book and the idea to be much more carefully argued than I had remembered, or been able to absorb at the time of first encounter. Bauman had troubles finishing his book. I also had some struggles completing my own book on Bauman. It is entirely possible that I was unable at that time to register the importance of the book or its animating idea. Reception, as we know, is also contingent, and the question of timing can be crucial. There was much to be unpacked in the book called *Liquid Modernity*, little excuse for the kind of lazy application that might follow in lesser hands. The issue of application is that those who follow are sometimes prone to using labels as excuses for the hard work of thinking, the legacy defined for us by Kant, that the hope of autonomy would mean thinking and speaking for ourselves. The work of critical theory is also inductive, not only deductive; you have to work at it. Great thinkers and great ideas are often turned into cartoon images. But the real treat I found in the library copy of *Liquid Modernity* was in its direct line to South Africa, literally to Somerset West, just up the road from Stellenbosch and yet a world away, depending on which side of the freeway you find yourself on: white, or black. There was a direct connect, in the opening passage of chapter 3, on 'Liquid Time/Space', where the story was of South Africa. This was the privileged dream of the gated community, a white utopia that, like South Africa at large, might in its imagination be free of black folk at the very same time as it depended on them for almost everything.

This was one line to Bauman I had found in South Africa. There were others. For this was a place to think about the state and violence and the other. My overseas friends thought I was still in metaphor when I emailed them that Stellenbosch was on fire. But no: it was literally on fire, as part of a worker–student alliance took to the local streets armed

with both ideas and incendiaries. I have sometimes thought that South
Africa needs its own version of *Modernity and the Holocaust*: 'Modernity
and Apartheid', so extreme a paradigm of modernity is it. Perhaps it is
too far away for people in the West to care. Perhaps it is too hard for its
denizens; but they also love the place.

There were other connections. Another immediately textual
connection I came upon was in that copy of *Legislators and Interpreters*
that I also obtained from the Stellenbosch University Library, and had
now carried to Leeds to share with Bauman. 'Did you steal it?' he asked
me. No; like others before me, I had borrowed it. Almost every page of
this library copy had been engaged with, keenly annotated. In this distant
land, so deeply imbricated in empire, it had also found its readers, who
were struggling to see the connections between his kind of claims and the
fibres of their own lives. This was Bauman's personal experience in that
crazy endless tour of cities, in which people wanted to talk to him, shake
his hand and thank him for some little insight, and to hear his views on
the signs of the times. How should we live? While the sociology discipline police were working on the case for prosecution against Bauman,
that he just made it up, the punters were lapping it up across the world,
not least in Italy and Spain, but as far afield as Scandinavia, South Africa,
China and Australia. Was Bauman careless regarding the rigours of conventional academic sociology? Maybe. Perhaps there comes a time in life
when it is necessary to speak, and to leave the conventions to others.

Along with impact comes the issue of finitude. How long could
the 'Bauman phenomenon' last? I wanted to mark his 90th birthday
publically, as well as privately. Together with Ian Varcoe I had conspired
a decade earlier to stage an event for his 80th birthday in Leeds. Together
with Richard Kilminster, Ian had successfully conspired earlier again to
celebrate Bauman in their *Festschrift*[10] and in a special issue of *Theory,
Culture and Society*.[11] Ian and I had Janina on board for the 80th party,

10 R. Kilminster and I. Varcoe, *Culture, Modernity and Revolution: Essays in Honour of
    Zygmunt Bauman* (London: Routledge, 1996).
11 *Theory, Culture and Society*, 15/1 [Bauman issue] (1998).

until Zygmunt got wind of the idea, and all bets were off. No parties! For his 90th birthday I decided to come in under the radar. I asked a number of friends and colleagues to write postcards or birthday cards for Bauman for our journal *Thesis Eleven*. This was a similar gift and gesture, if one he could not refuse. Janet Wolff, Keith Tester, Chris Rojek, Griselda Pollock, Magdalena Matysek-Imielinsk and I offered our best to him in capsule style. Janet wrote about his garden, and included a photo of the jungle. My own contribution included a photograph of Bauman and me from our visit from South Africa in 2015. It is not posed. We are in the sitting room at Lawnswood Gardens. I am showing him the library copy of *Legislators and Interpreters*, heavily annotated. He is teasing me, as usual.

Bauman gave away his own library, in happier circumstances of release than those in which I had had to part with many of my own books. He was happy to keep this story private. After the Charles University in Prague lost much of its holdings in the recent great flood, Bauman donated his collection to help make up the deficit. He was committed to the idea of use value. By the time we visited him on the occasion of his 90th birthday, the front room was once again full of books, tottering perilously in piles that you had to navigate around in order to get to the safety of a chair. Most of the titles were not in English but were, rather, in East European languages. I asked where they had come from, remembering that his library had been so thoroughly dispersed. Bauman had even, of course, given away his copies of my own books. So much the better, for their potential Czech readers. Sometimes he had to ask me what I had argued when or where, though I could barely remember. He looked at us, in apparent earnest, when quizzed about this new cornucopia of books in his sitting room, and whence it came, and answered with barely a smile: 'When I go to bed, they fornicate!'

We talked, and shared that meal, and drank too much. Cognac, which he was known to offer to travellers even in the morning; it would help settle you before your trip. He seemed to me again to be genuinely happy, in that way he liked to connect to Goethe's parable – I am able to have happy days, but never a fully happy week. Why? Because a week full of happy days would be unbearable. We never spoke about happiness. I do not think it was a core value or goal for him. I was also never persuaded that he was a pessimist, or that this was a central attribute of his thinking. He famously defined his values with Albert Camus: the belief in beauty, the hatred of humiliation. Life, for Bauman, was earnest, but it was never only that. It also rested on love, and loyalty to the other. Happiness mattered to him only inasmuch as you need enough of it to go on. He now seemed again to be happy; he was in love, and had a new wife, Aleksandra Kania, who was also a connection back to the long line of his own story, in Poland and in sociology.

Then it was time to go. There were wet eyes, and hugs and tears again as we left for sleep at Weetwood Hall.

It was the last time I would see him.

In 2016 we were unable to travel to Europe. We received visitors, our Swedish friends from STIAS, at home, and travelled locally. Later we were invited to Chengdu, to deliver keynotes on the Baumans and on the Budapest School by Fu Qilin, the leading Chinese authority on the work of Heller. George Markus, recently departed, was honoured in the opening proceedings. Sian was asked by Fu to read out loud the obituary that David Roberts had written for *Thesis Eleven*. East European critical theory, we discovered to our pleasure, had also found an addressee, and innovators of its own, in China. The intellectual culture was astonishing, and the canopy of East European critical theory one we were happy to share.

Later in 2016 correspondence with Bauman dried up, as it had done before when there was trouble. It was a bad omen when the emails stopped. Likely I played into this; when he backed off, I also backed off, gave him space. Keith and I were in touch with each other often, second-guessing. Bauman's penultimate email, to me and Keith together, is dated 9 September 2016. He rarely wrote to us together. He sent us the proofs for *Retrotopia*, his last work alive.[12] This was not a typical late gesture. Early in our relationship he would send me proofs in the post. The more he wrote, into the last years, the more dismissive he was of his own work, and the less inclined to share in these ways. There was something final

12 Z. Bauman, *Retrotopia* (Cambridge: Polity Press, 2017).

about the receipt of *Retrotopia*: 'Dearest Friends – perhaps you might be interested in the (attached) forthcoming (in January 2017) little book of mine … Love – Z.'

Z - full stop. Full stop. Hello and goodbye. *Do widzenia.*

There was at least one more, cryptic, message. John Hall reminds me that Bauman had written to me 10 December, anticipating the humorous prospect of his own immortality *avec l'Académie française*, the Pole amongst the Greats.[13] John was still working with Bauman on a text in the very late days before his death. I had felt Bauman's breath, and was awaiting the worst. There was further correspondence between Keith and me and then between Lydia and me. We waited. Feeling the air, I wrote him a last email message, in November, to thank him and say goodbye. I troubled the idea of a last, emergency visit. But, then, who was I? There were so many of us around him, who loved him in one way or another; and who were needy, at the wrong time, when his needs had to come first. There were some weeks yet. It was 9 January, Melbourne time, when I received the email from Lydia to say that he was gone. I was unable to say goodbye in any way that seemed appropriate or sufficiently appreciative.

He had sent me an email on 28 April 2000 telling me that he loved faxes, but was lukewarm towards email. Like the rest of the connected world, we had come to rely on the medium, even when it was infrequently exercised. It did not seem a sufficient way to say adieu. It was all I had. He was gone.

Later I still had the urge to send him a line, check in, say hullo. In similar manner, I wondered how Bernard Smith was long after his death, as a kind of reflex, every time I travelled by the aged care facility where he died, in Sumner House off Brunswick Street in Fitzroy. Wiser heads than me have put work into themes such as mourning and melancholy. Myself, I have long been wary of attempts to clinically distinguish between the feelings. We know when we feel good, and when we feel bad. Further attempts to catalogue and differentiate sometimes also seem like professional boundary work. As for me, I was lost. There were bad coincidences;

13 J. Hall, 'Liquid Bauman', *Socio*, 8 (2017).

a violent street massacre almost outside our window in the centre of the city of Melbourne, and the unspeakable inauguration that was stateside. The signs of the times were not good. And Bauman was dead.

I was depressed. Was this the deferred result of a somehow incomplete process of mourning for the death of my own father earlier? Anything is possible. My relationship with my father was distant. His formation and his life chances were dramatically different from my own. Born in 1923 in Stuttgart, he was taken as a babe-in-arms by his family to the Templer colonies in Palestine. These were dissident Lutherans, farmers and artisans whose tradition involved some utopian dimensions, including the idea of settling in the Holy Land, and striving towards the achievement of the kingdom of God on Earth. Not, as I later came to reflect, a bad idea; though they may have picked the wrong place. In 1939 the Templers were interned, fenced in within their own homes in Palestine; they were enemy aliens, German nationals in a British protectorate. They were in the wrong place, and world history moved them on, to Australia. Some of my relatives, the menfolk just older than my father, were called up to the German armed forces. They did not escape into compulsory exile in Australia, but were sent to the Russian front. It occurs to me as I write these lines that it is remotely possible that they were shooting at Bauman's troops at some point, and his troops at them. In 1941 the Templers still in Palestine were transported to internment camps in Australia, where they were imprisoned till 1947. At this point they were given an option: to return to Germany, in ruins, or to stay in Australia. My father and his family opted to stay. My father had met my mother during childhood in Lorch, outside Stuttgart. She was born in Lorch in 1924. Her family stayed in Lorch during the war, when my mother worked in the land army. According to family legend she came to Australia in 1949 armed with a £5 note, a salami and a proposal of marriage by proxy. Customs confiscated the salami, for which she never forgave them, though things got better with the passing of time. Some of the story of their people is told in *The Story of the Beilharz Family*.[14]

14 P. Sauer, *The Story of the Beilharz Family* (Sydney: Beilharz, 1988).

5 The moment of engagement.

Zygmunt Bauman was born in Poznan in 1925. His family fled Hitler into the Soviet Union in 1939. After some study, for he was still a youth,

Bauman joined the Polish army in exile, where he rose to rank of major. Returning to Poland he married Janina in 1948, a year before my parents were married in Melbourne. Janina Lewinson had been born in Warsaw in 1926. Her family on both sides were physicians. Her father was a victim of the Katyn massacre. The irony of the war for the young couple was that they would not have come together except for the war; their class backgrounds before 1939 were too different. Her station was well above his; their circles would not have connected, save for the war and then postwar reconstruction. Some of this story is told in *Winter in the Morning*, some in *A Dream of Belonging*, and in the text that combines them, *Beyond These Walls*.[15] The details of Bauman's life are less than fully clear; we await the publication of his biography by Izabela Wagner for Polity Press. Bauman usually refused to talk about the details of his life, as did my mother and father. Bauman did write a private family history for his children, which Wagner relies on to tell her narrative of his life and times. He showed this document to me once, overnight as I retired to bed on a visit to Lawnswood Gardens all those years ago, urging me to read it and then never to speak of it again. The publication of Wagner's biography, and the possible publication of the document in its entirety, will throw more light on these matters, though there will likely remain some controversy surrounding his postwar activities. My father wrote no such document that I know of. He had fine script, and secretarial ambitions, but no apparent need to write. He did say to me on one occasion that one of the good things about being interned was that nobody was shooting at you, and that being in the backblocks of Australia was not so different from being in Palestine. It was dry. But he lost part of his life there. He knew what camp life was. But this was very clearly an internment camp, not a camp of forced labour or a death camp. His story was not that of *Modernity and the Holocaust*, though his path was necessarily connected to the global reach of the Third Reich, which of course extended to Palestine, and even to the far-flung flat bush of Tatura. Nazism was a serious contender to become a world-system, even in faraway Australia.

15 J. Bauman, *Beyond These Walls: Escaping the Warsaw Ghetto – a Young Girl's Story* (London: Virago, 2006).

This was the generation that had to deal with fascism and communism, as well as the darkest days of capitalism – the Depression – and its halcyon days, of the postwar boom, into which I and my generation were born. Given this cleft of experience, hopes and dreams, it is not surprising that these generations often became conflicted. My relationship with my father was deeply conflicted, compounded by the arrival of hippy culture and the Vietnam War. He went right, in effect, worrying about issues such as obedience and decency. He used to worry a lot about doing the right thing. So, differently, did I. I went left, worrying about issues such as freedom and equality, though all this was likely overdetermined by the Oedipus complex. My parents were good to us. In retrospect, it seems likely that the household was dominated by my mother. My father spent his life in Australia working, extruding and selling electric cable, first on the factory floor as a process worker, then in the office: white collar. There was a strong Protestant ethic in the air. When I came later to read Weber in college, it all made immediate sense. I both shared Marx's concern with the problem of alienated labour and was deeply committed practically to the Protestant ethic. Like my father and mother, I spent almost my whole life working, though I now sometimes wonder why, or else why so unrelentingly. I was not knocking on heaven's door. And I did not think of the best parts of my working life as work, though they were also that. I understood work as labour, but also as creation. These spheres now seem increasingly to be bifurcated.

Did I, then, make of Bauman a father figure? I do not think so, though, as I have said, anything is possible. One is not always master in one's own house. In some ways Bauman reminded me, rather, of my grandfather, my paternal Opa; I never met my mother's parents. He had the same striking dark eyes, the same preference for silence and some of the same mannerisms: a particular pattern of humming his weariness with the world, a sense of calm, a fondness for birds. Bauman was not allowed to be close to his grandfather. I was not especially close to my Opa either. He was a reserved man, strict and distant. A carpenter, he taught us how to drive in a fair nail and how to clean up afterwards, but otherwise his workshop was verboten. Opa was stern, and silent. He smelled

6 Playing with jazz fusion band Serenity.

of coffee and sawdust or shavings. My father smelled of sweat, cologne and cigarettes. I remember his smell better; we must have been physically closer. Bauman understood the importance of smell, and, rarely for a sociologist, wrote about it.[16] Bauman smelled of whatever he was cooking

16 Z. Bauman, 'The Sweet Scent of Decomposition', in C. Rojek and B. Turner (eds), *Forget Baudrillard?* (London: Routledge, 2002).

and his pipe tobacco. He was not always shaven, later at least, and that stubble felt as though it might draw blood, though its touch was always endearing, and his embrace was complete and unhesitating – not a universal attribute among men, in my experience.

What did these friends and mentors mean to me? With the passing of my years I have become increasingly aware of my attachment to some of these leading members of the previous generation, who, unlike me, had experienced the age of extremes, as well as the age of austerity and the space called the bloodlands. They were European; they knew about rubble, and ruins. They knew about what came before liquid modernity. They knew about what came before solid modernity. This was modernity in ruins.

They had something I wanted, in terms of culture and understanding. I was deeply connected to Bernard Smith, but I am not sure exactly that I then felt love for him so much, perhaps, as an enormous admiration and an abiding affection. We worked together for years, and we remained serious friends in the time of his decline. I was among those who read to him out loud when he was past reading; he was never past thinking and talking. I read to him from his masterpiece, *European Vision and the South Pacific*,[17] and was still learning from him in those last days. I am not sure that we ever embraced, even though there was great good feeling between us. I developed strong feelings for Alastair Davidson, my dissertation supervisor and mentor, and before then for N. W. Saffin. But I felt no need for fathers; I had one already, and he had done a fine job in trying circumstances. I had spent years aggravating my parents when I was younger. They never gave up on me. I had feelings of love for Ágnes Heller, though perhaps the better category is the one she valued so much: gratitude. My affection for the Markuses, and for Castoriadis, was very deep. With Bauman, I notice from my correspondence that the language of love comes into play closer to the turn of the century. We might observe, in league with his arguments in *Liquid Love*, that the word has become much diluted in its everyday use, the most insipid being the

17 B. Smith, *European Vision and the South Pacific* (Oxford: Oxford University Press, 1960).

ubiquitous throwaway 'Love you!' – no subject, no author, no 'I'.[18] There was a sense of connection between us that, like the other emotions, I could never quite capture in words. Bauman and I both sensed and observed the intensity of our encounters. This seems to me to have been some kind of love.

Was this, then, some other kind of fixation on my part? Was I hopelessly attracted to leading figures of lost worlds of radical Marxism? I do not think so. They had the best ideas and depth of radical culture that were available to me. They were survivors of world history, messengers of the critical tradition that I identified with. They were my teachers. They had so much that I wanted, and were willing to give. My contact with them enabled and intensified the process of learning and cultural transfer between us. These were my mentors, then my friends in text and in the flesh. My advantage was to share in the ineffable moments of just being with them. In Bauman's case, as he often used to say, my job was to put order into the chaos of his writing, which sometimes seemed thrown off, in haste, and was capable of lurching from idea to idea. I had learned from the early Marx that humans were sentient, suffering subjects whose core need was creatively to labour. Early on, I had learned that to know thinkers like this, if it was at all possible, was to begin to think differently about the world of text, mind, idea. This possibility opened the sense that author was also subject, thrown into the world and seeking, like the rest of us, to adjudicate between theory and experience, wisdom and feeling. In the case of Bauman, it was for me the little things, the less directly cerebral things, that gave me insight and appreciation into this phenomenon, this writer's life spent in wonder and horror at this modern sublime, at what humans were indeed capable of, for better and for worse. These remain things that are not easily spoken, or committed to print. They remain real, and formative, nevertheless.

Thus Joan Didion: 'I know why we try to keep the dead alive: we try to keep them alive in order to keep them with us.'[19]

18 Z. Bauman, *Liquid Love: On the Frailty of Human Bonds* (Cambridge: Polity Press, 2003).
19 J. Didion, *The Year of Magical Thinking* (New York: Harcourt, 2005), 225.

But, as Didion adds, we also need to move on, to bury our dead. Our ghosts will ever also linger, however. Perhaps we need best to acknowledge them, thank them, listen to what they might have to say and move on. Too soon, we will join them. In the meantime, as Harry Blatterer, the sociologist of friendship, put it to me in conversation about the subject of this book, we continue to talk with our dead because they remain our interlocutors. The conversation never ends. Our ghosts never finally leave us, not until we leave them.

Part II

Ways of going on

Chapter 4

Entanglements

Our paths had crossed, Bauman's and mine; or perhaps they were parallel paths. He told me early on that the key coordinates of his work and thinking were socialism and culture. This was also true for me, increasingly so, as cultural sociology became as important a field for me as critical sociology, or historical sociology. In this regard my intellectual, if not my personal, relations with my other teachers were more intersectional. With Castoriadis and Heller there was much admiration, but I had never mastered either classical philosophy, economics or psychoanalysis. I could never know as much about art history or the visual as Bernard Smith. There was also a wealth of tradition available to Bauman that I did not possess. But I had, into the 1980s, made it my purpose to read the history of socialism and Marxism culturally, as bearers of a wealth of traditions of thinking about modernity. The postmodern then became a frame of reference for thinking this anew in what seemed very likely to be new times.

As I have mentioned, like others I was slow at first to recognize the importance of Bauman's project. Perhaps it was still a work in progress. Maybe it was me, always distracted by other things in the storehouse of possibilities of intellectual culture. It was a big toy box. In the case of Bauman, I was attracted to the combination of socialism and culture, and, via the Budapest School, I became more closely convinced of the value of East European critical theory. So I had solicited entries for my *Social Theory* book on Castoriadis and Heller, but not yet on Bauman.

I suppose there is also a possible chance that Bauman's best was at this point yet to come. Castoriadis had by this point published his magisterial *Imaginary Institution of Society* (1975) and Heller had published *A Theory of History* (1982). Castoriadis' classic is segmented, or assembled, though Heller's – if these are representative works of some highpoint – is more fully coherent. *Modernity and the Holocaust* (1989) is, in contrast, broken, a series of powerful essays thinking their way around the subject unveiled by Janina, and its culmination is arguably in the next book, which I have often thought his greatest or most powerful: *Modernity and Ambivalence* (1991). *Modernity and Ambivalence* contains the missing tail of *Modernity and the Holocaust*, in the argument concerning the doubly outcast, the *Ostjuden*.

Modernity and the Holocaust works as a kind of assemblage, almost like an exploded view. Some of Bauman's books, both before and after, display a more conventional academic narrative: beginning – middle – end, footnotes all the way. The Holocaust book is more like a work of sociological impressionism, or an approach of successive approximations. It seems as though the impossibility, or initial incomprehensibility, of its object indicates the necessity of a circling approach. How to begin to make sense of the Holocaust? The systematic nature of the regime of industrial killing does not here call out a systematic treatise to explain it. By the early 1990s I had also now known enough of Bauman to observe how at this stage he used to work, or, at least, what his writing habits were. He used to write at length, fond as he was of textile metaphors, warp and weft, and then cut it off. Not every idea was well placed, in this strategy, and there were already clear signs of what he later joked about as graphomania. Periods of intense writing such as this would then alternate with a dense programme of trips and visits out. He wrote at length, but not always, in my experience, systematically. Perhaps this was also because he was using writing as a way to think, to sort issues out, if not to resolve them. My sense was that he became increasingly impatient with his own ideas, and was always eager to move on. Ergo what he called my job, to put order into the chaos of his writings. He was the creator, I was the interpreter. Maybe I was the messenger; that would explain the odd angry shot in my direction from those others who invariably knew better than both Bauman and me.

The first serious practical bridge between us here was my study *Labour's Utopias*. This was published in boards in 1992. For the paperback, Routledge solicited an endorsement from Bauman, as related above in the story about Bauman's coat.

By 1992 I had at least worked out how to place Bauman practically. We were now collaborators on *Thesis Eleven*. We included his views on the postmodern in the MIT Press *Thesis Eleven* reader, *Between Totalitarianism and Postmodernity* (1992). There we also republished the views of other central thinkers for us – Fehér, Heller, Alain Touraine, Axel Honneth, Johann Arnason, Castoriadis – as well as work of our own. Our business in the Antipodes was export as well as import. We wanted to speak, as well as translate.

In 1994 I published *Postmodern Socialism*. This was the first book that I workshopped, co-developed with its Australian publisher, John Iremonger. This book would not have happened had it not been for this cooperation. John and I would meet periodically when he visited Melbourne from his base in Sydney and play a kind of publishing ping pong. He would tell me what he wanted to publish, where he saw the important gaps in the market; I would tell him what I was interested in, where I saw the arguments going. He wanted a book on the state for his innovative sidebar series, *Interpretations*. At some point he gave in, and I wrote a manuscript on romanticism, city and state. Its fields stretched across modern and postmodern, romanticism, socialism and enlightenment. It is likely the cleanest book I ever wrote, thanks largely to the tough editorial love put upon it by series editors John Frow and Ken Ruthven. There are three references in it to Bauman, to *Legislators and Interpreters* and to *Memories of Class*. At this point it is possible that I showed my irritation with the postmodern and its sometimes shrill, often ill-considered claims concerning the novelty of the now. Modernism looked to me like the now, in culture and art; and enlightenment looked rather richer and more historically thick and diverse than the newly arrived were able to detect. Romanticism, that current of modern self-criticism that also remains inescapable, had deeper echoes with the postmodern than its zealous pioneers were able or willing to recognize. All the same, the mere acknowledgement of the postmodern in the title of my book was inflammatory, as I discovered when I was attacked for the sin of fatalism in public. This was flattering attention, but misplaced, for the logic of the accusation was that what I said might make a difference to the prospects of socialism in Australia. I offered a two-word response; not the more obvious, but the more considered: 'Do better!' But there will always be those who know better.

I could not at first find in my correspondence any view from Bauman on this book. I made the mistake of imagining that any message would have arrived in 1994 or 1995. I found it later: 1996. Was he just busy? He wrote to me on 21 September that he had swallowed the book in one gulp. Others liked it. *Postmodern Socialism* became a bridge between Jeff Alexander and me. Jeff 'thought it really interesting' (16/5/96). Saskia Sassen wanted to use it as a text for her Columbia postgraduate class. It inspired a book by Chamsy El Ojeili on *Postmodern Communism*. Scholars of the stature of Patrice Higonnet used it in his book on Paris; thinkers as subtle as Leon van Schaik used it in his recent study of architecture. Don Levine, the leading expert on Simmel, wrote to me of 'what sheer pleasure it was …' (13/4/97). Chris Rojek wrote that it was a superb little book, saying: 'I wish I'd published this book' (5/12/94). Chris became a good friend, a fine intellectual whose achievement was perhaps under-recognized because of his dual identity as publisher. He was a different kind of antipodean, perhaps, for he always had a foot in each of two worlds, publishing others and writing himself. We routinely met up at ASA proceedings, or else in London or in Melbourne. For us, this was the basis of friendship, that we could move so easily between the world of ideas and the logistics of editing and publishing feasibility. Rojek was, of course, a long-term supporter and publisher of Bauman, mid-career, with the pioneering essays on the postmodern, and late, with the Sage Classics reprinting of earlier works such as *Culture as Praxis* (1973).

Postmodern Socialism even had its own Billy Bragg moment. Billy was a frequent visitor to Melbourne, in the charge of Vivian Lees, the leading rock promoter who was my best friend in primary school. Viv insisted I meet him, knowing that we had some things in common – not so much culture and socialism, as per Bauman, as, in this case, music and socialism. We met at Basement Discs, where Billy was to do an instore. The joint was packed. The doors had been closed for health and safety reasons: overcrowding, just too many fans. Billy was the milkman of human kindness, but also dead serious about socialism. I gave him a copy of my book, shook his hand; I wanted to thank him for everything that musicians such as he do. He began to quiz me on the spot, as the punters waited, their arms folded, feet tapping in anticipation; it was already past show time. The book looked great he said, and thank you, but had I managed sufficiently to establish the clear distinction between socialism and communism in these pages? Things lightened up when he spotted a Louis Prima disc on the racks nearby: 'You gotta listen to this!' Then he played, and sang, and kicked ass; Woody Guthrie, alive again.

And Bauman? It is possible that Bauman did not so much like my book, and did not care to tell me this. It is indeed possible that *Postmodern Socialism* overrates the potential and empirical legacy of enlightenment, and underplays the importance of romanticism or the potential novelty of the postmodern. Probably Bauman and I held differing, and mobile, positions on the spectrum that runs from what we call 'romanticism' to what we call 'enlightenment'. Following Ernst Cassirer, I was for my part happy to unsettle the hard distinction between romanticism and enlightenment – another A/B.[1] But I have no reason to deny any of my work. If this was a wayward child, it nevertheless remains a personal favourite. As with my Bauman book, I used to say of *Postmodern Socialism* that its best feature was the cover: the post-Soviet image by the collaborative couple Farrell and Parkin, *Red Squares*. I tried the image out on my six-year-old daughter, whose understanding confirmed our choice of image. What did it show? Fear, in face of the future. She had understood intuitively the look on the face of the pantomime proletarian: 'He's afraid' – as well we might be of modern times.

1 See E. Cassirer, *Rousseau, Kant, Goethe* (Princeton, NJ: Princeton University Press, 1970).

I was also busy at work in this period on my other antipodes, writing a book on the Australian Labor Party called *Transforming Labor*, which also appeared in 1994, cover courtesy this time of the postwar suburbanist Australian painter John Brack and the designer Chong. Here Bauman again appears only thrice, though you can see his influence in the design of my book as clearly as you can see Joseph Paxton's hand in the Crystal Palace, or Frederick Law Olmsted's in Central Park.

Bauman had laboured in this field at least twice, first in his own postdoctoral work for *Between Class and Elite* (1972), and again ten years later in *Memories of Class*. His research and its message across these years were continuous. The labour movement had lost its way as a social movement, by virtue of entering the state via the path of what his friend Ralph Miliband called 'parliamentary socialism' in the United Kingdom. (There's another research project: Bauman and Miliband … Bauman and Leszek Kołakowski; Bauman and C. Wright Mills, who visited Poland three times, 1957, 1959, 1961; etc.) The radical impulse of the earlier labour movement had been incorporated into the state but also, as Bauman would put it, into consumer capitalism. The pursuit of the 'good society' had given way to the pursuit of the 'goods society'. Labour was no longer outside or below the belly of the beast, but well and truly inside it. In more popular parlance, labour was now part of the problem of capitalism and modernity rather than of the solution to or transcendence of these problems or social relations.

This was a common new left critique of capitalism, or, as it was sometimes then known, neo-capitalism. Sometimes this line of critique was characterized as neo-Marxist. There was something 'neo' in the air, before the 'post' arrived. Its most eminent version came in 1964 with the publication of Herbert Marcuse's *One-Dimensional Man*. Bauman's sensibility echoed the diagnosis, if not the prognosis. In sociological terms, this was a version of the argument concerning embourgeoisement. Viewed from the perspective of consumption, the Western working class was now able to enter the cathedrals of capitalism, the palaces called malls, and to stay. Viewed from the perspective of politics, the two-party system was aligned around the centre. There were no serious electoral alternatives, which led some to portray neo-capitalism as indeed totalitarian, no choices: Coke versus Pepsi. Bourgeois democracy was a sham. This sense of closure took Marcuse, if not Bauman, in the direction of Third Worldism as a future or way out. The Western left was rarely able to confront the possibility that there was no future for socialism as we had previously understood it, as a state of affairs to be achieved. Bauman had understood, at least from his study of utopia, that socialism was a goal rather than an end state. Socialism was movement, not stasis. Others, seeing the incorporation of the proletariat into the Western system of spoils, and needing to identify an alternative revolutionary actor, looked to the peasantry or to guerrilla war, or, even more hopefully, to students, in their search for the revolutionary subject. The young Marx had imagined the proletariat as the negation of bourgeois society. Now the negation had to be located elsewhere, with the outsiders. As Frantz Fanon understood, this would involve violent revenge. As Bauman understood, this possibility would, however, lead to the endless reproduction of the dialectics of master and slave.

It is worth pausing for a moment to contemplate the available theoretical options for a thinker such as Bauman in the 1980s, the period when his own views became more prominent. This momentary detour can only be by way of a thought experiment, as Bauman's thinking was always already formed from the moment he became an intellectual in Warsaw. In retrospect, several movements or traditions nevertheless stand out. There was at the least humanist or Western Marxism; hermeneutics, a long-time echo across Bauman's work; both Marxist structuralism and structuralism itself; semiology; revolutionary Marxism, championed via the figure of Trotsky by *New Left Review*; cultural studies, the longer tail of which stretched from Raymond Williams to Stuart Hall; and critical theory, as exemplified in the work of the Frankfurt School but later pluralizing to take in the French, notably Foucault (the nuance here is apparent: Bauman was not influenced by Althusser, who he took to be a Stalinist version of Parsons, but he certainly was taken by Foucault and the critique of power and institutions). These were all, in a sense, invented traditions, like romanticism and enlightenment but even more pluralized; their key personnel often overlapped, for traditions are also ex post facto constructions. Thus, for example, some later surveys of Western Marxism came to include structuralism, even though the ways of thinking involved could be violently opposed. In Bauman's case, many of these currents combined and crossed, including existentialism, libertarianism and conservatism. Modernity, in his way of thinking, may have been selectively enabling, but it was also always deeply problematical, demanding a conversation without ending.

Bauman came to be known as famously eclectic, intellectually promiscuous even. This was consistent with his earlier record, when the cast of interlocutors was always abundant, and governed by a pragmatic sensibility. Culture was indeed an immense storehouse of possibilities. Signing up with one intellectual tribe and its *doxa*, on this way of thinking, would be the kiss of death, the very end of thinking. For many ideas or problems, such as the image of the socially dirty or slimy, there were thinkers such as Mary Douglas or Jean-Paul Sartre ready to hand. This was also consistent with the nature of his thinking; A is also B. When we drop down into the fine grain of any body of work in its texts, verse and line, there will be all kinds of crossovers and coincidences. Interesting thinkers are also contradictory, and eschew templates. This is one of the reasons why interesting thinkers are appropriated for different and sometimes hostile lineages. What we easily call 'traditions' are also classificatory conveniences or projections that are too easily fetishized. Bauman was sceptical about fads and fashions, and reluctant to see social theories as franchises, or tribal memberships. If in some sense Bauman was conservative, in others he was also libertarian, intellectually promiscuous.

As with hermeneutics, Bauman had a lifelong affinity with critical theory. With the passing of time the political logic of critical theory in the Frankfurt mode shifted closer to the tradition of liberal democracy, as is evident in the work of Habermas and then Honneth. Bauman did not harbour any significant expectations of this drift to liberalism. Liberalism will always be tied to the individualism that he found so problematical. His affinities were, rather, with the thinkers of the first generation. Within the tradition of the Frankfurt School, there were echoes of Theodor Adorno in Bauman, and certainly the classic *Dialectic of Enlightenment* was a clear presence on Bauman's horizon, especially after the appearance of *Modernity and the Holocaust*. Alongside these echoes in Adorno and, differently, Marcuse there were also affinities with thinkers such as Erich Fromm, for whom Having now stood in for Being, and for whom the art of loving stood central in everyday life. Into the 1970s, in Bauman's case, structure and the ideas of structuralism also still loomed large. Thinkers such as Lévi-Strauss gave Bauman important categories such as the distinction between anthropoemic and anthropophagic impulses. Some societies or populations were given to devouring the other, others to expelling them; some, for Bauman, combined both strategies depending on the political breeze.

More fundamentally, perhaps, and here anticipating the earlier project of the Alexander School, Bauman wanted to learn from both structuralism and hermeneutics. As he explains in his final but one Polity publication, the important and until now lost *Sketches for a Theory of Culture* (2018), structuralism was for him what Feuerbach was for Marx: a point of no return wherever the route was finally to go. This is a fascinating text for Bauman scholars. It was suppressed at the point of his exile in 1969, his own copy literally being confiscated as he crossed the border out of Poland. There is little subversive in it, except perhaps the aura of its Jewish humanist Marxist author, who, after all, had been sacked from his chair at Warsaw for that most noble of travesties: 'corrupting the youth'. In terms of social theory, this was a moment when culture or culturalism had not yet been set hard against the notion of structure; it was possible, indeed, to speak of both together. Culture and structure need here to be discussed together, as structure is also a practice, or, to put it differently, structure also always has a history. The period name for this was often semiotics, wherein structure and sign are configured together. Structuralization, for Bauman, also necessitates the discussion of individualization. Both these dimensions become more pronounced with urbanization; as for Simmel, modernity is best viewed through the prism of the city, and its radiation out, economically and symbolically. At a more abstract level, for Bauman, what we call urbanization is really an effect of industrialization and modernization. Bauman's was not an

7 Bauman in his office, University of Warsaw.

argument for the convergence of communism and capitalism after the Second World War, but it was indicative of an overarching interest in modernity, which would later give way to the term 'postmodern' and then, in turn, 'liquid modern'.

Structuralism was to remain a constant, if subordinate, theme in the work of Zygmunt Bauman. The structuralist movement in ideas was, after all, one of the most powerful in the twentieth century, reaching back as an invented tradition through Freud to Marx, and forward from Ferdinand de Saussure to Foucault. This would cross over with the notion of the critique of power, and what Ricoeur called the hermeneutics of suspicion, whose key thinkers he took to be Marx, Nietzsche and Freud. In its cartoon image, the key French structuralists were Roland Barthes, Foucault, Jacques Lacan and Lévi-Strauss (this was to leave out Althusser, who was the most influential among Marxist structuralists, but far less influential in the broader flows of French intellectual life). Its insights into notions of depth and representation, and its interest in language, remain formative for us who follow. Its repression and forgetting after post-structuralism remains one of the great ironies of modern theory. So soon as it appeared, it had been made to disappear. *Da! Fort!*

Yet the challenges of structuralism have not dissipated, any more than the idea of structures has ceased to have meaning in everyday life. We still know a structural encounter, when we meet race, gender or inequality, when we deal with institutions such as the prison or the hospital, or the university or the state. We have not escaped from the Freudian slip, or from the notion of symptom. Structure was, of course, like system, a necessary metaphor; and, like others, including the postmodern or liquid modern, it could always be used for lazy rather than rigorous thinking. Structure was, for Bauman, an activity, an ordering device whose application could result in terror or in mediocrity. Structure was also important for Bauman in this latter, more conventional sense. Structuring and structuralism were both ordinary and intellectual activities. Structuring, the pursuit of order, was an elementary form of human activity. Like the need for classification, humans could not do without the pursuit of order, even though its results could also be tragic and not merely humdrum.

Bauman's views on the future of socialism in the West were also inflected by this way of thinking. Although his was plainly a humanist socialism, it was also informed by the logic of Marx in the *Eighteenth Brumaire*: history is not a matter of acting just as we please. There are scripts, parts to play, constraints and limits on possibilities that ordinary folk are well aware of. So Bauman argues, in *Between Class and Elite*, against the intellectual projection of a revolutionary vocation onto the English working class. This is not, for Bauman, a matter of denying revolutionary spontaneity or the power of reforming zeal. The working-class movement has a great history of struggle and cultural transformation. But this working class is not Marx's working class, or the working class that finds itself choreographed, or even conscripted, into the dreams of various passing revolutionaries. The working class has no vocation, at least not one delivered from outside or above. Its self-activity may impress, from the communes and co-ops to the councils and little Moscows to Solidarity in Gdansk, but it will not happily follow orders from self-appointed generals. Viewed from the macro level of society, however, the drift of labour into the twentieth century was towards social partnership or corporatism, integration or incorporation.

The first English-language version of the argument, published in book form in 1972, got Bauman stick from no less a left hero than E. P. Thompson, a thinker from whom who you might expect more sympathy; but perhaps Thompson couldn't get it right with the Poles, or at least the East Europeans, whom he set out to straighten out, first, passingly, Bauman, then, at much greater length, Kołakowski.

There was something superior – even perhaps faintly aristocratic – about the treatment that could be meted out to the East European dissidents. I certainly have clear memories of the stiff Anglo superiority, or its puffed-up Australian version, being brought to bear on the members of the Budapest School in the time of their Melbourne exile. *Who were these people?* And by what right did they have the nerve to be so passionate about the ways of the world? How could they claim still to be socialists while insisting on their distance from actually existing socialism? And how dare they speak of *market* socialism, or of markets at all?

Janina touched this nerve later, when she wrote to me on 6 April 2004, bearing the good news of Zygmunt's recognition by the University of Leeds.

> Good news … On April 22 Zygmunt gets a Doctor of Letters honorary degree from his own University of Leeds – a rare honour in this country and a profound satisfaction: he had come here to be the head of the department as a complete stranger, a bloody foreigner from a little known eastern country with a communist regime and at the beginning met with the distrust of his colleagues and assistants. I feel happy and proud and want you to know about it.

Her message puts me in a mind of another story, relayed this time by Bernard Smith. In the 1940s Bernard was friends and neighbours with the refugee painter Sali Hermann, another Polish Jew whose final destination was not Canberra, or Leeds, but Sydney. As he relates the story, in Sali's voice:

> 'I've no trouble with Australians at all,' he would say in his rather throaty continental accent. 'I go to a pub with a friend and when I get too many curious looks I wait for a break in the noise, then I stare at my friend and say in a loud voice, 'The real trouble with this bloody country is that there are too many fucking foreigners in it.' He would then turn and greet everyone in the bar with a disarming grin. It never failed to work.[2]

This was not Bauman's style; and Leeds was not Sydney. Sydney's culture, as Hermann's story suggests, could be raucous and libertarian in its manners. It was an upstart port city, more democratic in temper even as it was also racist. Bauman conducted himself, rather, as John Carroll has observed, as a gentleman. Given his life path, it is likely that it was in fact recommended to avoid attracting attention, except by way of the word. Yet, like Sali Hermann, Bauman was also an outsider.

The Baumans were indeed strangers in the midst of the English and their left. Both Jewish and Polish, and with communist pasts, they came from the wrong part of Europe in terms of the cultural capitalism of the Anglo university system.

2 P. Beilharz, *Imagining the Antipodes: Culture, Theory and the Visual in the Work of Bernard Smith* (Melbourne: Cambridge University Press, 1997), 25.

The fact that they were awash in the thick intellectual culture of East-Central Europe was blurred in this imaginary hierarchy. Mixing up philosophy and sociology was viewed as a weakness here rather than as a strength. Conservatives kept their cold, analytic distance, while the Marxist left, obsessed with its own sense of Continental superiority by association, chose to privilege Paris and Frankfurt over other sources in its own display of metropolitan provincialism.

What, then, was this critical tradition? From a somewhat different position within English Marxism to Edward Thompson, Perry Anderson had announced in 1976 in *Considerations on Western Marxism*[3] that there was still, after a century, no decent map of the traditions. Then, in 1978, there appeared in English the magisterial mapping trilogy by Kołakowski, *Main Currents of Marxism*.[4] For Kołakowski, it included figures such as Kazimierz Kelles-Krauz; for Bauman, Polish pioneers of sociology such as Julian Hochfeld and Stanisław Ossowski, who stayed, and Florian Znaniecki, who went stateside. Earlier, and most famously, there was Rosa Luxemburg. Kołakowski somehow didn't quite make it for the new left, however. It is probably fair to say that Kołakowski's epic was occluded from left-wing sight because of his politics, which were beyond Marxism. Right kind of book – magisterial, in fact; wrong author. The East Europeans posed something of an embarrassment to the Anglo left, as they could justifiably claim to have seen the future, which did not work, which harassed and punished Marxists and then expelled them. This was also apparently what put Thompson in a state of bepuzzlement and rage: that these folk could no longer agree with us, we who, of course, knew better. The horizon here was not what had actually happened in Eastern Europe, but the dream of what might just possibly happen in England: the final triumphant arrival of socialism. Later this was to become the divisive issue around the peace movement, with its claim for unilateral American disarmament. The more orthodox sections of the English left could not remove themselves from the legacy of the Russian Revolution. The East Europeans, rather, agreed

3 P. Anderson, *Considerations on Western Marxism* (London: New Left Books, 1976).
4 L. Kołakowski, *Main Currents of Marxism*, 3 vols (Oxford: Oxford University Press, 1978).

with Max Weber's aperçu to the young hothead Lukács, that this experience would set the cause of socialism back by 100 years. East European Marxism owed at least as much to Weber as to Marx. Bureaucracy and the state loomed at least as large as the threat of capital, or of reification.

Bauman was a loyal Polish communist for a decade, in which time anti-fascism gave way to a serious commitment to the cause of socialist reconstruction in Poland. Within his own lifeworld, after the Second World War, there was no alternative. For better or worse, he was in the tent, whereas the English left were outside the carnival, cheering for intellectual heroes of their own choosing from across the Channel. So relations between the Western left and the East Europeans were complicated. The East Europeans despised the Soviet Union, who kept invading, and were themselves rather increasingly committed to what at that point was called market socialism. For much of the Marxist left in the West the only market socialism that might be tolerated would be Lenin's partial gestures under the New Economic Policy. These different Marxists had little in common, apart from their origins in Marx's work, and even over this they differed, as in the debate over the best Marx: young or mature.

It was as though the English new left, as represented here, always needed to know better. Thompson's 1972 review of Bauman's first book in English appeared in the *Guardian*.[5] It was radically and thoroughly dismissive, of the approach, of sociology, of the argument about labour incorporation, and even of style. Thompson left little standing. This may have seemed a small matter. It was not, as Keith Tester has shown – and we will return to this. It was a nasty piece of work, and it smelled of police action against the Pole.

Bauman told me that this review set back the reception of his work by a decade. That is all he said – a *sentence*: one sentence; ten years. Although he later presented *Memories of Class* as an exit, it was also very likely a return to an argument that had significantly more purchase than the baseless hopes of those who awaited salvation by Labour and were instead rewarded with new Labour. For most of the twentieth century in Anglo

5 E. P. Thompson, 'Boring from Without', *Guardian*, 28 December 1972.

cultures there prevailed the left hope that labour parties might somehow miraculously deliver socialism. This was, at the very least, the default position on much of the left: campaign for the election of a Labour government with socialist policies, follow the older strategies of entryism, and so on. Inhabitants of other cultures, such as those in Italy and France, put these hopes upon their communist parties. By the 1980s too many on the left were suckers for the allure of office, and its illusions of power.

The situation in the Antipodes anticipated the arrival of Tony Blair by more than a decade. In 1983 the Labor government of Bob Hawke had come to office, and with as much mystery as fanfare announced that its reign would take place under the combined banner of a social contract between the political and industrial wings of the labour movement. This document was to be known as the ALP–ACTU Accord, for the bipartite agreement between the Australian Labor Party and the Australian Council of Trade Unions. After the unceremonious sacking of the Whitlam Labor government by the Governor General in 1975, this looked to many, if not most, of the left as the best news since sliced bread. The peak labour organization, the ACTU, would have a place at the table – or so it seemed at first blush to the hopeful. Together with Rob Watts and others, I became a major critic of these developments and their false premises and promises.[6] The rush to new Labor was such that the Melbourne executive of the Communist Party resigned in order to swap horses, joining the centre-right of the Labor Party in 1984; not quite what Eric Blair had feared, but a surprise all the same.

Along with other, later pressures this led to the eventual collapse of the Communist Party of Australia, and to a revived hegemony for Labor and for New Labor. This was a moment in which the critical language of corporatism was revived in order to make sense of this new pursuit of the older dream of the prospect of harmony between the social partners of labour, capital and the state. Most of the critique of Labor took place in journals, monthlies and weeklies. Some of it occurred in *Thesis Eleven*.

---

6 See P. Beilharz, *Socialism and Modernity* (Minneapolis: Minnesota University Press, 2009).

Its best expression was in Julian Triado's 1984 essay 'Corporatism, Democracy and Modernity', which we then republished in *Between Totalitarianism and Postmodernity* in 1992. Triado also summoned Bauman to make his case, that the political imperatives of early labour had now been replaced by economic claims. General claims to the rights of citizens were replaced by claims to economic status or contribution, or productivity. Citizenship claims, here, were subsumed in claims to functional position.

The deep irony here was that, in Bauman's terms and in those of *Postmodern Socialism* and *Transforming Labor*, the formative claims of labour were backward-looking, and, indeed, romantic, rural and communitarian. Labour's utopia was that of the guilds. In Australia it became the utopia of the backyard, of the dream of non-labour rather than labour, and most recently of personal real estate investment as the best escape from the world of work. The ALP's project now was to steer and even to modernize capitalism, the latter through the strategy of industry development policy in the manner of what was then called the Swedish model. This, at least, was the template put upon the ALP by its left supporters. They were to be bitterly disappointed.

This was the context in which we fell again on Bauman's precedent in *Memories of Class*. Marx had claimed that the working class was both outside society, removed from it, and yet was potentially the last class, even the universal class. The golden years of the postwar boom ended that. The factory, for Bauman, receded as the primary site of popular life in Western capitalism, to be superseded symbolically by the mall, the life of production by the realm of consumption. The implication was clear. The immense accumulation of commodities upon which capital rested was now generated offshore. Production shifted from the heartlands of capital to what we used to call the Third World, these days the South. On a global scale, the Western working class was now in the tent – though this would not last, as any historicist would tell you. Patterns of inequality, as Bauman here observed, would increasingly become horizontal, regional. Capital and labour were crucial actors in this postwar compromise, but so was the state, and – as I have argued before – there is a libertarian streak in Bauman's thinking in this regard. There is no good reason to expect much of the state; if it takes one finger, as Janina warned in *Winter in the Morning*, it will take the whole arm.[7] They knew, because they had been too close to the state, and in socialist Poland the state was everything – or, at least, it aspired to be total, via the Soviet example. In the West, in the meantime, for socialists the labour parties subsumed the labour movements into themselves, and in turn became part of the problem.

These trends were also powerfully apparent in the Antipodes, which often followed global trends, but also sometimes pioneered their development. In my youth those around me had expected great things of Eurocommunist parties, this against all odds. Now their hopes had often been transferred to labour parties. In Britain, as in the Antipodes, these beliefs were based on illusion. I had never joined a party of any kind, believing, with the best of Marx and later Castoriadis, in the value of autonomy. By this point of life I had become convinced that it was time to move on, not from socialist norms and values but from the institutional forms and instrumental logics that had replaced them. The tease in the idea of *Postmodern Socialism* was that there was now little left at all. Socialism had struggled with the intertwined goals and ambitions of romanticism and enlightenment, nostalgia and progress. In its postmodern phase there was a risk that socialists no longer knew what to think at all. There would always be resistance; the struggle never comes to a conclusion. But this process is largely defensive, and constrained within the dialectic of masters and slaves. As Bauman had put it earlier, in 1976 in *Socialism: The Active Utopia*, perhaps the best way to hold on to the tradition was to think of it as a counterculture. It, and we, might persist as a cultural subdominant, those who need to say 'No' to a world that, by all appearances, remains out of control.

7 J. Bauman, *Winter in the Morning* (London: Virago, 1986), 89.

Chapter 5

Heads up from giants

For many years it had been my practice in teaching social theory, and especially in supervising postgraduates, to suggest that there were three most elementary routes to encountering a field. You could think with problems, think with thinkers or think with theories. Each approach had strengths and weaknesses. Thinking with thinkers could be productive if you chose with care, selecting those whose work was a delta or series of tributaries. What was my own exit from this mess that socialism was now in? I changed Antipodean feet for a spell, and chose to cool my heels working with two great thinkers, first Smith, then Bauman. Although they were rather different thinkers, the two-step was a necessary one for me. I had to work through the thought of one to make thinking with the other possible.

What might this mean? As I have suggested, a strength and a challenge of coming from Australia is that you need to know both the local and the global. The anxiety about the danger of provincialism here is unhelpful. What we know, and the lifeworlds we inhabit, are constituted by the movements and cultural traffic that make up our lives. We, in the southlands, cannot *not* know something about both centre and peripheries and their mutual patterns of engagement. The classical definition of Antipodean is having the feet elsewhere. Under the influence of the British Empire, it came to refer to folk from the southland, Australia and Aotearoa/New Zealand. The term has a history of stigma, making of us the freak, the other, and a reprise history of reversal, including Bernard

Smith's observation when asked on BBC radio about the Antipodes in the 1950s. 'These – here, the BBC, London – these,' he said, 'are my Antipodes.'

I came upon the work of the art historian Bernard Smith in a serious way in the 1990s. This was a major moment for me, but it was also a necessary precondition of moving on to work on and with Bauman. Culture and socialism were two of the switch points. The key work in Smith's writing is, and remains, *European Vision and the South Pacific* (1960). I had for some time been writing essays on Australian intellectuals, checking out their archives and their published work, and when possible interviewing them. These essays are now gathered in *Thinking the Antipodes* (2014), echoing François Furet's study of the French Revolution. I had never been persuaded of the early *New Left Review* foil, that the only interesting thinkers came from the Continent. The Australian version of this attitude came to be known, after A. A. Phillips, as 'cultural cringe'. I was entirely persuaded, rather, by arguments such as those of Paul Hirst: that there was a local Anglo tradition also worthy of radical recovery; and this seemed to me to be true of the Antipodes too, from William and Maud Pember Reeves to Marjorie Barnard Eldershaw to Robert Hughes to Kim Scott and Alexis Wright. There is a long list of brilliant Antipodean writing (Mexican writing, Czech writing, South African and Afrikaans writing – 'writing in minor languages'). Phillips had argued that there was also a converse Australian view to the cringe, which he called the 'strut' – or, as the Americans would say, the 'booster'. I was no strutter, but I wanted to know the local traditions and give publicity to them as resources for thinking, understanding and hope.

Together with Trevor Hogan and Sheila Shaver, I was later to write a study of the founding mother of Australian sociology, Jean Martin, entitled *The Martin Presence* (2015). But what detained me in the 1990s was the exquisite panorama of Smith's work. It offered me the prospect of an education in the visual, and a learning opportunity without parallel, as I visited him weekly for some years, researching his own archive before it was dispatched to the NLA. Neither of us drove, so we did not talk in the car, but we spoke weekly in the kitchen and sometimes, later, over a drink. He taught me a great deal. I cannot claim to have taught him anything much, except perhaps one thing. We shared a fondness for Irish whiskey; and, as it happened, we also each enjoyed a bath. My contribution to Bernard's development in his later years was to draw to his attention to the pleasurable habit of combining the two, of the possibility of drinking in the bath. He seemed impressed by the idea, and made it his own. Otherwise I was his publicist, his interpreter, and he was my educator and my friend. My job was to connect up the dots across the path of his thinking, and to remind his audience of his existence as a major and lateral thinker.

Perhaps as with Bauman, though differently, I became Bernard's interpreter. The prospect of making sense of Bernard's work was a different kind of challenge. I stacked it all up chronologically, read it through, looked for continuities and ruptures (none, really) and then spent years of these Fridays working through his archives at his home. I did not have any especial claims to personal originality in this project, seeking, rather, to map out this life's work from its genesis in the 1940s, not least as many of his readers had grown up with him and consequently did not know his work at all in this systematic sense, having read it (or not) in serial instalments as life went along. For my purposes, there were two big and connected claims that I wanted to give voice to. The terminology may have been mine, but the ideas and their originality were his. The first was that thinking the antipodes was a matter of relationship rather than place. The antipodes was not an idea stained indelibly by Eurocentrism. Like Bernard, I might have my own antipodes in England or the United States, he also in Ireland, me in Germany, and so on. Here I was also consciously manoeuvring the claim of Marx in the final chapter of *Capital*, that capital itself is a relationship rather than a thing. This echoes the now well-exercised image of master and slave from Hegel, and revisits its sense of asymmetrical reciprocity between them. Master and slave are never to be equal, yet the slave, or the subordinate culture in imperial relations, also has some cultural effect on the master. What is negatively referred to these days as 'cultural appropriation' is, in this way of thinking, more fruitfully understood as a matter of 'cultural traffic'. Cultural traffic, following the thinking of anthropologists such as Fred Myers and Nicholas Thomas, is not equal, but it does involve transaction and entanglement. The image works better than hybridity as it is constituted in movement, rather than biology, and has no end point, nor any easily recognized point of origin. It moves.

The result of our relationship and my labours was a book called *Imagining the Antipodes,* this frame combining references to Smith's earlier and controversial *Antipodean Manifesto* and his later, and magisterial, *Imagining the Pacific.* This book of mine also generated a mixed response: hostility from the disciplinary police; indifference from others who were unable to entertain the proposition that Smith's work might contain a social theory, or a way of thinking about the world. Revisiting my files 20 years later for the research on the present book, I am still shaken by the violence of some of this criticism. Why was there so much at stake? Various superior types made it clear that I was the wrong person for the job, or that I had written the wrong book, that it was the wrong job, as in *The Wrong Trousers.* This was not a charge I could take seriously, except for the confidence with which it was delivered. This, incidentally, was then a difference also between Bauman and me. Bauman never responded to criticism. When I did, back then, he offered the counsel that it was a waste of time; nasty criticism said more about the critic than the subject or the author. Probably he was right; and I never warmed to the sense of combat that many of my colleagues seemed to think was the defining manner for the seminar room. I had already worked out that Habermas was wrong, that the better argument rarely won. So various critics came out of the woodwork to straighten it, and me, out. The odd intervention was likely useful in giving me a chance to argue back productively. Randolph Stow spat at my book in the *TLS,*[1] which gave me my only ever opportunity to appear in the pages of said august weekly, here in the letters column.[2] Stow accused me of putting words

1 R. Stow, 'He Made His Own Luck' [review of *Imagining the Antipodes*], *Times Literary Supplement,* 3 October 1997.]
2 P. Beilharz, 'Imagining the Antipodes' [letter to the editor], *Times Literary Supplement,* 24 October 1997.

in Smith's mouth. I had not; Bernard was busy making them up himself, as in 'Formalesque'. There was a much more gracious review from Greg Dening, whose image was that as the beachcomber. He had often come upon Bernard's footprints before him, as he was so often there first; and Zygmunt Bauman reviewed the book for *Thesis Eleven*. I do not remember whether this was his idea or mine – probably mine, as when I think back across the years I do not remember a single occasion when he ever asked me to do anything. The review represented a kind of meeting of minds, my teachers reaching across their own antipodes, in which I was merely the facilitator – a role I was more than happy to play. It was a rare moment in other ways, too: the master reviewing the student. He worried that this might raise eyebrows. I liked the image, and the possibility. This was a nice reversal: Bauman on Beilharz. Bauman wrote:

> Peter Beilharz has done for Bernard Smith what Bernard Smith has done for Australian art. After *Imagining the Pacific,* no thinking about art could omit Australian art. After *Imagining the Antipodes,* no thinking of art may omit Bernard Smith.
>
> Bernard Smith's life work thus far has been a journey of self-discovery. Peter Beilharz's biography of Smith is an expedition to discover the sources and the trajectory of that particular self-discovery, undertaken with a view to learning something of value about self-discovery. Self-discovery being the most infuriatingly seductive but (or *because*) elusive of arts, both *oeuvres* have a lot to offer also to those among us who do not count any arts, let alone Australian arts, among our major concerns nor intend to make the thinking of arts our major pastime.
>
> Smith's self-discovery was an important part of another process – that of the self-constitution and self-assertion of Australian art. Art is a laboratory in which floating or liquid meanings fall out of their solution in social life and become visible, are sedimented, crystallized and otherwise solidified. The self-assertion of Australian art was, in its turn, a crucial part in the process of self-constitution of Australian identity. In both those processes Smith was, so to speak, simultaneously a bird and a major ornithologist; arguably, the founder of the most consequential and authoritative ornithological school. Smith's life can be read as the story of knowledge and of its object. 'Smith was, in effect, bringing the eyes of a stranger, an outsider, to the inside' – says Beilharz. To narrate Smith's life work is to discover how

the two, the knowledge and its object, come to life together and guide each other through the life they share. *Imagining the Antipodes* being a study in the sociology of knowledge, the object of that study could not be more felicitously selected. And Beilharz does his best to prove that this is so, and to exploit in full the opportunity which his choice has offered.

'Imagination' is the crucial category in Smith's critical history of Australia and its art. It has, as Beilharz points out, two major components – *imaging* and *imagining*: 'Imaging involves the construction of an image in the presence of its object; imagining is a more abstract process, where an image is constructed in the absence of the direct sensory contact with the field from which the imagery of the imagining is constructed.' Both components of imagination are potent, but their true potency is fully revealed in their cooperation. 'Imaging' is what re-casts the objects of experience into objects of knowledge. But it is the imagining, operating as a rule on the raw stuff left over by past imaging, that informs and instructs the recasting. For years artists painted their memories of blue English lakes and green willows while staring at the brownish Australian rivers and grey gumtrees, and went on portraying the natives in the likeness of noble or ignoble savages. Smith's lasting contribution to sociology of knowledge is to wrest the imagining out of imaging, its favourite hiding place and most secure shelter – and thus to lay bare perhaps the most insidious, ubi-quitous and on-going self-deception and cover-up perpetrated in human perception of the world. Beilharz's lasting contribution to sociology of knowledge is to image that process of wresting, and so, in reverse order, to render the secret and surreptitious labours of imagination into the object of knowledge.

The imagining buried in the imaging of the antipodes was the work of the modern mind. Modernity and the antipodes are two main characters in the drama which Smith's life work unfolded. They are also the two main foci of Beilharz's study. Two – or one? Are they thinkable at all apart from each other? Could any other but the modern mind muster enough cheek, guts and stamina to cast its distant colonies as *antipodes* – simultaneously refuse-dumps for its nightmares and treasure boxes for its daydreams? Could any other but modern powers be powerful enough to exile its inner demons and secret desires to the Botany Bays of the world (in Beilharz's poignant and juicy phrase: 'The antipodes was all that the English made it up to be: the other, the subordinate, the bodily and vulgar; below the equator and below the belt')? Could any other but modern practice be con-fident and resourceful enough to attempt to elevate its imagination to the rank of the sole legitimate imaging and then try to re-make its object in the likeness of its portrayal? To translate the task of 'explaining Australia' as the task of explaining Australia *in relation to Europe*, and render that translation official and binding? Modernity implies antipodes just as the antipodes imply modernity. Disentangling the two is another of Smith's feats, unravelled carefully and with utmost skill by Beilharz – just like the other one, the disengaging the imagining out of imaging. Between themselves, Smith and Beilharz set an example of learning about one through scrutinizing the other.

Page after page, Beilharz works his way through the thicket of senses which the antipodes keep in store, have for those inside and outside alike – the meanings which sediment into the phenomenon of antipodes and the meanings gestated by antipodean existence ('the antipodes must be understood as a *relation,* not a place' – this crisp phrase grasps beautifully the essence of Beilharz's project). It would be impossible to convey in a few sentences the wealth and profundity of Beilharz's findings: whoever decides to follow Beilharz's exploration, page by page, will be richly rewarded for the effort. Let me point out that the antipodean condition, like most other social locations, is both socially produced and self-produced – individual life by individual life. One is born in the Antipodes, but one also grows into that condition – one *becomes* an Antipodean. What from the individual perspective appears an objective determination of choices and their constraints, has no other substance than the choices made and the constraints they set for the choices yet to be made. The dialectics of the social and self-production is anything but straightforward or transparent; we owe to Smith and Beilharz an insight into its uncanny complexity.

Being Antipodean is a case of a much wider condition: that of being on the receiving end of a culture seen by the insiders and outsiders alike as superior. And not just superior, but the peak of humanity, indeed, the synonym of human, a pattern to be emulated by others and to serve as the yardstick of their maturity. Being cast on the receiving end however offers an advantage: joining the superior culture reveals itself as a task to be performed, a target to be reached – and whenever there is a target there is also puzzling over whatever those who hit that target without actually trying never had chance to notice, let alone seriously to consider. Being on the receiving end is a thoughtful sort of being-in-the-world. It is also a perpetually becoming kind of being – nothing follows anything just by itself and without effort, life is a series of steps on a never ending road and each step must be planned, backed by a lot of home-work and have a purpose. No wonder that most of the useful knowledge about themselves which superior cultures receive comes as a rule from those whom they cast on the receiving side and who try to make sense of their being there: from the up-and-coming intelligentsia of peripheries and of the populations charged with the duty of assimilation. That intelligentsia may have been compared by Toynbee to the moons reflecting the shine of the sun, or to the planets kidnapped by the pirate suns – but the reflected light does not dazzle or blind, and it is the orbital rhythm of the planets which allows us to measure the sun's power of gravity.

Being on the receiving side of a superior culture, and so also being antipodean, means to embrace the superior culture's values while knowing better than those who live by them unreflectively what these values are. It means that for the antipodeans values are, for once, *vorhanden* rather than merely *zuhanden* – objects to contemplate, examine, evaluate and handle. Life here must be *given* values or gain them – even when appropriated, the values remain forever a *property*, with a memory of their purchase lingering forever. That makes the thinking antipodean a 'permanently displaced person' (Smith), a 'perpetual outsider'. An outsider will never turn into an insider; she may at best become a *former outsider*. Two thoughts come therefore to an outsider 'naturally', prodded by the experience of freedom – which itself is no freedom, since it is not a matter of choice. One is the thought of absolute truth and absolute values, which would stay put when one runs to reach them, rather than moving elsewhere when finally, they seem within reach. Another is the suspicion that values and truth are never extemporal nor exterritorial, that all foundations are laid in moving sands and that instead of principles set for all there are but rules of the game set by some for others. The two thoughts are, of course, contradictory. But this contradiction is not a flaw of antipodean mind; it is but a reflection of the endemic ambivalence of the antipodean condition.

They resemble the strategies which the antipodeans are likely to resort to resolve that ambivalence. These strategies are also twofold, and also in contradiction. One is the 'black is beautiful' strategy; nativism, born-again ethnicity, inventing traditions, tribalism, victim complex or 'put the wagons in a circle' – all calculated stratagems or gut reactions. Another is the stance of *plus catholique que le pape* category; we are the sole guardians of the values abandoned, forfeited or otherwise betrayed where they have come from; banished from the centre, they may only count on shelter in the periphery. The two strategies do not always stand apart. More often they mix, in all sorts of proportions. The results tend to be as ambiguous as the situation which feeds them.

What thoughts set Smith on his journey, what strategies guided his own itinerary? For Smith in 1940, the insider and the acute observer of antipodeanism, 'western civilization has experienced a breakdown and is now undergoing a process of degeneration'. Under the circumstances, 'the new art forms which arise after a period of surrealism generally flourish upon new soil away from the older cultures which originally fertilised them'. No wonder, Beilharz comments: 'it was around 1936 that surrealism, already in its old age on the continent, arrived in the antipodes'. This is a problem which before the time compressing electronic revolution the antipodes could do little about: stimuli travelled slowly, it was a long and tiresome journey to Botany Bay, not just from Whitby but from Paris as well. All thinking people on the receiving side of superior cultures found themselves time and again fighting the new disguises of the 'mother civilization' in the name of yesterday's worn clothing; or, what amounts to the same, trying to pass today's entry exams by writing last year's exam paper. In such actions the two strategies met and blended. Yes, we can be relied upon, we took the values seriously and defend them tooth and nail, come what may; but yes, it is us, and us alone, who are uniquely predestined to be loyal and victorious in the defence of what truly counts – our apparent curse is in fact a blessing.

What can one make of that ambivalence? Its cognitive repercussions are, as it were, equally ambivalent. The receiving side is a good place from which to contemplate the world and to describe the view; vistas opened there are wide, visibility is excellent, the contours of things are sharp, visible details remarkably plentiful. That clarity of vision may be however all too easily ascribed to an 'objectivity of the standpoint', rather than to a particularly felicitous particularity of a particular condition. And then – as is, apparently the case with Smith at the time of *Antipodean Manifesto*, one may be not quite clear about the reasons which prompted the fight against the current metropolitan heresy in the name of yesterday's metropolitan orthodoxy.

As I said before, however, Bernard Smith happens to be in the Antipodean bush both a bird and ornithologist, and in his work he manages to juxtapose and blend the two in most excellent a fashion, squeezing the best out of each casting and succumbing to the limitations of none. It is Peter Beilharz's great achievement to meticulously analyse this compound and to take an exhaustive inventory of its chemical properties. This is a difficult job, considering that benign compounds are sometimes made of explosive or poisonous ingredients.

Alongside the antipodean phenomenon, modernism – in its complicated stance of peace-war with modernity – is another thread running through Smith's studies. Smith likes most modernist art, and he is, moreover, a modernist by character and temperament. His statements about the nature of modernist endeavour read like reports of autobiographical self-scrutiny. Modernism, he insists time and again, 'is not a reflection of modernity. Instead, it set up a penetrating critique of modernity. Modernism is the dialectical twin of modernity'; 'the artistic tradition has been consistently antagonistic to the values and structures of modern industrial society'. Elective affinity between the subject and the object of study is certainly a blessing. Like most blessings, it risks, however, to stand as a mixed one. In the opinion of the undersigned, this is the case of Smith's reluctance to admit the decline of the twilight of the modernist adventure. Modernists were indeed highly critical of modernity; but they criticized modern reality in the name of modern promises, they accused modern practice of having betrayed modern values. They were impatient, they would not wait, they rushed *ahead* to the land of modern values fulfilled – they were *avant-garde*, the forward units capturing footholds for the rest of the army to advance (they – like Smith himself – wrote *manifestoes*, a typically modernist need and urge). None of these characteristics holds today, though. There is no avant-garde without an army to follow, and there are no forward units without a clear idea where exactly the 'forward' is. Modernism was a particular, time-bound form of innovation and critique – not its only conceivable form, and certainly not an extemporal one. Both innovation and critique have every chance of surviving the modernism's decline. But it will take some innovation and a lot of critique to secure this survival.

Imagining the Antipodes – this reflection on how reflection is and can be done – will provide enormous help to anyone wishing this innovation and critique to survive.[3]

There was even more going on here. What strikes me in retrospect is how completely engaged Bauman was with a text, and a world so distant from his own; except that he was a Pole and a Jew. Clearly, there were some shared curiosities, and axes. Antipodes; modernity; self-discovery; empire and art; and culture, here and there. We found ourselves, somehow,

3 Z. Bauman, 'Imagining the Antipodes', *Thesis Eleven*, 53 (1998).

in the same labyrinth; he, also, in mine. Once I had foregrounded the idea
of the Antipodes, Bauman made it clear to me that he wanted to join in.
On 17 December1997 he wrote to me about the Festschrift for his friend
Piet Nijhoff, which was also called *Antipodes*, in the Dutch, *Tegenvoeters*
(1997). This time the outside view came from the Netherlands. As the
Dutch historian Johan Goudsblom once put it to me, being outside the
centres was like being on the back side of a one-way mirror: we see everything they do; they see nothing of us at all. As Bauman now put it to me,
'You see, you do not need to live in Melbourne to be an Antipodean.'
Part of this may have been a tease, as in the endless jokes about liquidity.
But there was something else going on, too, a willingness to engage
with this way of thinking that was outside the metropolis, yet umbil-
ically connected to it. He understood about empire; he was a Pole. He
understood what it meant to be positioned, as a Jew. He understood that
I needed to visit Whitby, even though my lineage was German, rather
than British; he suggested the trip, and urged us on to visit the place from
where Cook had set sail. It represented an Antipodean loop. The notion
of 'former outsider' was an interesting twist on subsequent claims that
Bauman had become a kind of 'honorary insider'. Bauman was at the
very least prepared to think about what it might mean to think like an
Antipodean. His status was always conditional, even when he became
a reluctant celebrity. There would always be those looking to shoot him
down, get him off the stage.

His celebrity was indeed looming, even if his presence remained awkward. The prizes and doctorates stacked up: the Amalfi Prize for the
Holocaust book; the Asturias Prize, taken together with Alain Touraine;
the Adorno Prize, from the city of Frankfurt; and the rest. I was invited
to the Adorno event: 13 September 1998 in the Paulskirche, Claus Offe
delivering the laudation, Frank Wolff performing his *Fantasie für Cello
und Papier* to a delighted recipient. Wolff played off the music sheet,
played with the sheet, and finally presented the sheet to Bauman. It was
evidently a perfect moment. I had to miss the event, but was represented
by my student Fuyuki Kurasawa. It gave me great satisfaction, even at this
distance. As for me, I have received no name prizes, and expect none.

There was also a charming snap to this moment, however. The same day Bauman had his letter from Frankfurt, 17 September, I had a phone call from my vice chancellor, informing me that I was to be awarded a personal chair. The process had been rather more rigorous than Bauman's morning coffee interview encounter in Canberra in 1970. There were many more tripwires; somehow I had managed to dance around them. But the category, personal chair, is doubtless now also redundant. Universities used to have lots of students, and fewer chairs; now it is the other way around. Professors, at any rate, rarely seem to profess. They are too busy dealing with the university imperatives of making contacts and contracts and money. Everywhere the old currency is devalued.

Were we now thinking alike? Maybe not, though the resonances remained uncanny. The extent of his achievements always towered over mine. The breadth of his culture and experience were bound to be beyond me. My life with Bauman was a prolonged learning experience. We also had some disagreements, Bauman and I; this was one of them: the hard distinction he wanted to draw between birds and those who study them – between actors and arguments. The critical point or reservation was clear enough: in the ever-expanding age of celebrity, there was too much talk of persons, or style; too little of ideas, or substance. He told me directly that I should have less interest in ornithologists. By this he also evidently meant that my interest in his life path was less pertinent than our shared interests in the problems of our worlds – culture and socialism, modern and postmodern. We should be looking outwards, not in. Yet, for me, these matters of substance were also connected to us as sentient, suffering, creative human beings. I had perhaps met this view, or a weaker version of it, first all those years ago in 1971 in E. H. Carr's *What Is History?* (1961), and the advocacy that to place an argument you needed also to place its author. If you want to know poets, follow their place and path. It mattered, for me – and I am sure for my audience – that Bernard Smith was born a bastard in 1916, when it really mattered. It certainly mattered for Bernard Smith. This meant that he felt the need to write his own biography, not once but twice; that his biography of the social realist painter Noel Counihan was also in a sense a proxy for his own life, and a path not taken as a communist artist. It mattered that he was a lifelong Marxist, as this was also in a way the lifeline he had given me, as I needed myself to move away from a socialism in tatters and yet maintain some continuity with the tradition that had formed my thinking. Smith's work enabled me to move more fully into matters of culture via the visual. As he put it of himself, Smith was a cultural historian with a primary interest in the visual. I could not define my work in such a precise capsule. Socialism still seemed to me to have a strong critical claim to the project of making sense of modernity. Culture seemed to me to have the greater elasticity, not least as, for all this suffering, creativity nevertheless persisted, even through this suffering. I was still working around the coordinates that Bauman had taken as his own: socialism, and culture.

I put *Imagining the Antipodes* to bed in 1996; it appeared in 1997. I posted Bernard the manuscript, like a coward, as I was about to board a plane for Manchester on my way to Leeds. He was delighted with the result and with the spur my book gave to the fresh consideration of his own work, though it is not the kind of book he would have written. As Stuart Macintyre and Terry Smith put it, the book represented a new point of departure for Australian intellectual history. Little wonder it got stick.

Although I continued to write about Smith's work, and still do, it was now time to take on Bauman's. My approach was the familiar. Begin at the beginning, with *Between Class and Elite*, recognizing the importance of the Polish pre-life and apologizing for my inability to engage directly with it. Stack up the books, read through them all, locate all the available essays, look to discern continuities and ruptures. Here, in Bauman's work, there were, arguably, two, or three: the turn into the Holocaust; the postmodern, then liquid modern, turns; the turn to little books, the deliberate turn away from writing for imagined colleagues in the social sciences in the university system. I wanted to interrogate these shifts, but also to look for the continuities across the path of Bauman's thinking. My more fundamental purpose was to establish something of the rich diversity of his work. The work of social theory is perennially given to reduction or truncation, as though each thinker or theory has only one thing to say. Ergo, in this way of operating, Bauman is the liquidity person. It all ends up in a kind of mediocre smorgasbord, like the kind my family had confronted in Vegas. The work of theory, too, becomes McDonaldized mash, and theorists learn to rely on their elbows rather than their better senses, including their ears.

So I began at the beginning, with a massive pile of stuff to read and digest. I had published my scanner on Bauman in *Thesis Eleven* in 1998, and had a sketch map of the project in my head. This was the year that Bauman published *Work, Consumerism and the New Poor*, which I now see acknowledges my own prodding about class. My purpose in this scanner, as later with the *Bauman Reader*, was to place text in context, and to insist that Bauman's thinking had a history and a historicity. You might associate this with the German notion of *Entwicklungsgeschichte*, a history of the development of thinking, or with Heinrich Wölfflin's maxim, via Bernard Smith: vision has a history; every concept has a history. This approach could be criticized from different perspectives, but at the very least it helped avoid the perils of what Bauman called the Columbus complex, after Pitirim Sorokin (even that idea had a precedent). By the time that I came of age, intellectually, there were even more serious pressures on us to innovate, to claim originality, a 'new big thing', an immaculate conception that would put us under the spotlight, or get you on TV. Credit went to the *arriviste*, the Columbus who claimed to have first seen the light, or named it.

As Robert Dessaix observed of my radio discursive style, which he helped bring out in conversation on his ABC shows on *Books and Writing*, I tended to keep moving. The light, if it shone at all in my direction, had to struggle to follow. This was partly because, like Bauman, I endorsed the centrality of the conversational model. The problems facing us were never really resolved. The idea of innovation needed to be tempered with that of repetition and rediscovery, reinvention. The conversation never ended. This was a view that Robert shared. He had escaped from the academy, but remained a Russian. He taught me a great deal about performance and presentation. For, if writing is a way of thinking, then so is speaking. He taught me about intonation, spacing, timing, but also about precision. The way you think about speaking then may also affect the way you write. He used to send me postcards when travelling. One was of a Matisse paper cut-out. On the back he wrote, in congratulations at something I had written, 'Be careful with those words! You'll cut yourself!' He teased me about a piece I had written about Bauman and the notion of security, *Sicherheit*. I had said something about the German word being a sensibility you would know from the German safety flight card when you flew Lufthansa. Not 'when', he said to me: 'if'. Make each word matter, and the silences in between. It is a lesson I am still working on.

My scanner in *Thesis Eleven*, which then grew into the introduction for *The Bauman Reader*, began from the proposition that there were two most obvious markers in Bauman's work to that point: the Holocaust, and the postmodern. I wanted to insist that it was vital to look back, to consider Bauman's sources before examining his own contribution. I did not use the word at that point, but my claim was that, even more so than others, Bauman was a *bricoleur*, a thinker who worked through a team of interlocutors to achieve different forms of assemblage. This feature of his thinking made it annoying, to those looking for clear axioms and ready to apply theories, but it was also educative and, in its own way, exemplary. There was no Bauman app, no go-to Bauman, no Bauman made easy. You had to work at it. If there is an arrogance or a prejudice in this way of thinking it is to do with senses of available time and cultural capital. As we used to say in more radical days: 'No research, no right to speak.' Otherwise, the intellectual conversation would literally be dominated by those who did not know what they were talking about (it happens, not least in public life, but also in universities, where distorted communication often rules). Bauman's approach served as a constant source of resistance to the narcissism of the pose of intellectual as hero. He always presumed that we routinely entered into a conversation that precedes us. And when our time is up, we step aside.

My reservation about the prominence given to the Holocaust and the postmodern in the Bauman reception, then, was that it missed out all the other bits: class, culture, socialism, waste, surplus populations, hermeneutics, intellectuals, ambivalence, ethics, the others, consumerism, and more. Coming out of the matrix of a kind of East European crit-ical theory, or a Weberian Marxism, Bauman's work increasingly became reactive in the literal sense, a reaction to new 'signs of the times' as they came to public prominence. Much of the latter work, however, was to follow, as Bauman changed the form of his essays into the *Buechlein,* or little books, which later followed on identity, community, globalization, migration, and so on.

There was an already existing literature on Bauman when I arrived, but it was fledgling. If I had arrived, so to say, too early, then they who came before me had arrived even earlier. None of us could have guessed at that time how long the tail of Bauman's work would become. He was already 70 at this time, approaching the phase of late style. Primary among the early actors were Ian Varcoe and Richard Kilminster, who had the advantage of having worked with Bauman for years at Leeds. Theirs was pioneering work. There were others who arrived closer to me, such as Keith Tester and Dennis Smith, and then Michael Hviid Jacobsen, who always did fine work. There emerged something of a tradition of Scandic enthusiasm for Bauman. Anthony Elliott both generated strong work on Bauman and went on to apply it in different ways in the broader field of liquid modernity. Tony Blackshaw added a useful book and a cleverly conceived *New Bauman Reader.* Mark Davis wrote a fine monograph on Bauman and freedom and added others on metaphor and liquidity. The industry was cranking into gear. Younger hands and heads were in the wings.

Bauman had given me his road map of Yorkshire in 1999. I still have it, in tatters: it is in the Bartholomew GT Series, no. 6, 'Northern England'. We had used it to navigate Yorkshire. My job now was to gen-erate a map of his work. My task in *Dialectic of Modernity* (the title of which echoed the German translation of Bauman's Holocaust book, *Dialectic of Order,* which in turn echoed *Dialectic of Enlightenment*) was to expand the canvas sufficiently for newer readers to at least have a mapping sense or back catalogue of how this project of Bauman's had emerged. The working title for my book was *Modernity as Ambivalence,* which was also the name of an honours course I taught in order to get the project moving, until I decided that ambivalence did not capture it, or indicate the extent of the canopy. As to the more literal sense of canvas, I had always admired the different works of Lydia Bauman that checkered the walls of the Bauman home at Lawnswood Gardens. One in particular had caught my eye, *Flax Fields in France*, a beautiful combination of sand and lavender, palette and paint, spots of flower fading to middle ground, the heavier blotch of the other at the darker horizon. As I said to my friends, and to Lydia, even if my words were disposable, the cover was worth keeping the book for.

First, it had to be written. Once I had digested the materials, the presenting issue was, as in my Smith book, how best to organize it. Some sense of historical development seemed obvious, but there also needed to be sufficient attention to themes and to thematic development or change. The development of Smith's work was more predictable; there were few surprises. Bauman's trajectory became characterized by surprise, or lateral shift, which is one thing that made his work appeal to a popular audience at the very same time as it infuriated the professional experts. Bauman's thinking was mobile. I settled upon six chapters: 'Class and Labour'; 'Culture and Sociology'; 'Intellectuals and Utopians'; 'The Holocaust and the Perfect Order'; 'Touring the Fragments'; and 'Following the Human Condition'. The resulting book is a kind of postmodern tapestry. *Dialectic of Modernity* was a challenging book to write, partly because of the task of putting chaos into order. The strong sense I had from Bauman was that he had no interest at all, as some do, in seeking to choreograph the reception of his own ideas. If he was a careerist, as some have suggested, then he was not a very good one. For so soon as he had finished one thing he was on to the next. There was a kind of controlled frenzy, or even carelessness, to his working and writing style, while at the same time his work was always associative and richly suggestive. He was pleased with the result. On 18 January 2000: 'It's arrived. WOW WOW WOW WOW WOW [etc.].' There was the added pleasure of presenting Zygmunt and Lydia together in word and image. Lydia was also delighted. I made some enquiries with contacts in the art world about bringing Lydia and an exhibition of her work to Australia, but these failed. Finally, I had also managed to do some small justice to the importance of Janina's work.

'What you write about me is honey to my heart. Do I really deserve it?' (21 January 2000).

The materials for *Dialectic of Modernity* were difficult to marshal and to integrate. Bauman's publications were spread widely, and they were more than usually diverse. The writing was also a challenge. I had begun to doubt my capacities. As Coetzee says somewhere, if writing were easy, why would you bother with it? But I was blocked and frustrated, and this was no fun at all, except that on a good day I would put my biro down sensing that I might have understood a little more than on the previous encounter. Eventually I had to force myself to write every day in self-imposed solitude at the Research School of Social Sciences (RSSS) at the ANU. Barry Hindess, Judy Wajcman and Frank Jones held the door open for me as I scrambled into the Coombs Building. I was desperate to finish. It was a monastic existence, and I was lonely. But Bauman and I were in different ways in trouble. Our emails twist and turn around busyness, his of emerging celebrity and an incapacity to say 'No' to requests, mine to do with the transformation of university life and the expansion of teaching and other duties. As I confessed to Bauman, apologizing for the slow progress on my Bauman book, on a good week I might have a half-day to read or write, and increasingly I was knackered, tied to what my German relatives called the *Hamsterraedle*, less elegantly in English the rat's wheel. Travelling momentarily into the RSSS was an escape route, for which I was grateful. Solitude forced me to work, as did the ghost of Max Weber, though sometimes the prose seemed to suffer from the sense of coercion, self-incurred tutelage.

There were some long-distance connections between Bauman and me here. The ANU was a special place for Bauman. Bauman had a history here. He used to tell the story of how, while visiting in 1970, he had been invited to a meeting of dons over coffee, the vice chancellor, Sir John Crawford, presiding. As he walked into the room he was offered a chair. After two hours of conversation he was offered a chair. But, although he and Janina were taken by the place, it was too far away – not from the metropolis, but from the worlds of their daughters. They relished the local landscape and wine, travelled north by coach and discovered the wine box, which could even be savoured en route, like schoolchildren on the bus. A loose page of notes from an interview we conducted with Jerzy Zubrycki for our later biography of Jean Martin recalls that there was serious local support for his appointment. It was not to be; the place and time were out of joint. Occasionally someone will say to me on hearing this story that this was a loss. Imagine if Bauman had stayed in Canberra! My reply is generally in the negative. Bauman remained a European, of a particular kind. Yorkshire was his proper fate, or destination. He was his own kind of antipodean.

Part III

Talking the days

Chapter 6

Working together, at a distance

Dialectic of Modernity is not my happiest child. When I look at it, it seems to me to bear the marks of a difficult time and arrival, though this may not show to its readers. I am happy, however, with the tapestry effect. I think it manages to combine the two interpretative ingredients central to its project: text and context. More than anything I had written to that point – perhaps until the book you are holding now – I was finding my way. Like Bauman, I think, I was reading my way into writing, and writing my way into thinking. In retrospect, the result looks tentative to me, though this is also likely a matter of hindsight. At that point, we had no idea what might come next, for any of us.

There were also, as ever, other things to be going on with. Family, *Thesis Eleven*, teaching, and all the rest. There were more books to come, for both of us, some of these together.

Blackwell had for some years been publishing a *Reader* series, covering thinkers as diverse as Bourdieu and Parsons (later I put forward proposals for Heller and Dan Bell, neither of which flew). There was to be a string of others, from Jean-François Lyotard and Julia Kristeva to Walter Benjamin, Castoriadis and Fanon. Steve Seidman, one of the few American sociologists apart from my close friends who took Bauman seriously into the new century, helped connect me to the Boston office of Blackwell, which, despite Steve's apprehensions, was keen to spread the word across the Atlantic. There were fans in the

Boston office, such as Susan Rabinowitz. On my 2000 visit to Leeds I took materials and lists for the *Reader*, which was to follow on my Bauman book. He had written to me earlier, 'You are permanently welcome at Lawnswood Gardens' (27 April 2000). There was talk, but also work. Together we discussed the table of contents, issues of inclusion and exclusion and issues of order and sequence. We shared in all of this to the extent that the Italian edition listed us as co-authors … not quite. He generated the ideas, I sorted and ordered them. He insisted that we split the royalties.

He was a generous and responsive man. More recently my son, who works for ABC Radio, became friendly with Waleed Aly, the most prominent Muslim public intellectual and media personality in Australia. As a party game, Waleed asked his dinner guests to guess his favourite author, offering a number of elusive hints. Nikolai identified Bauman from these hints; easy. 'How can you know that?' 'Well, I know him … ' So we asked Keith to procure a fresh copy of *Liquid Modernity*. He conveyed it to Leeds, where the sage warmly inscribed it to this new admirer and posted it, like a kipper in a bag, to Waleed in Melbourne. Why would the cartoon careerist Bauman do something like this? He was capable of great kindness. He did not need to do this. The idea of Bauman as a man on the make never made any sense to me. I never met that man.

When it came to the *Bauman Reader* (2001), he was happy to approve but not to direct. I alone decided what to cut, what to leave out, when – inevitably – we came in over length. Here the bias was also historical, both because this was necessary background and because the new views were still in print, or even yet to appear with Polity. At this point, into the new millennium, there was no discernible Bauman industry, and it would have been proleptic to speak of Bauman before Bauman. There was no Bauman, in terms of the larger popular reception, until the year 2000 and the arrival of *Liquid Modernity* and its sequels. The *Reader* thus focused on 'Socialism', 'Class and Power', 'Hermeneutics and Critical Theory', 'Sociology and the Postmodern', 'Figures of Modernity' (a strikingly Baumanesque theme), 'Ambivalence and

8 In thought, à table.

Order' and 'Globalization and the New Poor'. Likely its most frequently cited section, as in Dan Stone's scanner on *Genocide*, was that entitled 'The Century of Camps'. For what Bauman and the rest of us had failed fully to anticipate was that this, and not only the twentieth century, would also become the century of camps.

Bauman was pleased with the *Reader*; perhaps it was a better carrier for his work than my own study. Here our labours were mixed differently. As he wrote to me on 14 August 2000,

> I mean Bauman Reader … I am tremendously impressed by the thought and force you put into it. I would never be able to repay you in kind – no skills, no wisdom, no determination to match yours …

though he protested, bittersweet against the significance I had put on his work in my opening lines – modesty forbid.

And he was, in fact, modest, as well as weary. He wrote me on 2 January 1996: 'My sole consolation is the hope that the truth that I have nothing to say will soon be discovered and the travels stop.' On 17 November 2001: 'Beilharz's Bauman seems to be making sense.' The implication was evident, here and elsewhere: Bauman did not always feel in control of his writing. The world was beyond us. Everything we offered by way of explanation was on further notice. He did not always make sense to himself, though if you asked him a question there would always be an answer back, even if it took the form of another question in return. The energies between us were good, and mutually supportive. He pushed ahead, regardless; I followed, looking to make sense of it. Neither of us would ever be able to finish our work. Every day we swept, every day the dirt would return.

There was no rush of publicity for the *Bauman Reader*, but there were some good conversations. One occurred on ABC Radio with Michael Cathcart, Bauman on relay from Leeds. The distant Polish voice now entered Australian airwaves talking about the life of sweeping up. Another took place when John Carroll launched my books at Readings bookshop in Melbourne. My son Nikolai filmed the event on video, which we sent to Lawnswood Gardens in a padded bag, just as I had earlier posted him a kipper from Whitby in a padded bag ('Succulent and tender!'). Bauman emailed on 26 November 2000 to inform me that the tape had become compulsory viewing for the extended family. He waxed lyrical about John and me as 'strong poets'. And he lamented the death of his Amstrad, his own personal means of production, the dinosaur computer he was so deeply bonded to. He took pride in its redundancy; it had served him well. And, although he hoped for a world of repair, there was no such prospect, neither for his computer nor for the new global order. He was now increasingly given to talk of the evil empire. I was always a bit twitchy about anti-Americanism, which on the Australian left was often simply phoney – bag the Americans, then go home to listen to some kind of blues or *Kind of Blue*, watch Hollywood noir sipping their bourbon, dreaming of Venice Beach and Manhattan. It was as though they expected the North Americans to deliver on their dream, rather than be prepared to accept that it might indeed represent the best and worst of modernity.

These projects, my Bauman book and the reader, led to another. Rojek invited me to construct that box set, the four volumes of which appeared in 2002 as *Zygmunt Bauman* in the *Sage Masters of Modern Social Thought* series. As with the Blackwell readers, there were already box sets on Bourdieu and other leading thinkers.

It took some years to assemble and edit these essays, which at the time represented everything strong that we could locate on Bauman's work. Internet retrieval devices were less sophisticated then. Suzi Adams, Karl Smith and Vince Marotta conducted much of the location and copying of work. Veteran sociologist Peter Hamilton coordinated the project for Sage and happily joined in the detective work. We came up with sufficient good material for four volumes, a total of almost 1,600 printed pages, these from the materials almost entirely in English, some few in German. But there was sufficient for four volumes, not five. Today, I guess, you might fill 50 such volumes. These days it would be difficult to read everything on or around Bauman and still be home for Christmas dinner.

I divided these papers into eight parts. The first part included profiles and surveys. Bauman's work was not yet at this stage especially well surveyed. So there were 14 surveys or introductions, or interviews, followed by seven papers on or by Janina, as I had come early to the conclusion that there was no understanding one without the other. Part II was entitled 'Socialism and Intellectuals', and connected back to Bauman's life and work in Poland as well as to the substantive questions of what intellectuals might do or be. This section included the best surveys of East European revisionism; everything had a history. Part III collected materials on the Holocaust. At this point the response to *Modernity and the Holocaust* was still settling, some of it resolutely negative, as Bauman was often construed as identifying modernity with the Holocaust and refusing the achievements of Western civilization and progress. Distorted communication reigned, then as now. But there were some probing papers on the question of genocide, on comparison and on geography; for, if the Holocaust had a history or a time, it also had a space, a demography and a geopolitics, as well as historic precedents and ongoing echoes. Part IV was slim; only 11 strong papers on the postmodern. This was the place that the Americans joined in: Douglas Kellner, George Ritzer, Steven Seidman. Part V was given over to 'Ethics', Part VI to 'Death and Religion'. Part VII was dedicated to 'Sociology and Marxism'. This section included issues of class, consumption and bureaucracy. The set concluded with a section called 'Extensions', or applications: work by others that took the scholarship further, into matters of hybridity, as with Bulent Diken, or law, with Jock Young, or Joanildo Burity, taking us to Latin America, or Jon Stratton, connecting up to the colour of Jews. This latter was the section that most interested Bauman; not his own work, but what might come afterwards.

The project of the box set was to restate the importance of context and complexity in the reception process of social theory, in this case via the work of someone central such as Zygmunt Bauman. To begin to know Bauman better it would be necessary to know who his teachers, such as Hochfeld, and contemporaries, such as Kołakowski, were, at least by impression or engagement, and to have some sense of the fibre of Janina's work. In order to get further with thinking the Holocaust or the post-modern or ethics it would be helpful to know the terms of debate and disagreement. There may also have been some hope in this project to help secure a hearing for Bauman across the Atlantic. North American contributors to the box set could be counted on the fingers of one hand. The next project I worked on for Rojek was, in my mind, called *American Postwar Critical Theory*, though the last word finally came out as *Thought*

(2006). The contents of the two box sets were, essentially, mutually exclusive, even though the Frankfurt School had been so centrally mediated through the United States in its own reception via the work of Jay, Wolin, Kellner, Calhoun, McCarthy, Poster, Ben Habib, Cohen and Arato and many others around important journal projects such as *Telos*, *New German Critique*, *Constellations* and *Philosophy and Social Criticism*. Bauman, in any case, remained at this point largely invisible in the United States. I also wanted to suggest that there was a tradition of local inflection that might be characterized as critical theory, including most significantly the work of Richard Sennett and Christopher Lasch. Steve Turner jokingly accused me of inventing a tradition, literally making it up, but others chose to run with the idea, such as Patricia Mooney Nickel in her book *North American Critical Theory after Postmodernism* (2008). In retrospect I am not so sure, but I did want to argue for the pluralization of critical theory, so that it might be seen not only as German and then French, but also as East European and even just possibly as American, Antipodean, and so on.

Some East Europeans who moved to the United States had a serious effect there – Ivan Szelenyi, as an entrepreneur and institution builder, perhaps more than Ágnes Heller, who became an increasingly public figure in Europe but had less direct public impact in New York, where she worked for many years. Bauman and the North Americans remained in a sense mutually indifferent, with exceptions of admirers including Craig Calhoun, Jeffrey Alexander, Seidman and Ritzer. There were certainly sympathies with others such as Rorty, and clear affinities with thinkers such as Sennett. Bauman's influence remained more significant in Europe, though in these earlier years, before liquidity, his influence was also peripheral.

Janina assisted me in the production process for the box set; Zygmunt was not involved in the process, and may have been bemused by it, not least with reference to the notion of mastery. As he put it later, in dialogue with Alain Touraine at Asturias, he saw himself as a follower rather than a leader or pioneer. The contents of the box set suggested that this was changing, however slowly. Popularity is not the same as leadership or innovation, but as I write the Wiki hits are a million and a half for

Touraine, closer to 3 million for Bauman (the winner is Foucault, with almost 16 million). The satisfaction of metrics!

Bauman was busy writing and speaking at this point, and worrying the grim reaper. I concluded the preface with the 'You want to put me in a box' reference, and added one line directed personally to Bauman: 'So here it is.' The first time he saw the results of our labours was when the set was published, and the box arrived at Lawnswood Gardens. I think he was surprised by the extent of the results. For my part, I was pleased by the breadth and width of the findings. Our net was full to bursting at four volumes. And these were still early days: 2002.

This was an especially intense period in our relationship. They were dense and productive years. The language of love begins to appear in its prose. There had emerged a strange sense of connection between us. It was particularly intense when we were together, yet also at our antipodean distance, him in Leeds, me in Melbourne. On 24 August 2001 he welcomed receipt of my inaugural address as professor. 'It has arrived. Superb piece. How can you say anything new about Marx and Weber?' On 3 January 2002 he wrote to thank me for the piece I had written on his other totalitarianism, communism. 'You are a genius,' he wrote me; or at least, I told myself, a half-decent cobbler. 'How uncannily closely we think,' he said. Earlier, on 26 November 1994, he had anticipated this line of thinking and its echoes: 'It seems that similar curiosities make you and me tick.' Sometimes we would reverse the flow of information and I would post him a pile of my stuff, or even a case of wine. 1 April (!) 2001 he wrote to me under the subject heading 'Drunken banter'. I had sent him a different kind of box.

> I can't even thank you – I am completely drunk on superb Australian wine … Your faithful, even if inebriated Z.

On 12 December 2002 he wrote thanking me for a

> huge pile of goodies of highest quality (which) has circled the globe and landed on my doorstep. Hugest thanks, Peter the Great! […] You cannot hold your fingers off touching every sore spot of our world!

He would draw on his stock of Anglo vernacular, as in 'bullseye!', 'full to the brim!', 'piping hot!', and so on. His English vocabulary, like that of my German mother, sometimes seemed pickled in aspic. She would use phrases such as 'happy as Larry!' and 'good as gold!'. Sometimes my German relatives would call her on the phone just to hear her speak this argot. For there were powerful period Anglo influences, in each case. My mother was *Schwab*, but when I was little in Croydon she used to buy me *Playhour*, where I learned about the foibles of cartoon characters Harold Hare and Uncle Oojah – characters who did not resonate easily with German or period Australian culture, yet who were also part of my lifeworld (they still are; at least they were bumblers or dreamers, better role models than the tragic figures of discipline in *Struwwelpeter*).

Australian culture, too, was a puzzle, even if not the oxymoron that some of my English acquaintances like to rag me about. Bauman was especially pleased with my interrogation of periphery and metropolis, not only Australian or Mexican but indeed also Polish, and with the notion of North American culture as a potlatch culture – again, not only American but symptomatic of modernity's ease of comfort with, and even celebration of, waste and excess. Waste was to remain a constant concern of his work; human and other. Perhaps that is why the sense of the absurd never quite left his work. As the graffiti in Melbourne dictated: 'Work. Consume. Die.' These days we might add: 'Drown in Your Own Waste.' I had argued that Bauman's was indeed in sympathy with what Joel Kahn had called for as an anthropology of modernity. We, the insiders, nevertheless often did not feel at home in this world.

For some time now Bauman would announce each new work, an average of one a year, as his last. 'This is my last book.' It is possible that I sometimes could not keep up, juggling my antipodean obligations and responsibilities in both research and teaching. It is also possible that, having become his interpreter, I imagined, falsely, that there would be nothing new to come. There was.

A new sense of foreboding sometimes entered our relationship, or perhaps a new sobriety. Janina wrote to me 18 May 2005, as I anticipated a later visit, 'As Zygmunt said, "Old age is risky." You can no longer take us for granted. November seems far away.'

On 21 July 2006 he wrote me a sad, or bittersweet, message about my most recent visit as a *Blitzbesuch*. My visit, it seemed, was too rushed. I was tired, and distracted. Often there were third parties visiting at the same time, full house: '[W]e hardly talked, you did not tell me much – perhaps I am not an attractive conversationalist any longer … ' It is possible that, in our different moments of life and in different ways, we were both depressed. He was sad, increasingly, as Janina declined. His world was shrinking for a moment, as Rudiger Joppien said of Bernard in decline. Life gets smaller as you grow older. I was somehow losing my way, feeling morbid after the death of my in-laws and my father, wondering what was left, feeling as though I should also be fixing to die. I was not immediately able to push away the sense of the impending immediacy of death. Janina died 29 December 2009; my father had died 18 July 2007, and both my parents-in-law in the same period. Bernard Smith died in 2011, Robert Hughes in 2012, followed by Stuart Hall, John Berger and so many others who also crossed Bauman's life; Lobby Loyde and Billy Thorpe, formative rock musicians of my youth, both known to me personally from my teens, had gone in 2007. There was a demographic pattern to all this. These were musicians I had played with, at the funkiest club in Melbourne, when I was 15. The musicians went before the scholars. The dreams of youth were receding. The dominant musicians and artists and elders of my youth were going down like flies.[1] Are we ever ready?

The process of mourning and recovery was so difficult for Bauman that he stopped travelling for almost two years. I suppose that it took some passing of time, a recovery of the will to live, and one more special ingredient; he fell in love again, for a second time. This was yet to come.

1 See P. Beilharz, 'Lobby and Me', *Thesis Eleven*, 91 (2007); 'Rock Lobster: Lobby Loyde and the History of Rock Music in Australia', *Thesis Eleven*, 109 (2012); P. Beilharz, and S. Supski, 'So Sharp You Could Bleed – Sharpies and Artistic Representation: A Moment in the Seventies History of Melbourne', in A. Michelsen and F. Tygstrup (eds), *Socioaesthetics* (Leiden: Brill, 2015); 'Tricks with Mirrors: Sharpies and Their Representations', in S. Baker, B. Robards and B. Buttigieg (eds), *Youth Cultures and Subcultures: Australian Perspectives* (London: Ashgate, 2015).

In the earlier moment we published a special section of *Thesis Eleven* remembering Janina, and we carried a fine review of the latter version of *Winter in the Morning* and *A Dream of Belonging*. There was a pervasive sense of sadness in the air across those years.

Despite all, there were still outbreaks of humour. On 23 February 2006 he wrote me that he had just received his copy of the Danish book *Om Bauman*, which included my essay connecting his thinking to that of Foucault, Castoriadis and Giorgio Agamben. 'Relished your exquisite Danish style!' By this stage I had become notorious among my friends for telegraphic email style. My student Anthony Rodriguez, from Colombia, called me 'the Mies of the email'. *Minimalista*! Keith said he had forgotten how cryptic my style was. Like Bauman, I was often less than enthusiastic about email, except as a message system. Email often seemed to be the enemy of thinking, so much did it gobble up of the day. We were all increasingly caught up in what Hartmut Rosa calls the acceleration of modernity.[2] There was also a physics to this. I could not type, unlike my mates who went to private schools or took typing classes, and my fingers went sideways; osteoarthritis. The results could be comical, as, at my hands, a 'Q' on QWERTY could well come up as an 'E'.

Bauman was also often funny and cryptic at the same time. Even email could be put to his purposes, though he was likely most mischievous in person.

Once as I sat in the wingchair in his front room, reading, he bustled in bearing an offprint from the morning mail. 'Are you interested in sex?' he demanded of me. His query was disinterested. The offer was a paper on postmodern sex for the *Zeitschrift für Sexualforschung*. He was indeed interested in sex, necessarily, as he was interested in life and love. He understood how important sex was, to life and love and to humour itself. Perhaps the best expression of this came with the essay on 'Postmodern Uses of Sex' in *Theory, Culture and Society* in 1998, though there are also other appearances, such as his voice-over on Erik Gandini's 2016 documentary *The Swedish Theory of Love*. As Eva Illouz was later to put it in

2 See Rosa, *Social Acceleration*.

Why Love Hurts, the shift from solid to liquid modernity also involved a move from love/sex to sex/love, the latter coupling remaining contingent.[3] Sex was, so to say, getting easier, or at least more readily available, at the same time that love was becoming more elusive and difficult. Who these days had the time for love?

In the meantime there was still work. Likely we were both using work to push death away, only with different senses of urgency. I sent him a copy of the textbook that Trevor Hogan and I had developed out of the inspiration of Bernard Smith's first, 1945 study of Australian art, *Place, Taste and Tradition*. We called ours *Place, Time and Division*, and commissioned more than 80 writers to write short, direct entries on things that mattered, from incarceration and masculinity to sex and kitchens and rock music. Rather than thinking of this project as the brick or telephone book of student first-year handbooks, we wanted it to be an innovative introduction for any interested reader, combining always geography and history with sociology more conventionally defined. We workshopped the project with writers across the larger Australian cities. Jeffrey Alexander was visiting with us across this period, reading mainly Australian literature, so we asked him to act as reader. Like Bauman, he was delighted with the resulting book. Along with 40 years of *Thesis Eleven*, our textbook remains the single most important or exemplary project I have worked on.

In all this I was driven, by my own ghosts, by the Protestant ethic or whatever. I certainly had some sense of having something to say, though this has also likely eased. These days I am often inclined to prefer listening. I suppose that there have been graphomaniac moments in my life, though as I have grown older I have become more sceptical of the value or the political significance of books and writing. Although Bauman was often accused of pessimism, he seems never to have wanted for something to say, though it is evident that in his later life it was often literally conversational, involving a new party as an interlocutor. To register all this is to leave one key agent out of the picture, however. This is Polity Press, first and foremost in the figures of Anthony Giddens and John Thompson.

3 See E. Illouz, *Why Love Hurts* (Cambridge: Polity Press, 2012).

The story of Polity Press needs to be told, but not here. The achievement of Polity is absolutely extraordinary. Giddens and Thompson, and David Held, are well known for many achievements; if they had only established Polity Press, this would surely be sufficient a monument. Polity has been responsible for translating and commissioning some of the most important contemporary academic writing. It has become a filter, a first port of call for all who read or work in social theory in the English language. Habermas, Bourdieu, Castoriadis, Lefort, Giddens, Beck, Barthes, Adorno, Elias, Alexander, Bobbio, Honneth, Luhmann, Ricoeur, Todorov, Offe, Agamben … on and on and on, and these are only the boys – too many boys; and then Bauman. Polity helped make Bauman, and liquidity, a brand name, a trade icon. There would be no Bauman as we know him without Polity, and likely no liquidity either.

When the Polity story is written, it will need among other things to look into the creative role of management in the publication record. As in Brian Epstein and George Martin and the Beatles, Chas Chandler and Hendrix or Cream and Robert Stigwood and Ahmet Ertegun, it is insufficient to imagine that the artist alone is responsible for the output. Certainly, Polity played a major role in marketing and distributing *Liquid Modernity*. The summer before the publication of *Liquid Love*, likely the most expressive of these liquidity arguments, I visited Bauman in Leeds and read a manuscript, his 'last book' for that year, then entitled *Love, Death and Eternity*. Later he referred to it as *Love and Death*, or as *Together Apart*. It subsequently appeared in 2003 as *Liquid Love*. In my copy of *Liquid Love* I find a loose note, written on the back of my Manchester to Leeds train trip receipt for 13 August 2002. This contains a summary of the table of contents for the typescript I read at Lawnswood Gardens. The last two chapters are the same as the final product; the first three chapter titles diverge. There were five chapters in the typescript, four in the book. Apparently there was some serious project development going on. As Iremonger and Rojek and others had brought me on, so did Giddens and Thompson surely help bring out and deliver the liquid brand. There was the editorial work together, but then there was also the closest critical sociology got to its own Bee Gees – Bauman, Beck and

Giddens, often triangulated together in the literature on the diagnosis of the new modernity as the go-to boys in sociology today. (There was, of course, another, fourth 'B. G', central to Beck's work: his wife, Elisabeth Beck-Gernsheim, as in *The Normal Chaos of Love*.)

Bauman was evidently fond of both Thompson and Giddens. Of Giddens he said that he was 'gentle yet relentless' in the preface to *Postmodernity and Its Discontents* (1997). He was also given to wax lyrical there on the contribution to his work of another David Roberts, who again is thanked for ten years' editing collaboration in the preface to *In Search of Politics* (1999). Editing, like publishing, remains vital to yet largely invisible from the performance of social theory. Perhaps Bauman's correspondence in the Brotherton will cast further light on these collaborations. We all know that knowledge production is not a matter of immaculate conception, even if in everyday gossip we are suckers for the idea of romantic genius. Life is staged, even in social theory. It takes two, or more.

I asked Giddens about Bauman and Polity; he was unable to help. From John Thompson I had no reply; I understand that these are busy people. Bauman wrote to me occasionally that he was under pressure to deliver, though externalities alone can be no sufficient explanation for the incredible levels of output that he achieved: four books each for 2013, 2015 and 2017, for example. Did he, then, write too much? Probably, though this was part of a strategy in which a steady, serial audience of academic readers was no longer to be taken for granted, and he had developed a serious or even compulsive need to write.

Bauman's audience was also mobile. Amidst the extraordinary proliferation of information, he, and we, could no longer presume that we had faithful readers to follow us. This was the whole point of the claim about liquid modernity, that the accepted postwar patterns of making and receiving intellectual culture were also being transformed. After solid ideas, good or bad, there was Twitter. This, in turn, is one of the reasons that Bauman was sometimes given to repeating himself. A good idea is worth repeating in times of liquid modernity; you never know if anyone is listening, or reading. More, as Keith Tester argued in his last essay for

Thesis Eleven, there is more than one way to understand repetition, which can be multifaceted and creative rather than simply boring or tediously cyclical in nature.[4] We all remain creatures of repetition. For some of us, the process is additive.

This may be one central aspect and irony of the 'Bauman phenomenon' – that at the moment of his death we knew him both very well, in terms of public exposure, and yet hardly at all, in terms of the finer fibres of his thinking and his purpose. Into the first decade of the new millennium liquidity had become the mantra. Perhaps its tail was the conversations published together with the Mexican Citlali Rovirosa-Madrazo as *Living on Borrowed Time* (2009) or with David Lyon in *Liquid Surveillance* (2012). Surveillance was a new theme for Bauman, though it had been following him since Orwell and Foucault. He also returned to classical concerns in sociology with Tester and Jacobsen in *What Is the Use of Sociology?* (2014) and in works on inequality, consumption and the newly prominent figure of the refugee, as stranger and enemy for those within the walls of apparent safety and security in the West.

At the same time, something new was emerging. This took a new form, as the conversation with different interlocutors, but it also took on the immediacy of new times, the interregnum, and the status of literature as sociology or a window to social understandings in these new and terrible times. In the face of these urgent and pressing signs of the times, and facing the immediacy of his own sense of mortality, Bauman was also trying to push death and fear away.

4 K. Tester, 'On Repetition in the Work of Zygmunt Bauman', *Thesis Eleven*, 149 (2018).

Chapter 7

Last decade: Bauman writing, reading and talking

Perhaps I was mistaken never to have asked Bauman more fully about how his published work was project-developed or edited. There were always other things to talk about, and he did not like to talk about himself or about his writing. Perhaps he enjoyed the element of surprise in our relationship, or perhaps he did not actually know what he was going to do next. Perhaps I made the mistake of thinking I knew him, or of knowing that what might come next would be more of the same, or somehow continuous at best. Perhaps my mistake was to imagine that I had sorted out the coordinates that he might continue to follow. In any case, there were surprises to come, as well as continuities to attend to. We were in the flow of our own historicity. There would always be innovation, though by this late moment of his life it may well also have been the case that Bauman's thinking was already sedimented. Who among us thinks anew into their 80s?

My box set on Bauman may have had little effect in seeking to contextualize and historicize Bauman's work. The set still falls into the earlier phase of Bauman reception. Recent work, such as that of Ali Rattansi, ignores it, as well as my other work on Bauman; *c'est la vie*/this is not an iceberg. Collections such as these disappear into the libraries at which they are pitched, or else just disappear into thin air. They are not intended for mass consumption but as resources for scholars working in the field. For context and historicity matter, especially when major thinkers depart, and there is a kerfuffle of repositioning, some wanting to claim the ideas, or the body or the mantle, some wanting to hasten the burial and dismissal. *Out of my sunshine!*

Rattansi was one such who wanted Bauman off the stage. This may have been unfortunate timing, as Bauman was about to take his own exit. Rattansi describes his interest in Bauman as an obsession. *Let us straighten the crooked timber of humanity!* What his critique, in *Bauman and Contemporary Sociology* (2018), stirs, among other things, is the question of his own subject position. Here Bauman is charged repeatedly with failure, with flaw, with weakness and guilt. This is the language of interrogation: the verb 'to indict', the noun 'verdict'. As though failure is not the precondition of success; as though there are no flaws in our own glass. As though we are in the magistrates' court, or the Office of Corrections. As though sociology needs to be defended against those, such as Bauman, who are alleged to sully its professional reputation. *Books without footnotes!? Where is your index?*

Social theory, too, is like showbiz. Rattansi is shadowed by Inspector Clouseau; he is the officer of the flaw. For as long as Bauman has had a presence on the stage, there have been those who wanted him off. *Out of my light, sunshine!* As we have seen, this was a pattern going back to Edward Thompson's attack. This was one oversight from my box set; the Thompson review should also have been there, though, before Keith Tester wrote his superb assessment of this episode and the peculiarities of the English idiom, I am not sure that all this had sufficiently fallen into place for me.

Keith's paper was published in the *Polish Sociological Review* in 2006. It was called 'Intellectual Immigration and the English Idiom (Or, a Tale of Bustards and Eagles)'. Its cast was actually a threesome – Thompson, Kołakowski and Bauman – for Thompson had also taken Kołakowski to the cleaners in that notorious and notoriously long piece in the *Socialist Register* for 1973. Thompson had animus against sociology as well as theory. But the main issue, proving Bauman's response that you don't argue back because it is not about you but about something else, was that Bauman was some kind of potential obstacle in the path of revolution. How dare these Poles take any kind of distance on revolutionary

Marxism? This was presented as some kind of version of ratting. There was a complete incapacity to extend empathy to those who were stuck inside Soviet-type societies, until it was time to vomit them out, to expel them to the West, where they did not belong either. Bauman was no stranger to stigma; now there was a new version of it, where even the right to speak in a Polish accent was under threat.

Kołakowski had himself engaged in criticism of Bauman, in 'A Pleading for Revolution' in 1971. These two also had differences, though Bauman held Kołakowski in the very highest regard, both before and after they parted ways politically. Such matters were brought to bear by Tester and Bauman in their *Conversations*, but also contextualized with care and detail in the two volumes edited by Tester and his colleagues in two more invisible volumes published in 2005 and 2007: *Bauman before Postmodernity*; and *Bauman beyond Postmodernity*. The first volume is close to our immediate interests here. It is intellectually sophisticated, but also bibliographical, textual and contextual in scope. Its title is like the joke that once came up from a young student of mine: Paul McCartney was in a band before Wings? Yes, there was a Bauman before the postmodern. Bauman had been intellectually active for 30 years before the postmodern. Tester and his colleagues included interviews and supporting essays in their dossier, but also summaries of 1,000 words or so apiece on the early works – on young folk in Warsaw, 1962; the social structure of the Party in industry, 1962; innovative and conformist personality, 1965; mass culture, 1966, the limits of 'perfect planning', 1967; Polish youth and politics, 1967; and so on, through to papers on semiotics, 1968, and the Polish Jewry, 1969. Similar sections follow for later decades, as, for example, with 'The Structuralist Promise' in 1973, to the essay on Elias in 1979. Further interviews take us into the 1980s, with more synopses to follow. The volume, and its sequel, are labours of love, an invaluable source for those interested in the nuanced interpretation of Bauman rather than the cartoon cut-out. The second book, *Bauman beyond Postmodernity*, has a similar sense of detail and attention to difference. These books deserve much wider attention as keyhole optics into the Bauman still largely unknown to the later audience, or, at least, to those who claim to take ideas seriously.

Bauman's earlier work on socialist Poland deserves further scholarly attention. It may well be the laboratory of his much later distinction between solid and liquid modernity. It brings to mind some of the most powerful period Polish writing, for example, of Ryzard Kapuściński, especially with reference to the issue of consumerism and emergent youth culture. Here it is as though there was already a prefigurative version of the symptomatology of liquid modernity at work, for the transition from war and austerity to reconstruction to early consumerism also raises questions about the transformation of second nature. The point is obvious, if insufficiently recognized. Whatever categories we choose to describe our moment, the ways in which that moment is experienced will be highly differentiated, by place and region, race, class and gender. Whether solid, liquid or modernity in ruins, the modalities of experience lived out by groups and subjects will be highly variegated. Whatever our need to generalize, there is never a moment in which one size fits all.

Yet there is also the need to characterize the spirit of the age, as we see it; and this will always be subject of dispute and difference. By 2005 Bauman had shifted from modern, to post, to liquid. The liquidity show was now well under way. If the year 2000 was a marker, with the appearance of *Liquid Modernity*, then there were other patterns of development to follow. In the first decade of the new millennium Bauman was producing a book a year, including the little books – on identity, community, individualization, *Liquid Life*, *Liquid Fear*, *Liquid Times*, works on consumption and consumer ethics. There were two books in 2011, one translated by Lydia, and two in 2012, but I think the signal of changes to come is flagged in *44 Letters*, in 2010. *44 Letters from the Liquid Modern World* points to *This Is Not a Diary*, which represents some kind of shift in style or voice, after the death of Janina at Christmas 2009. In 2013 there were four books, three in the form of conversations, which becomes the new preferred mode of discourse, representing the conversational model taken to its logical conclusion. The exception, in 2013, is *Does the Richness of the Few Benefit Us All?*; Bauman never gave up on the basics, or on his commitment to socialism and culture, beauty and dignity, and followed this later, in 2016 and 2017, with solo volleys on refugees, in *Strangers at Our Door*, and on the revived will to political nostalgia, in *Retrotopia*. In 2014 there were two volumes of conversation, one in 2015, two in 2016. Keith and I proposed a shared volume in 2016 on film, art and photography. Maybe we were too late; maybe it was too late. He did not pick up on the idea. As he said elsewhere, he was getting sick of listening to his own voice. Others were more interesting. And the Reaper was ever near.

Clearly, there was something for Bauman that was after the postmodern, or even after liquidity. A number of patterns and clues emerge across this brace of books. There is a renewed enthusiasm for the literary as a form of understanding. There is a sense of the urgency of the immediacy of global politics, dispossession and crisis. And there is an extended openness to the views of others, not least those who are elsewhere in the global room or at work near or far, in Mexico, Italy, Lithuania, Warsaw, Finland. The interlocutors now are peripheral, in terms of the Paris–Frankfurt axis or the transatlantic hegemony.

Let us scan some of these horizons. *44 Letters from the Liquid Modern World* is a gesture to his romantic Polish forebear, Adam Mickiewicz. The number 44 was a symbol of freedom, unlike 84. Bauman dedicated the copy he gave to me 'To Peter – with invisible hundreds I intended to write to him … '. But these 44 were written also under pressure, this time from *La Repubblica della Donne*, which asked him to send its readers a letter once a fortnight, over almost two years. So there was an archive here, too. Letters – an older format, in a world drowning in messages and information. Our own patterns of private contact had always been epistolary. Now there were public epistles, a sharing of private and public issues and worries. These were travel reports, longer postcards from a moment when he did not budge from Leeds. He claimed to be following Benjamin, and his distinction between sailors' stories of the fantastic and peasants' stories, which were closer to home and therefore homespun. These days, as Bauman observed, the distinction was no longer so plain. The fantastic might live next door to us. The themes roamed wide and far, from the crowded solitude of the girl today who sends 100 text messages a day, looking ever outwards rather than inwards for strength or affirmation, to Twitter, to net purchasing sex – as easy as ordering a pizza, even easier than the Vegas strip, where the hustlers promise a girl to your room in 20 minutes. Some of these themes are old: David Riesman, the difference between outer- and inner-directed personalities; or even older, as in the Marxian lament that quantity swamps quality. These are also in a sense Simmelian impressions, the feuilleton flashes of insight that you might associate with the most powerfully condensed writing of journalism. Indeed, Bauman is in a sense the end of a long line of critical journalists, from Marx and Simmel to Robert Park and Habermas. Likely this is one undeclared reason for the disciplinary hostility towards Bauman: 'Oh no! Perhaps he was a journalist.' Certainly, he wanted to be a messenger. Health, illness, education, time, calculation, the unpredictable, Depression and depression, interregnum, crisis … something, apparently, for everyone, or for many, on the screen in the West, increasingly, perhaps also in the East, not least in China.

Was this not, then, at least in form a concession to the speed of liquid modern times, these emissives? I think not, though it can always be argued that we too are insinuated in the problems we wish to explain and to criticize. Nothing, contra Thatcher, is outside society or immune from dominant social trends. Yet the writing here is too thick, too suggestive, too substantial to resemble what today are called texts, or text messages. As in *This Is Not a Diary*, which it evidently is – a diary, just as Magritte's pipe was not Bauman's pipe – the *Diary* begins with a confession, that at 5 a.m. on 3 September 2010, already at his desk, Bauman is painfully aware of the risk of having nothing to say, but needing still, like a habit or addiction, to write … But there is also pleasure in this need to write, and not only a need or obsession. As others have demanded: 'Roll over, Descartes!' Writing is a way to think. Maybe writing is primary, before thinking; or perhaps *A* is also *B*, after all. The spectre of graphomania is a joke; the need to write is serious. The first sight of his day is the image of Janina on the screensaver; he is not alone, or at least not entirely. So the postcards, the images and issues unfold, snippets from the news pages, problems of the lifeworld and deathworld, problems of refugees, stimulants from Michel Houellebecq, Milan Kundera and José Saramago, responses to the daily bad news and attempts to think all this mess. As usual, he is all over the place. This is the world as it emerges from the computer – it no longer has the apparent coherence suggested by the morning newspaper to Hegel. And yet Bauman is present, and fully focused: '29 December 2010 – On Selected Quandaries. One year ago Janina left me.' Bauman is in a tunnel, waiting.

Perhaps the conversations came as some kind of lifeline. They began with *Borrowed Time* in 2009, though as we have seen there was always time for interviews, across the decades, even if never for replies to various assembled critics. Probably the serious precedent for the various later conversations was the encounter between Bauman and Tester published in 2001, which remains a fine portal into this complex. Tester and Bauman are likely the most productive or intensely engaged of these conversationalists. In 2012 there was *On Education*, in collaboration with Riccardo Mazzeo in Italy. Here the imaginary interlocutors include Marcel Proust, Edgar Morin, Sennett, Gregory Bateson, Saramago and many others, these great thinkers brought to bear on the apparently impossible presenting issue of how to get education to work, this not least in a multicultural, globalized and terrified world. It is as though we, folk like us, still persist in expecting everything of education, residue of the Enlightenment, and yet simultaneously expect our institutions to deliver nothing.

Moral Blindness, with Leonidas Donskis, followed in 2013. Now we are in Lithuania, back plumbing the depths of the human condition. But of what can we speak? What might we claim to know, or even to judge? For in everyday life we engage in such activities freely, and they all have consequences. In the academy, in the university and on the left the stringent measures applied to language use can be more difficult. For some time now it has been a norm to privilege position or direct experience over other claims to understanding in radical debate. This culminates in the controversy over cultural appropriation, in which it is presumed that no one from outside a culture can enter into it or legitimately borrow from it without doing violence to that other culture. There is some power in these claims. To walk in the shoes of others may well be a good starting point in the conversation of humankind. But these arguments also threaten to foreclose on the possibility of engagement. If I may speak only of what I directly know of, the conversation will be short indeed. More, this kind of view runs the risk of denying cultural traffic; it presumes that cultures and even subcultures are closed and hermetic vessels, which seems counter-intuitive. Globalization has been with us at least since 1642; imperialism for much longer.

This is one ambient issue for Donskis. As he relates, as Bauman said in his Kaunas lecture, for writers there is nothing harder than writing about situations that you not only have not experienced but wouldn't even want to experience.[1] Yet these horrors of modern times are also in some sense universal, common human property or responsibility. To talk about evil means being willing to talk about the Devil, and in Bauman's case, and in Janina's, being prepared to talk about demons and the process of demonization. Modernity, in all its forms, relies on the exercise of Faustian pacts. All this is set in the context of Eastern Europe today, where – to modify Heller's view of the United States – there has been both the worst of communism and now the worst of capitalism. These possibilities of understanding are often still lost on the Western left, or on its academic traces. East European margins so rarely seem to count, in the big cosmopolitan conversation.

In 2014 Bauman published *State of Crisis*, working together with Carlo Bordoni, his old friend from the Italian discussion journal *Promoteo*. This volume is, as it observes in opening, an essay written by four hands, doubling Escher. Here the script is apparently tighter. Bauman and Bordoni were brought together by common concerns and respect, but also by the mutual curiosity in breathing new life into Gramsci's throwaway line about the interregnum: the idea that we, like Gramsci in the 1930s, were caught between two worlds, the old dying, the new as yet unable to emerge. Whereas the conversation with Donskis is more excursive, that with Bordoni is more

---

1 Z. Bauman with L. Donskis, *Moral Blindness: The Loss of Sensitivity in Liquid Modernity* (Cambridge: Polity Press, 2013), 9

focused. It also resulted, later, in Bordoni's own book, *Interregnum* (2016). Crisis here, as in the critical theory tradition, connects the prospect of collapse with that of the turning point. So the conversation travels over the state in crisis, modernity in crisis and, finally, democracy in crisis. There is crisis everywhere, not least in terms of those who struggle for bare life.

Bauman's conversation expanded into 2015. Although Bauman was becoming open to the charge of repetition in these times, what is refreshing about the two conversations with Stanislaw Obirek is how sharp and new they are. They have travelled very different paths, one Marxist, the other Jesuit; maybe they are not so different, or at least parallel. The two find themselves obliged to play devil's advocate, even if these are two different devils. *Of God and Man* (2015) begins with Pope Francis, but travels wide and far. The history of theology looms large – Judaism, monotheism, polytheism. Kołakowski appears here, and Emmanuel Levinas, but also a new conversationalist: J. M. Coetzee. For we might also be agnostic about agnosticism. Bauman and Obirek play with the idea that they each have been tempted by different historic prospects, the first by the Promethean, the second by the messianic. Many insights and observations follow from both conversationalists, including the personal. Bauman laments that, although Obirek had a close narrative relationship with his own grandfather, he, Bauman, found himself in a situation in which his grandfather gave up on telling him stories, likely because the youth was insufficiently wise to take it all in. (My recall is that, as for me, his was a mother-dominated household, a sense reinforced by Wagner in her biography of Bauman.) Bauman also shows his own, much later intellectual preference for writing over speech, however, as with Jacques Derrida. So the two talk about religion for days, a more civilized version of waiting for god, and Obirek allows Bauman the last word: 'Amen.'

Another volume with Obirek followed: *On the World and Ourselves* (2015). Discussion continues on good and evil, with class, the precariat, Guy Standing and the question of dignity, the Polish Solidarity and Stalinism here jostling with Augustine and the Bible. Bauman and Obirek also offer differing sensibilities as to what it might mean to be Polish, or a Polish Jew. As Bauman says, his status as a Pole was always conditional, subject to possible withdrawal or suspension. Jews were construed as thieves, even to the extent that their identities could be cast as stolen. During his six years at primary school in Słowacki Street, the boy would have to take refuge indoors, away from the playground, where blows and kicks would rain down on him. Even the lending library, unlike mine in suburban Croydon, had put up the 'Not Welcome' sign.[2] His Soviet school experience was different, allowing him to be both Jewish and Polish. One thing led to another, and the end point was his own adoption of communism. Then Poland expelled him, and then he was invited back after 1991. Poland escaped from communism, and turned into something else: hatred and skinheads, no right to speak.[3] As Bauman was to mutter to me, this was another unrequited love affair, this one even deeper than his love of the French, who were late to pick up on his work. Maybe they had heard it all before in its local inflections. Perhaps they had no need of this messenger. His loss of Poland was another matter.

By this point Bauman seemed, like Kołakowski, to have views on absolutely everything. Why not *management*, then? Evidently he had long harboured interesting views on organization and bureaucracy. *Management in a Liquid Modern World* (2015) brings Bauman together with Jerzy Kociatkiewicz, Monica Kostera and, most interestingly perhaps, Irena Bauman, who might be the one here who disagrees with him most. The interregnum is an opening gambit. For, if the world is caught, stuck between orders, then this will also have consequences for management. Some will be stuck in the old world, others looking forwards but unable to make the leap forwards. The resulting conversation shifts to the meso level of analysis, and to the city as a unit of analysis. There is also a politics here, past or emergent. Kostera is author of a book called *Occupy Management!*, and the tradition from which Bauman comes has more than a passing interest in the idea of self-management. The particular inflection that Irena Bauman brings to the conversation, as an architect and urbanist, is reflective of a need fully to factor in environment. This move

2 Z. Bauman and S. Obirek, *On the World and Ourselves* (Cambridge: Polity Press, 2015), 108–9.
3 Bauman and Obirek, *On the World and Ourselves*, 110–11.

promises to change everything. The implicit dispute between daughter and father here concerns what these days is called post-humanism.

As I have noted above, the status of humanism in Bauman's own thinking remains ambivalent or unresolved. He emerges as a socialist and socialist humanist, yet a fundamental part of his thinking in the 1980s involves taking a distance from Enlightenment. He embraces socialist construction after the war, and then steps back from the model of social engineering in the 1980s, as in *Legislators and Interpreters*. Irena Bauman wants to insist that humanism may be the inner circle of the cosmos, but that there are others concentric outside it. The idea of interregnum, in this light, may miss the point. We are not just in between, but in a scene more given to catastrophe than Gramsci's was between the wars. Our present crisis, in her way of thinking, is not a repeat. Irena refers outwards, instead, to C. S. Holling's theory of 'panarchy'.[4] This is a way of thinking like long waves of technological development, except that it insists on the vital place of ecology as constitutive rather than secondary to humans and technology. The present crisis is made by humans, but humanism alone cannot capture the extent of the process. In terms of response, it may be less cities than networks and communities that matter here. This way of thinking follows on from Irena's own urban practice, as anticipated in *How to Be a Happy Architect*. The movement onwards and outwards is suggestive.

There are many other fascinating excurses here, including Kostera's ruminations on the image of Eastern Europe – Chekhov, Dostoyevsky, Kieślowski, Emil Cioran – as the guardian of darkness, in contrast to the bright Western light of *les Lumières*. If only the two could be manoeuvred together. Yet it is the practical level to which conversation returns: the new energy for artisanal work, for local production and consumption, for the good life as it might just possibly be enacted by those fortunate enough, under the radar of Fordism and factory farming. The grounds for hope remain here small, and local. The absent third party to this conversation between daughter and father might again be Richard Sennett.

---

4 Z. Bauman, I. Bauman, J. Kociatkiewicz and M. Kostera, *Management in a Liquid Modern World* (Cambridge: Polity Press, 2015), 35.

Bauman's next interlocutor is again intriguing: Rein Raud, professor of Japanese studies at Helsinki, via Tallinn. Together they speak of *Practices of Selfhood*. How do we think about subjectivity in these times? Fragmented, multiple, open to endless reinvention. Here the dramatis personae range wide and far, from Blaise Pascal to his old favourite, Mary Douglas, through to Coetzee and Jonathan Franzen and the post-Soviet satirist Vladimir Voinovich as well as the performance theory of Jeffrey Alexander. Literature always looms large in the conversation, as the image of performance from Shakespeare to Goffman itself suggests. Much of the open-ended discussion concerns the most central issue, the transformation of what we used to call human nature at the hands of technology: the enormous global proliferation of screens. Ours may well now be the age of screens; we are in need of a new Hobsbawm to begin to make sense of all this, after the *Age of Extremes*. Screens change the way we conduct our affairs, the way we negotiate each other and intimate space, private and public. Yet Bauman also, always, is given to insist on the maldistribution of these life chances. In order to discuss culture it is also necessary to discuss resources. He quotes Joseph Stiglitz: 'We have empty homes and homeless people' – people with more space than they can properly use and others with no durable space at all. Some live in cardboard boxes, while others have crises of storage: too many homes, too many boxes. Suffering persists, outside the roseate halo of the smiling selfie.[5]

In 2016 the focus returns to Lithuania, and his conversation partner Donskis. This volume is entitled *Liquid Evil*; the theme of liquidity has not yet been exhausted. Here light and dark return, via Mikhail Bulgakov and *The Master and Margerita*, the letters between Paul Auster and J. M. Coetzee, and those old companions, Kafka and Orwell. The hulk of Vladimir Putin looms large, as do the parallel stories of Lithuania and Poland. Of particular concern here is the question of the lifeworlds entered into by new generations. Bauman refers to the work of Roman Pawlowski, and his distinction between Polish 'children of the transformation' and 'children of the crisis'. These are, as he observes elsewhere, two

---

5 Z. Bauman and R. Raud, *Practices of Selfhood* (Cambridge: Polity Press, 2015), 122.

different versions of the precariat, which itself can be cross class. Precarity is not socially choosy. 'Until further notice' is universal these days, after the passing of the illusion of solidity and the further erosion of solidarity.

Perhaps there is a pattern, some kind of consistency across many of these works. Some others, such as *44 Letters* or *Not a Diary*, seem to take a different tack, to make a break or pause for thought. And so it is with *In Praise of Literature*, from 2016. Here the epigrams are from Adorno, though the cue is suggestive rather than substantive. It is well to recall Bauman's occasional distance from the thinker he jokingly called 'Theodor the Obscure'. Lyotard once wrote of Adorno as the Devil. Bauman was not a puppet or Mephisto of Adorno, however. He was not an aristocrat or an elitist in the cultural sense. There are always too many in the room for a single thinker to offer the master key to making sense of Bauman. This applies to all the thinkers in Bauman's house of many rooms, Adorno included.

There are, of course, affinities between Bauman and Adorno. One of them, traced with sensitivity by Keith Tester, evokes the image of 'late style'.[6] Themes no longer emerge anew, in late style, so much as they return and are subjected to rumination. As Adorno suggests, late style beckons history, or repetition more than perhaps growth, or innovation. Late style may be suggestive of death, of awaiting the final exit, of the final reconsideration. Late also suggests dead, as leftists used to joke about Ernest Mandel's category of late capitalism; capitalism is many things, but it is not yet late! Such rumination also evokes the association of love and death, as essayed by Bauman's second wife, Aleksandra Jasinska-Kania, who echoes Bauman in wanting to connect love and death as much as love and its usual co-term, hatred.[7]

The conversation on literature between Bauman and Mazzeo in a sense extends that with Jacobsen and Tester, on the lasting legacy and remaining project of sociology. It goes further back, to Bauman's conversations with

---

6 K. Tester, 'Sociology: The Active Catastrophe', *Revue Internationale de Philosophie* 3/70 (2016).

7 A. Kania, 'The Fluidity of Love and Hate: Zygmunt Bauman on Death, Love and Hatred', *Revue Internationale de Philosophie*, 3/70 (2016).

Tester and the query regarding desert island discs. In that earlier moment, Bauman nominated his favourite as Borges. The question of course goes much further back again, and has been well plotted in the classic work of Wolf Lepenies, *Between Science and Literature* (1988). Bauman's purpose is at the least to align literature and sociology, and therefore to visit again the conversation regarding the respective strengths and weaknesses of the liberal arts and the social sciences. It is a well-ploughed field, in which views, and interests, are bound to remain essentially contested. Its critical horizon, which will also remain contested, is the question whether sociology or literature can change the world. The short answer to this question is likely 'Yes', but only indirectly, not when it is pursued as a conscious strategy or project. Sociology and literature change little worlds more than big ones.

Bauman's case is that literature and sociology feed off each other. There is indeed a place for facts here, as Bauman indicates with reference to the work of Arlie Russell Hochschild on changes in marriage and family structure, or in Göran Therborn's indices of the different lifechances that result from structures of national and global inequality. This is less a matter of an advocacy for literature than one of showing where it joins in on the conversation about everyday life in postmodern times. Only sociologists would imagine they have primogeniture here. So the writers who wander through Bauman's house and are beckoned to join in are the likes of Coetzee, Robert Walser, Robert Musil, Elias Canetti, Susan Sontag and W. G. Sebald. These are, like the best of sociologists, diagnosticians of the times. The form of writing that they choose may not resemble that of the social sciences, but the messages remain evocative, and may even be more powerfully disseminated via what is presented as fiction. As Janet Wolff has argued in her appreciation of Bauman's tropes, the case for reading sociology and literature together is less one of identity or possible merger than of this possible alignment. This is an approach that seeks out value, empathy and insight. It would suggest what Wolff calls a poetic way of doing sociology.[8]

8 J. Wolff, 'The Question of a Sociological Poetics', in M. E. Davis (ed.), *Liquid Sociology* (London: Routledge, 2013).

Bauman suggests here that there is nothing new under the Sun. This is not his usual temporal sensibility, that of liquid modernity. It is not new. Mazzeo suggests, after Stefano Tani, that there are three key metaphors for our times, in addition to liquid modernity: screens; Alzheimer's; and Zombies. These, Tani argues, are exemplary symptoms of our times. The triad seems random. Ours remains the topsy-turvy world anticipated by Marx, however, as the domination of the world of commodities, or the world of things. For Bauman persists in arguing that there is little new under the Sun. Screens represent a serious change in prosthetic culture; Alzheimer's and Zombies may, rather, be cultural symbols or symptoms. For Bauman, as for Marx before him, ours is, as I suggested earlier, a potlatch culture taken to modernist extremes. We are drowning under a surfeit of stuff, as surely as those who work through our garbage in poorer countries are at risk of disappearing under the mountains of our waste even as they comb through it. Again, the discussion here is open-ended, from sex and karaoke to avatars, mobile phones and fascism. It ends with a more frontal turn to literature and sociology, again via the conversation between Auster and Coetzee. Can either literature or sociology change the world? This may be a necessary question, but it has no answer apart from the obvious: 'Yes'/'No'/'Maybe'. And then there come the implicit questions that follow: who are proposing themselves as the agents of change, and in whose interests? For this world is always changing, whether in ways that are consciously directed or not. One of the first lessons of either literature or sociology may be that the dominant forces might, rather, be those beyond our control. Poets may have been imagined by poets as the unacknowledged legislators of the world, but all this has been taken wildly off course by the engineers of the human soul, and the dictators at whose pleasure they may now play.

This is a motif that arcs all the way back to *Legislators and Interpreters* in 1987. There Bauman wickedly suggested that perhaps the appeal of Weber's Protestant ethic was to the self-image of the intellectuals. Sociology was unable to shake off the dream of the salvation of society. We, the sociologists, would remain somehow invisible in the process. Forty years ago Bauman made the choice to value interpretation over the will to legislate. Now the cat was out of the bag. Intellectuals may well be social ventriloquists, aspirant social engineers. Or, they simply talk too much, and cannot tell the difference between word and deed, between the seminar room and the world outside, looking to set things aright indoors and out. Bauman at least imagined his audience to be outside the halls.

This leads to the opening motif of the 2016 volume with Ezio Mauro, another translation from the Italian. *Babel*, Babylon, the endless recycling … Perhaps this text is especially mimetic, as its subject matter is the babble, the endless proliferation of voice and volume, which is accompanied by a near-universal incapacity to listen or to learn. Everything seems random and uncertain. There is too much information, too many facts, too much noise.

Babel does, indeed, repeat. It also includes some new and blistering observations on the overproduction of knowledge, or, at least, of publication. This is more Babel, a throng of so many voices and writers that no one any longer can truly aspire to mastery of a field, including that of Bauman studies. We are caught in a vortex of 'Publish and perish'. Yet each word that we write is one that we do not read, each word we speak one that we do not hear anew. As Bauman put it earlier, in the nineteenth century we – people like us, on the left – imagined that the world could be put to rights if only we had the facts, the information, the data. Now, into the twenty-first century, we have so much information that we are completely overwhelmed by it. There is too much data, and too much stuff. Too much of nothing.

And there is always another book. This book on Babel is followed by a last series of short commentaries edited by Neal Lawson. *A Chronicle of Crisis 2011–2016* (2017) consists of 24 short cameos on inequality, solidarity, Facebook and the precariat, neoliberalism and Trumpetry. The firmer message of exit comes with *Retrotopia*, his swansong in 2016, this to be followed by two posthumous books with Polity, and we know not what to follow, as the stakes in the Bauman industry rise or decline. He will have the last joke with his 'last book', for we do not know what it will be or when it might arrive.

Retrotopia was a good finale for Bauman. It carries a dedication to Aleksandra, 'companion of my thought and life'. It opens under the world-weary sign of Walter Benjamin and Paul Klee, where the 'Angel of History' is also overwhelmed by a mounting pile of debris, and then Svetlana Boym's work on nostalgia. The worse the decline of the West becomes, the more desire there is for returns to imaginary pasts. These are not properly utopian, as they lack the futurist element that is constitutive of so much modern or modernist utopia. Four key chapters, or returns, follow. The first is back to Hobbes – nasty, short and brutish, or, the new *Leviathan*. There is an inescapable sense in which social life becomes more and more violent, angry and aggressive. These days we do not so much avoid the eye of the stranger on the street out of indifference or the blasé attitude as out of fear. We lock our doors and pray for strong leaders. These are not good precedents, the memories of what came before in such times.

Bauman now engages with Umberto Eco, which is apposite, as Eco closes his last book, *Chronicles of a Liquid Society* (2017), by engaging directly with Bauman; it makes a wonderful epitaph, or circle. Next Bauman takes us back to tribes. Under these real and imaginary pressures that make up modern times, our fears and anxieties, we draw around the wagons, or pull up the ladders. We believe our nations and the planet to be full. So we are also, and here Bauman returns to Benjamin Disraeli, back to inequality, to two nations or more. The last, and most provocative, chapter suggests that we long to be back in the womb. This would be somewhere warm and safe, where there is struggle, no anxiety, no pain, no steep learning curves, no disappointment. Long-term optimist, short-term pessimist, that he was, Bauman concludes that our fate is simple: we face joining either hands, or common graves. As he knows from work such as Therborn's on lifechances, class and health and longevity, what comes before that end point will be highly asymmetrical. The prospect of death is not selective, but that of misery is. This is one of the consistencies across the work of Zygmunt Bauman. Inequality matters; and we are always capable of doing better.

Bauman had his share of suffering; not that there is any proper ethical calculus for this. Bauman understood something of stigma, of racism and anti-Semitism, and he never would give up on the issue of the loss to humanity generated by unnecessary inequality. In this context, it seems strange that, among many of the accusations that were delivered against him, one should be an alleged insensitivity to suffering. How would we know? How would we fathom the motivation of another? Would this not be the God's-eye view? Whatever, it was not the view he took for himself. After his life in Polish postwar reconstruction, he did not want to legislate, but to interpret. He had hopes for reform communism into the 1960s. But after 1968 he could no longer be a communist, nor communitarian, nor yet liberal. Perhaps he ended his life in a corner. Perhaps he is not alone there.

Chapter 8

The 'Bauman phenomenon': signing out

There were to be more volumes, after *Retrotopia*, and there will doubtless be more again to follow. There were to be two final books, published during the writing of the book you are holding. The first was *Sketches in the Theory of Culture*. This is an important work of serious conventional scholarship, especially of interest to those with a strong curiosity in Bauman, because of its history as a lost and suppressed text from 1968. Structuralism was a significant influence on Bauman, not least because of his fascination with Lévi-Strauss and what Bauman called 'the structuralist promise'. This work is reminiscent of Bauman's earlier work in both the scope of its interests and the breadth of the texts and authorities brought to bear on them. It chases theories and ideas wide and far, but also engages with data concerning, for example, the situation of postwar youth and education in Poland. In this it might be said to anticipate some of the later theorems concerning liquid modernity, though it is also likely that the continuity of Bauman's sociological interest is in the staple issue of social change, or at least in the fact of turbulence. If there are some constants in the way Bauman thinks, then the academic density of this classic 1968 text also suggests a world that, for Bauman, is lost to us.

The last book – to date – is a small volume of conversations with Thomas Leoncini, entitled *Born Liquid* (2017). As younger generations of black South Africans were said to be formally 'born free', so had the last generation been born in the West and elsewhere into liquid modernity. Substantively, the interest in being born into this new world meant taking on what others might regard as the fads and fashions of these new times: crafting the self, tattoos, cosmetic surgery, hipsters, bullying, online dating, gender transitions, and so on. Methodologically speaking, this would involve the challenge of the new normal. Phenomena such as these might raise the odd older eyebrow, at least some of the time, but for younger folks they are routine, already naturalized or normalized as second nature. No biggie. This was an important field for Bauman to offer as his finale, but the results remain suggestive. If we were to follow his cue, rather than his text, we might instead turn for elucidation to a work of fiction such as Sally Rooney's *Normal People*.

Perhaps the surprise here in Bauman relates to perennials, such as bullying, on which Leoncini asks Bauman point-blank: 'Were you bullied?' And Bauman answers: 'Yes, directly; I was, permanently, daily.' This is what it meant to grow up as a Jewish boy in Poznan. This was not a conversation I ever had with Bauman, who would always steer away from the personal, though as I have mentioned he did choose to share with me the detail of his memory text written for his daughters. The unspoken remained central, figuratively.

Friendship, of course, has no particular model, and no obligation of self-disclosure, though it does involve something of this willingness to share. Doubtless there were also things I chose not to share with him. Ours was not a confessional relationship. But it has now become clear to me how deeply the bonds of friendship mediated our work, and the other way around.

So, how did this work, this intellectual relationship between Bauman and me? Zygmunt Bauman was my friend, among others. Was this a special relationship? I do not know. Our personal relationship grew to be something based on respect, mutual interest, friendship and love. Our work and our projects were entangled. In terms of the Bauman reception I came in early, though not at the very beginning, which belonged to Kilminster and Varcoe. I came in together with Dennis Smith and then Keith Tester. I was unpersuaded by Smith's tale of Bauman's careerism and by the pitch of the claim that Bauman was a prophet of postmodernity; it seemed to me that he was neither prophet nor postmodern. Tester's approach, then those of others such as Jacobsen and Elliott, seemed more congenial. The arrival of the liquid modern generated more heat than light, in the first instance. But there would also always be debate; these were essentially contested concepts, and the argument never ends, not even when we do.

Bauman and I were also drawn in other directions, by personal and family life and by work obligations, which in my case involved institutional obligations. We achieved a kind of intensity together into the new millennium that seemed to need little work of maintenance later; it was rekindled when there was something we worked on together or when we spent time together. It reopened as easily as email, or as our meeting at his door.

Bauman and I were different, with some shared sympathies and perhaps with some complementary competences. If we were both antipodeans we were evidently not the same kind of antipodeans. What, then, was our textual relationship, beyond the correspondences indicated above, where his work had influenced mine, as in the sociology of labour movements in Britain and Australia? Bauman wrote so much that I was compelled in the research process for this book to make lists – spreadsheets, even. What was I looking for? Correspondence, concordance. What I found was non-correspondence. There is no causal relationship between his own publication history and mine. In the twenty-first century I worked around his project, rather than mapping each new move he made. For better or worse I now imagined that I had the big map sorted, and that what followed would be variations on a theme. Perhaps I was also now following the path of the older man, late style, moving from growth to history.

Across the path of our time together I published more than 20 papers on Bauman, in addition to those six volumes. I published my first paper, the scanner of his work to date, in *Thesis Eleven* in 1998, the same year as *Work, Consumerism and the New Poor* and the little book on *Globalization* appeared. It was translated into other languages, including Portuguese and Chinese. In 1999 I published a piece on McFascism with George Ritzer, who was taken by the connections between McDonaldization and that murderous Fordism. I also joined in Harald Welzer's interview with Bauman at Lawnswood Gardens, later published in translation in *Thesis Eleven*. Into the new century I published various reviews of Bauman's books as they appeared, in scholarly journals and in dailies such as *The Age* and *The Australian* in Australia. I had always thought of reviews as a good way to sharpen your wits and to keep a balanced perspective; those who wrote books put so much of their lives into them, even if the results might disappoint. As a wiser head said to me when I was cutting my teeth on reviews, you always needed to think twice; disappointment on the part of the reviewer suggested expectations. It was a similar point to the one that Bauman urged upon me; when someone butchers a book in public, there may also be a certain pathology, a particular symbolic violence involved. In order to do any justice to a book under review you need to consider the task that the author has set for him- or herself.

In 2002 I published the materials on and with Bauman in *The Bauman Reader*. The Italian translation of the *Reader* published by Armando presented us as collaborators, Bauman/Beilharz. That same year I published the paper on Bauman's modernity, as well as that on Bauman and communist modernity – the other modernity that had to be read with and against fascism. I also wrote a new series introduction to Bauman and the Bauman reception in that box set. In 2005 I penned my survey of his work in Ritzer's two-volume *Encyclopedia of Social Theory*. I also wrote a paper on George Seddon and Karl Marx, where the antipodean bridge on the issue of second nature was Zygmunt Bauman. In 2006 I published a paper on Bauman and some of his interlocutors, here Foucault, Castoriadis and Agamben, in the *Polish Sociological Review*. This piece found another home in *Om Bauman* in 2006 and in the Filipino journal *Budhi* in the same year. I greeted Bauman's 80th birthday with 'To Build Anew' in *Thesis Eleven* in 2006. For he was the *Bau*-man, the builder as well as the Bauer, the peasant, the man of the simple life, which his was at Lawnswood Gardens when he was left alone by curious visitors or invitations to speak from afar. The year 2007 saw the publication of 'Bauman's Coat'. I also published the new scanner in Tim Edwards' *Cultural Theory*. This essay looked to thinking cultural studies into sociology, via some central figures: Marx and Weber, Freud and Foucault, to Lévi-Strauss, the structuralist promise and the structuring activity. 2009 was just a fragment, 'Therapy with Bauman', a direct response to his own views, in *Anthropological Psychology*, though I did also deliver a 'Key Thinkers' lecture at the University of Melbourne for Ghassan Hage, which made its way onto YouTube. There were too many other things going on to read, or to write. In 2010 I developed another introduction to Bauman for Jon Simon's own clever 'A' to 'Z', *Agamben to Žižek: Contemporary Critical Theorists*, this time pulling out the thread of surplus populations as a major theme from the Enclosure Acts to the tourists and vagabonds and refugees of modern times. I also published a small piece on the 'Another Bauman', as in the anthropological imagination. Ritzer commissioned a substantial new survey for his major, two-volume *Companion to Major Social Theorists* in 2011; this included a scan of themes and also some engagement with the context and reception of Bauman's work. I always wrote these surveys from scratch, though it is also entirely possible that I was by now repeating myself as well. My purpose, however, was to use each fresh opportunity to write about Bauman, to reread and rethink Bauman, for there was inevitably something new to learn or to discover, about me or about him. Call it mimesis, if you will; it involves transfer, learning, and not only repetition.

In 2011 I bade farewell to Janina Bauman, together with Sian Supski and others in *Thesis Eleven*. Our paper followed a line from Janina: what remained after all world-historic hopes had expired was the need 'to love and to be loved'. In 2013 I acted as reader for the volume edited by Mark Davis on *Liquid Sociology*, as a result of which I was asked to add a concluding chapter to the book working around the themes of liquidity and metaphor as engaged by the writers gathered there. Bauman remained fond of Goethe; without metaphor, we could not speak at all. In 2016 Carlo Bordoni invited me to write on Bauman for the *International Revue de Philosophie* and later to write on Bauman and the interregnum for his journal *Prometeo*. In 2017 Magda Matysek-Imielinska asked me to write on the power of culture for *Prace Kulturoznawcze*, and I brought together Bauman with Jeff Alexander and Raymond Williams as three iconic thinkers of culture. This was a flag of my exit from sociology via cultural studies at Curtin. Culture was one line of strong connection across those two fields. The result was published together with unexpected responses from Dominik Bartmanski and Sławomir Magala, and a final reply from me. In 2017, with his departure, I wrote three obituaries: one for Michael Burawoy in *Global Dialog/ISA*, one for *Thesis Eleven* and the final for Steve Matthewman at the *Journal of Sociology*. Each piece was in turn different; these were always fragments, or impressions. Then there was 'Lunch with Bauman', a special section of issue 149 of *Thesis Eleven* (2018), including his own views and Aleksandra's along with mine and Keith's – perhaps *his* last word, this time on that irritant called repetition, here understood creatively as revisitation rather than as more and more of the same.

Most recently I wrote on Bauman and Heller for the Chinese journal *Comparative Literature: East and West* in 2017. This piece was a kind of coda to those days we shared together in Jena in 2012. I am currently researching the reception of Bauman in China, where his work has been translated at least since 2004. For, if hypermodernity has a home, then it may well be in China. Bauman touches on this in the 2012 preface to *Liquid Modernity*, in which he puzzles over the hypermodern logics of state-directed capitalism steered by a one-party state. When I work together with my students at Sichuan University on issues such as liquid modernity they cannot quite see themselves in it, or not yet; their sensibilities are, rather, closer to the idea of modernization, that category we on the Western left rejected earlier for other reasons. They see China as socialist, not state capitalist. They see abundance, and development, futurist cities and full shelves more than surplus populations and massive regimes of waste. After a generation of jaw-dropping development they see the achievements of development more than its costs. If this is not socialism, then it is modernity with Chinese characteristics. As Weber understood a century ago, there is no causal relationship between capitalism and democracy. As the state capitalist tradition in Trotskyism showed, there may be other ways of interpreting modernity. And, as the Hungarians suggested, there may be something in the idea of dictatorship over needs, except that, here, abundance of a particular kind trumps the shortage economy of Soviet-type societies. Our conversations continue. But Bauman, and Heller, have an audience in China, which is a space to watch. It is the engine house of modernity. There is work here for critical theory. We still have our work cut out, though this will involve at least as much listening and looking as writing and judging.

If Bauman wrote too much, was this also, then, too much, on my behalf: too much writing, too many wasted words? I do not think so, and this for two reasons.

First, as I have repeatedly emphasized, Bauman's work presents itself as a tapestry or kaleidoscope of issues, fields, themes and problems. Bauman was a promiscuous thinker, and this trend accelerated as his writing proceeded. The spread of his work is not universal; how could it be, like the map of the world that has as its scale 1:1? Yet he responded to the signs of the times, drawing on the work of thinkers he had grown up with and leavening this with the work of others later, especially in literature. We used to joke, he and I, about the importance of stimulants: tobacco and alcohol; coffee and tea; food, books and ideas; thinkers and projects. Stimulants were, as Lévi-Strauss had it, things that were good to think with, 'a little glass of rum'. So Bauman was always busy thinking and thinking with, as in thinking, for example, with Castoriadis. Castoriadis once said of his own work on *Socialisme ou Barbarie* that he just pulled the thread of bureaucracy, and kept pulling. It was an unhappy line through the labyrinth. The corpus of Bauman's work has many loose threads, and I have been happy to pull at them: modern, postmodern, liquidity, love, violence, conformism, anthropology, critical theory, Eastern Europe, Weberian Marxism, surplus populations, maelstrom, whatever. There has always been some point of access, some door or window that is new to me. I still do not feel that I have exhausted this body of work – at least, not for myself. I do not think that I have done with Bauman or his cast of thousands yet. But that is not the point of this book, whose purpose is, rather, to momentarily settle accounts, or to say goodbye.

Second (and the two points are connected), I have come to be ever more persuaded of the virtue of the practice of writing in order to understand.

Every time I write about Bauman (or anything else) I either understand something better, or understand it anew. I seem to be thinking with or alongside Bauman even when I am thinking anew, or now alone, for myself. It is a fallacy, in my view, to imagine that we ever understand anything fully, most especially on first encounter. Writing and understanding are circular, and open-ended. Writing is not a second-order discourse; it is constitutive of thinking. This was the idea that Michel de Montaigne signalled as the strategy of the *essai*, the essay, the attempt. It was central to Bauman's way of thinking, but not only to his. The same, for me, can be said of teaching. It has its own purposes, but it is also a way to think. At the end of my path, it is my Chinese students who make me think. And it is the task of writing that brings the prospect of release.

What, then, was the 'Bauman phenomenon'? The word is chosen carefully; part of the answer to this question is that I do not know. The 'Bauman phenomenon' appears, and we can describe it, or track it, across all those publications, YouTube sequences, and so on. Explaining it is a more open-ended process, not least as it is also a phenomenon in the everyday sense – an event, a spectacle. The interests or coordinates of Bauman's project can be mapped or catalogued, but there is no privileged point at which we can detect its true essence or inner purpose.

And what was the Bauman effect? The issue of reception is difficult to track, though some estimates might be made. Opinions will vary, as, for example, do those of Rattansi and myself. For Rattansi, Bauman was a good man of largely negative effects. The implication, finally, is that Bauman was out of date, out of time – somewhere between milk and yoghurt, as Bauman used to joke, too close already to the use-by date. As for me, I am unsure about how best to measure time when it comes to social theory. What seems more apparent are differences in terms of place. Bauman may have become most prominent in the United Kingdom, where he found himself, and where he was abundantly promoted as a go-to theorist by Polity Press and *Theory, Culture and Society*. In the United States his effect was negligible. In Southern Europe and Latin America there was an enthusiastic following for his ideas. In India and China his work is well known. In Australia, in contrast to the United Kingdom, his reception has been selective and partial, via *Thesis Eleven* in company with the Budapest School, and via the work of individuals such as Anthony Elliott, Adrian Franklin and me. In Australia, it seems fair to say, Bauman was not treated as a guru, and in consequence there was no need to kill the father. There was crossover between *Thesis Eleven* and the Bauman Institute, and collaboration with individuals such as Keith Tester, all of whom had differing affiliations. Yet Bauman could in this context also be treated as he treated others, as one thinker among many others in the rich storehouse of intellectual culture that might be available to us. This remains a perennial challenge to those who work in the human sciences: how to innovate and adapt to the new, while maintaining a sense of continuity with the traditions that we adopt and adapt or make our own. Like our subject matter, we are now trapped between tradition, modernity and the postmodern.

Who was Bauman writing for? For us; for posterity; for himself, as a need. The path of Bauman's writing itself suggests that he could not think except through the act of writing. It seems clear that he wrote to keep away despair, and to stave off death. But he also wrote to think, and to keep thinking. This is why I should have understood better the old joke about the last book. It was not just a tease. So long as I breathe, I hope; so long as I write, I might hope to understand. This is also, then, my last book.

It was, and is, time to say goodbye.

I wrote several obituaries for Zygmunt Bauman on request. As with my other papers on Bauman, each gave me the chance to learn something new by writing it out. This, the obituary that follows here, is the best of these pieces, the most satisfying, though it also confirmed my sense that there was more to be said before I was done. Perhaps it might serve as a summary here, of these pages and their ruminations. After knowing him for 30 years I was still learning, thinking here in terms of symptomatology and a hub and spoke structure to make sense of his work. I needed to write it out, as I have sought to do in this book. So this is how it came:

Zygmunt Bauman died January 10, 2017, aged 91. He was one of the most influential sociologists of our times. Go Google, or check a Polity catalogue.

The 'Bauman phenomenon': signing out

What did he come to say? What is his legacy?

There are some interesting ghosts hereabouts. Rumours about plagiarism, or even more hilariously, self-plagiarism (otherwise known as repeating yourself, not a bad idea if you have something interesting to say). Allusions to the dirty hands of a communist past, for which the only evidence seems to be that there is no evidence. One, more frequently claimed sighting is of the spectre of pessimism. Heaven forfend, in these times of endless progress, that a Polish sociologist might arrive in the happy West with the bad news. In what is likely his last interview, with Al-Jazeera, Bauman repeats his self-description, that of the person who combines long term optimism with short term pessimism. The terms of reference, even when we resort to Gramsci, pessimism of the intellect/optimism of the will, are less than helpful. Pessimism is an attitude, or a temperament; the practice of sociology depends rather on conversation, debate, theory, evidence and argument, appraisal and critique. In fact, Bauman was an anthropological optimist: he believed that human beings could always do better. But he also followed the image of hermeneutics, where we seek to act as messengers; and nobody welcomes the visitor, just as fewer of us these days are happy to entertain the idea of welcoming the stranger.

But why the bogey? Why the image of the grumpy old man? The prophet of doom? He was indeed old, but, we might instead say, wise, and worldly wise. Everyone you can find who met him or worked with Bauman will tell you other stories, of generosity and curiosity, engagement and inquiry. He was a remarkable, open personality, even if he was increasingly to become attached to the mantra of liquid modernity.

His was an untidy prominence. He was the unwilling celebrity, the outsider/insider. He was a moving target, or, he liked to ask questions about moving targets – love, loyalty, modernity, identity, refugees, strangers, inequality, globalization, glocalization, media, consumption, literature, individualization, TV, mobile phones, body enhancement, death, social media, whatever. Perhaps this is one reason why his audiences admired him as much as some of his institutionalized colleagues abhorred him. He had the capacity to connect; he was interested in big picture issues, and in small stories about them; he was not a professional sociologist, in the Anglo sense, but came to be a popular intellectual who had no particular interests in defending disciplinary boundaries.

In a world where the practice of sociology becomes more and more narrow and specialized, each of us digging our own furrow and needing to please our employers and institutional masters, Bauman was a maverick.

Even those who admired him had troubles making sense of this. Some just despised him, like the senior British sociologist who apparently thought he just made all his work up. Bad for business; bad for the profession. Others, for example, Neil Gross, writing in *The New York Times* 9 February 2017, described Bauman as weak on method and in effect all over the place. That sounds to me like a good place for sociologists to be, all over the place. And there is, of course, a method in any sociological madness. In fact (in *fact* …) as I shall suggest here, there is a clear pattern in Bauman's trajectory. This may at first sight be difficult to discern across the crazy quilt of 58 or so books in English, but it is there.

So to begin at this beginning, in English … no, let us begin earlier, with just a glance at his Polish pre-life. There is always a world before us. For the data of Bauman's sociology was also the data of experience, and he experienced all three major world forces of the twentieth century, Nazism, communism and capitalism, which also means he experienced empire and race at least three times over. A Jewish communist, twice the victim of institutional anti-semitism, his life takes him from the Polish army to the University of Warsaw, where he discovers sociology. This is Continental sociology, or what he would later call critical sociology, the kind that presumes that most interesting questions open up also onto matters of philosophy. Ought matters as well as is, and working for the state or for statistics always needs some distance, a cautionary note. But bear in mind, he never gives up on the promise of sociology, defending the project till his last days.

After some contact with American and British scholars, and after the development phase of a critical or humanist Marxism in Poland, he and other leading Polish professors like Kołakowski are sacked for corrupting the youth. They have no alternative but exile. Bauman and his family take a one way exit visa via Tel Aviv and Canberra, and finally settle in Leeds. This is where the English language story begins, with a book on the British labour movement in 1972. The deluge of writing begins, but it is more measured until his retirement in 1990.

What follows the book on the British labour movement is a series of not altogether obvious sequels: books on culture and socialism, two early leitmotifs; then the idea of critical sociology, hermeneutics, class; then, from 1987, what was later identified as a postmodern turn. Bauman is indeed one of the first sociologists to take the postmodern seriously, though as he says, as a problem to be addressed rather than as a privileged way of explaining the present. The postmodern needs to be taken seriously because it seems to represent significant societal changes, or at least the sense that intellectuals imagine that these kinds of changes are upon us. Then, in 1989, there is what in retrospect looks like a rupture: he published *Modernity and the Holocaust*. The initial response to the book was hostile, though it has by now become a standard reference. In other words, the critique of modernity has since become normalized, because critics like Bauman were prepared to look into its dark side. This book seeks to throw light not only on the Holocaust but on its necessary modern preconditions; and it is his living *femmage* to the work of his first wife, Janina Bauman, in her astonishing memoir *Winter in the Morning* (1985). It also opens the door to his further interest in ethics, for as he puts it, the most chilling thought about the Holocaust is not that this could have happened to me, but that I could have done this.

So more books were to follow, on *Modernity and Ambivalence* (1991), one of his most intellectually powerful works; books on mortality, ethics, life in fragments, freedom, more on the postmodern and globalization, work and poverty and the new poor, tourists and vagabonds, the end of politics, and so on.

But there is a broader seachange at work here, too. Bauman has by now retired, and has changed his writerly strategy. He decides no longer to write for us, for his global colleagues, who might in principle be expected to follow the work of a leading thinker serially, instalment by instalment. He begins rather to write for an imaginary punter who reads the odd book, maybe on the tube or bus, or who stumbles over a book on a vital topic while browsing a shop or the net or somebody else's shelves. One of the most striking books here is *Liquid Love*, 2003, though the real turning point is the prequel, *Liquid Modernity*, 2000.

What is the liquid modern? By this point, the new millennium, the energy of the argument about the postmodern was fading. Probably there was too much enthusiasm for the putative postmodern, as retrospectively there was for the glossy global, and too much lazy dependence on the use of neoliberalism as a spray-on, the latter yet to come. The argument in *Liquid Modernity* is, like that in his other books, multiple. There are claims that there has been a serious cultural shift in the way we see each other, our significant others, our institutions and loyalties. This is a matter of contrasting the postwar, solid modern Western world of Fordism with the way we live now, where the principle of disposability rules, for employees and lovers, for each other as humans as much as for takeout coffee cups and plastic sushi packs. Humans do not go directly into landfill, but their lives can just as directly be wasted. And everywhere others are sorting our Western trash. Redundancy, waste, excess surround us.

Liquid Modernity was a kind of transitional work for Bauman, in content if less so in format. For he had decided also from around this point to focus on an imaginary popular rather than academic audience, and the flow of little books, like Penguins or Suhrkamps or 10/18's followed. And the range spread, too, to take in matters as diverse as surveillance, management, education and literature. And his style became even more conversational, as in *44 Letters from the Liquid Modern World* or *This Is Not a Diary*, which was, of course, complete with jokes about Magritte and pipes, exactly that: a diary on these great and terrible times.

Liquid Modernity mapped all this out, or at least opened this optic. For there Bauman was entirely methodical. After some excurses on the idea of liquidity and on metaphor, there followed chapters on emancipation, individuality, time/space, work, and community, with a postface on the challenges of writing and of writing sociology. He always persisted in seeing this vocation as sociological.

And then the tide of little books followed; on waste and wasted lives, on surplus populations, on the art of life, on liquid times, on fear and liquid fear, on so many things that perhaps Bauman did appear to be all over the place. The point, however, is that there is a kind of symptomatology going on here. Each little book is a spoke to the hub, a sign of the times. Each allows the interrogation of a different aspect of liquid modern life, for which the general diagnosis is that sketched out in *Liquid Modernity*. For each of these little books discuss the big issue through one symptom, community, identity, globalization, love, and so on. The big issue persists. The illusory self certainties of the postwar west are evaporating before our eyes, after the postwar boom and the machine of modernization has offered everything to everybody, and guess what? failed to deliver. In result, we turn, as *Retrotopia* has it, to dreams and nostalgia for allegedly simpler worlds, before it all went wrong. Ergo Trump, Brexit and the whole new deal. Only we can actually never go back, so instead we board up the gates, talk about walls, pull up the ladders. Because we, or some of us, feel entitled and now spurned, or because we cannot even begin to imagine sharing our western good fortune. We live in fear, for Bauman: liquid fear.

Is Bauman then a theorist of decline, even if he was not a grumpy old man? The presenting question is not about him but is rather a question for us. Some of Bauman's messages in bottles were, indeed, delivered in the form of cautionary tales. He spoke of the postmodern as the prospect of a modernity without illusions; and he often spoke of the need to defamil-iarise the familiar. Like most of us, he hoped for a more fair and just world, but sensed that the fear that weighs so heavily on us, the fear of losing the privilege that we have or have had, immobilizes us politically, makes it easier to hide at home, lock those doors, pull up those ladders. There are no longer serious alternatives in the existing political system, but we are locked into it as firmly as into any other iron cage. These are collective problems, which need shared discussion before we are even to think of any possible move to resolution. But we can always do better.

***

And me? And us, he and I? I got to know Zygmunt Bauman around 1988. I had reviewed this amazing book, *Legislators and Interpreters*, for the *Australian and New Zealand Journal of Sociology*. I posted him a photo-copy, to his home in Lawnswood Gardens, suspecting that this little flag would not otherwise come his way. We had already published his views in our journal *Thesis Eleven*, and continued to do so over the next decades. I began to visit the Baumans annually in Leeds on my way home from the ASA proceedings, and did so annually for more than twenty years. At this point, into the nineties there was very little published engagement with his work; his was not yet a household name. He had not yet retired or begun to do those little books, strong on argument, lean on footnotes, or at least as likely to quote the *Guardian* as Marx or Weber. I published one of the first works on Bauman, *Dialectic of Modernity*, in 2000, and my *Bauman Reader* in the same year. This meant that I came in just before the so called Liquid Modern turn. I then published the four volume collection of crit-ical assessments, *Zygmunt Bauman – Masters of Critical Thought*, in 2002; and I have published twenty or so essays on his work since, up until the present, for I have not yet been able to exhaust the interest of his work.

There are at least two aspects to this ongoing curiosity, for me: first, the moving target approach, always a new problem or issue to chase, right down to his last, *Retrotopia*, into this year. Second, his was always a conversation with many interlocutors, so that most of the thinkers who I found interesting over the last thirty years, from Sennett and Simmel to Mary Douglas and Levi-Strauss, Derrida, Foucault and Sebald, Heller and Arendt, Habermas and Bourdieu, Rorty and Musil, Cioran and Levinas, etc etc, all showed up here at some point. This was, as he liked to say, a house with many rooms, though he actually also lived an exemplary life, in a modest, detached home, where abundance came only in books, wine, and hospitality. What this plurality of reference points signifies is not namedropping but a democratic recognition that there are always others who have stories to tell about the issues presenting, that we always enter existing and plural fields of discourse, and that the cult of innovation *ex nihilo* is the worst kind of academic conceit. There is always a conversation that precedes us. Our voices are small; our interlocutors abundant.

Increasingly these interlocutors also became literary, as in Calvino and Perec, Orwell and Huxley, Saramago, Borges, Kafka, Kundera, and also East European, as in Mickiewicz. The point here is that Bauman had no obsession with personal originality; his was a world of many voices, where writers of all kinds offered an immense storehouse of possibilities for us all to think with. Thus one of his last books was entitled *In Praise of Literature*. Would this please Mr Gradgrind, the Dickens character who bluntly demands 'Facts, sir, nothing but Facts!'? Let us remember, as we remember Zygmunt Bauman, that Gradgrind was also a literary figure, and that the image credited to Marx, all that is solid, seems actually to come from Shakespeare. The imagery of choice may have been liquid, but Bauman's legacy is firmer, more critically engaged, and finally, more hopeful than that. It indicates, still, the need of a place to stand, to orient ourselves in this great and terrible world. The legacy of Bauman is to help us seek out these bearings. Map, compass, pencil ... Bauman (pipe and matches), a book or two. Like all great intellectuals, he led not by exhortation but by example.[1]

---

1 P. Beilharz, 'The Legacy of Zygmunt Bauman', *Journal of Sociology*, 54:3 (2018).

Ending

How, then, shall I finally end a book about ending?

Sweet Peter, Everything you said about the joys of being together – works both ways. Janina and I go on missing you with an intensity growing by the day.

23 September 1997

We are waiting to see you, up or down the staircase …

19 February 1998

Sweet Peter, we are already looking through the window – are you approaching? August is so far ahead, as yet … yours ever Z.

11 April 1998

Janina and I wait at the window.

21 April 1998

You must have constant hiccup, we think of you so often … since Peter joined that couple, there have been three after all!

18 February 2000

So now loving Peter is a favourite pastime for almost all the extended family!

27 February 2001

Let's love each other as thus far – day in, day out – till the very last.

18 March 2005

You made the old couple happy. We are both grateful beyond bounds …

25 August 2006

Als immer … yr. Z.

9 November 2006

Your desolate Z.

22 June 2009

***

Dear Peter, Janina died tonight.

29 December 2009

Hello, old friend. I hope you will allow me the impertinence of this message, which is entirely selfish in motivation. I want you to know that I love you, Zygmunt, and that I need you to be around. I wish you all the strength in the world in the next days, and I hope that it will not be too long before we embrace, sit and talk again. With love from Peter.

1 January 2010

Dear Zygmunt, please accept this as my last letter to you. It is, alas, public rather than private or truly between us, and it is too late. It is my message to you, in a bottle sent from a distant land, when you have already left us … This is, then, my very last, until there is another time to think with you, and after you.

Did you ever notice that we, each of us, alone and together, used the language of love when we wrote? I suppose that I did notice, but without understanding what it meant. So that I am still thinking, about love, death and friendship. And I am grateful – graceful? – grateful. Thank you for everything. Goodbye. See you soon.

Peter

28 May 2018/15 May 2019

Acknowledgements

This project took more time and inner turmoil than I might have imagined. It gave me further reason to contemplate the nature of friendship as the necessary precondition of thinking and writing, or doing sociology at all. I took advice from many people across this time. The draft was read by Tim Dolin, Harry Blatterer, Trevor Hogan, Evelyn Juers, Glyn Davis, Chris Rojek, Keith Tester, John Hall, Izabela Wagner, Jeffrey Alexander; by members of the Bauman family: Aleksandra Kania, Anna Sfard and Lydia Bauman. The years travelled here were held up by Dor, Nikolai and Rhea, by Sian and Savannah. My friends in and around *Thesis Eleven* made all this possible, across the last four decades, as did the wider circles of those working on and with and sharing around Zygmunt Bauman. Three of my Melbourne friends might also see their influence here: Ghassan Hage, Nikos Papastergiadis and – alas, too late – Patrick Wolfe.

I thank Curtin University and my immediate colleagues in media, culture and creative arts for their support across these years of work, and La Trobe University for many years of support and stimulation – indeed, for that original affirmation and kick-start from 1988 and for the capacity to work with Bauman over the decades that followed. I thank my students and colleagues in literature and journalism at Sichuan University and my immediate colleague Fu Qilin, who has given me many things, including a last chance to team-teach and learn anew. I thank the National Library of Australia for accepting, storing and giving me access to my personal papers in Canberra.

Acknowledgements

Last, and first, Sian Supski and Caroline Wintersgill made this work possible. Tom Dark and Alun Richards saw it through Manchester University Press. Rebecca Willford and Mike Richardson edited and finalized the text. Alonso Casanueva Baptista created the Index.

Finally, amidst so much that looks back, there is also the warmth and light offered by the new arrival: Theodore Beilharz, aka Ted, 2018–.

The following texts are reproduced and acknowledged with thanks to Sage Publishers and Aalborg University Press.

Bauman, Z., 'Review of "Imagining the Antipodes"', *Thesis Eleven*, 53 (1998), 136.

Beilharz, P., 'Review of "Bauman, *Legislators and Interpreters*"', *Australian and New Zealand Journal of Sociology*, 24:5 (1988).

Beilharz, P., 'Bauman's Coat', in M. H. Jacobsen, S. Marshman and K. Tester (eds), *Bauman beyond Postmodernity: Critical Appraisals, Conversations and Annotated Bibliography 1989–2005* (Aalborg: Aalborg University Press, 2007), 375–8.

Beilharz, P., 'The Legacy of Zygmunt Bauman', *Journal of Sociology*, 54:3 (2008), 294–9.

Peter Beilharz, Chengdu, 20 September 2019

Bibliography

Alexander, J., 'Marxism and the Spirit of Socialism (1982)', *Thesis Eleven*, 100 (2010).

Alexander, J. (ed.), *Remembering the Holocaust* (New York: Oxford University Press, 2009).

Alexander, J., *Theoretical Logic in Sociology*, 4 vols (Berkeley, CA: University of California Press, 1982–3).

Alexander, J., and P. Smith (eds), *Cambridge Companion to Durkheim* (New York: Cambridge, 2005).

Anderson, P., *Considerations on Western Marxism* (London: New Left Books, 1976).

Baecker, D., 'The Hitler Swarm', *Thesis Eleven*, 117 (2013).

Bauman, J., *Beyond These Walls: Escaping the Warsaw Ghetto – a Young Girl's Story* (London: Virago, 2006).

Bauman, J., 'Demons of Other People's Fears', *Thesis Eleven*, 54 (1998).

Bauman, J., *A Dream of Belonging* (London: Virago, 1988).

Bauman, J., *Winter in the Morning* (London: Virago, 1986).

Bauman, Z., *44 Letters from the Liquid Modern World* (Cambridge: Polity Press, 2010).

Bauman, Z., *Alone Again: Ethics after Certainty* (London: Demos, 1996).

Bauman, Z., *The Art of Life* (Cambridge: Polity Press, 2008).

Bauman, Z., *The Bauman Reader*, ed. P. Beilharz (Oxford: Blackwell, 2000).

Bauman, Z., *Between Class and Elite: The Evolution of the British Labour Movement: A Sociological Study* (Manchester: Manchester University Press, 1972).

Bauman, Z., *A Chronicle of Crisis: 2011–2016* (London: Social Europe Editions, 2017).

Bauman, Z., *City of Fears, City of Hopes* (London: Goldsmith's College, 2003).

Bauman, Z., *Collateral Damage: Social Inequalities in a Global Age* (Cambridge: Polity Press, 2011)

Bibliography

Bauman, Z., *Community: Seeking Safety in an Insecure World* (Cambridge: Polity Press, 2001).

Bauman, Z., *Consuming Life* (Cambridge: Polity Press, 2007).

Bauman, Z., *Culture as Praxis* (London: Routledge & Kegan Paul, 1973).

Bauman, Z., *Culture in a Liquid Modern World* (Cambridge: Polity Press, 2011).

Bauman, Z., 'Dictatorship over Needs', *Telos* 60 (1984).

Bauman, Z., *Does Ethics Have a Chance in a World of Consumers?* (Cambridge, MA: Harvard University Press, 2008).

Bauman, Z., *Does the Richness of the Few Benefit Us All?* (Cambridge: Polity Press, 2013).

Bauman, Z., *Europe: An Unfinished Adventure* (Cambridge: Polity Press, 2004).

Bauman, Z., *Freedom* (Philadelphia: Open University Press, 1988).

Bauman, Z., *Globalization: The Human Consequences* (New York: Columbia University Press, 1998).

Bauman, Z., *Hermeneutics and Social Science: Approaches to Understanding* (London: Hutchinson, 1978).

Bauman, Z., 'Imagining the Antipodes', *Thesis Eleven*, 53 (1998).

Bauman, Z., *In Search of Politics* (Cambridge: Polity Press, 1999).

Bauman, Z., *The Individualized Society* (Cambridge: Polity Press, 2001).

Bauman, Z., *Intimations of Postmodernity* (London: Routledge, 1992).

Bauman, Z., *Legislators and interpreters: On Modernity, Post-Modernity and Intellectuals* (Ithaca, NY: Cornell University Press, 1987).

Bauman, Z., *Life in Fragments: Essays in Postmodern Morality* (Malden, MA: Blackwell, 1995).

Bauman, Z., *Liquid Fear* (Cambridge: Polity Press, 2006).

Bauman, Z., *Liquid Life* (Cambridge: Polity Press, 2005).

Bauman, Z., *Liquid Love: On the Frailty of Human Bonds* (Cambridge: Polity Press, 2003).

Bauman, Z., *Liquid Modernity* (Cambridge: Polity Press, 2000).

Bauman, Z., *Liquid Times: Living in an Age of Uncertainty* (Cambridge: Polity Press, 2006).

Bauman, Z., *Memories of Class: The Pre-History and After-Life of Class* (London: Routledge & Kegan Paul, 1982).

Bauman, Z., *Modernity and Ambivalence* (Ithaca, NY: Cornell University Press, 1991).

Bauman, Z., *Modernity and the Holocaust* (Ithaca, NY: Cornell University Press, 1989).

Bauman, Z., *Mortality, Immortality and Other Life Strategies* (Cambridge: Polity Press, 1992).

Bibliography

Bauman, Z., *Paradoxes of Assimilation* (New Brunswick, NJ: Transaction, 1990).

Bauman, Z., *Pictures in Words, Words in Pictures* (Leeds: Bauman Institute, 2010).

Bauman, Z., *Postmodern Ethics* (Malden, MA: Blackwell, 1993).

Bauman, Z., *Postmodernity and Its Discontents* (New York: Blackwell, 1997).

Bauman, Z., *Retrotopia* (Cambridge: Polity Press, 2017).

Bauman, Z., *Sketches in a Theory of Culture* (Cambridge: Polity Press, 2018).

Bauman, Z., *Socialism: The Active Utopia* (New York: Holmes & Meier, 1976).

Bauman, Z., *Society under Siege* (Cambridge: Polity Press, 2002).

Bauman, Z., 'Stalin and the Peasant Revolution: A Case Study in the Dialectics of Master and Slave', Occasional Paper 19 (Leeds: University of Leeds, Department of Sociology, 1985).

Bauman, Z., *Strangers at Our Door* (Cambridge: Polity Press, 2016).

Bauman, Z., 'The Sweet Scent of Decomposition', in C. Rojek and B. Turner (eds), *Forget Baudrillard?* (London: Routledge, 2002).

Bauman, Z., *This Is Not a Diary* (Cambridge: Polity Press, 2012).

Bauman, Z., *Towards a Critical Sociology: An Essay on Commonsense and Emancipation* (London: Routledge & Kegan Paul, 1976).

Bauman, Z., *Thinking Sociologically. An Introduction for Everyone* (Malden, MA: Blackwell, 1990).

Bauman, Z., *Wasted Lives: Modernity and Its Outcasts* (Cambridge: Polity Press, 2004).

Bauman, Z., *Work, Consumerism and the New Poor* (Maidenhead: Open University Press, 1998).

Bauman, Z., I. Bauman, J. Kociatkiewicz and M. Kostera, *Management in a Liquid Modern World* (Cambridge: Polity Press, 2015).

Bauman, Z., and C. Bordoni, *State of Crisis* (Cambridge: Polity Press, 2014).

Bauman, Z., and L. Donskis, *Liquid Evil* (Cambridge: Polity Press, 2016).

Bauman, Z., and L. Donskis, *Moral Blindness: The Loss of Sensitivity in Liquid Modernity* (Cambridge: Polity Press, 2013).

Bauman, Z., M. Jacobsen and K. Tester, *What Use Is Sociology? Conversations with Michael Hviid Jacobsen and Keith Tester* (Cambridge: Polity Press, 2014).

Bauman, Z., and T. Leoncini, *Born Liquid* (Cambridge: Polity Press, 2017).

Bauman, Z., and D. Lyon, *Liquid Surveillance: A Conversation* (Cambridge: Polity Press, 2012).

Bauman, Z., and E. Mauro, *Babel* (Cambridge: Polity Press, 2016).

Bauman, Z., and T. May, *Thinking Sociologically*, 2nd edn (Oxford: Blackwell, 2001).

Bauman, Z., and S. Obirek, *Of God and Man* (Cambridge: Polity Press, 2015).

Bauman, Z., and S. Obirek, *On the World and Ourselves* (Cambridge: Polity Press, 2015).

Bauman, Z., and R. Raud, *Practices of Selfhood* (Cambridge: Polity Press, 2015).

Bauman, Z., and C. Rovirosa-Madrazo, *Living on Borrowed Time: Conversations with Citlali Rovirosa-Madrazo* (Cambridge: Polity Press, 2009).

Bauman, Z., and K. Tester, *Conversations with Zygmunt Bauman* (Cambridge: Polity Press, 2001).

Bauman, Z., and B. Vecchi, *Identity: Conversations with Benedetto Vecchi* (Cambridge: Polity Press, 2004).

Bauman Lyons Architects, *How to Be a Happy Architect* (London: Black Dog, 2008).

Beilharz, P. (ed.), *Alastair Davidson: Gramsci in Australia* (Leiden: Brill, 2020).

Beilharz, P., 'All that Is Solid … Maelstrom and Modernity in Zygmunt Bauman', *Revue Internationale de Philosophie*, 3:70 (2016).

Beilharz, P., 'Another Bauman: The Anthropological Imagination', in M. Davis and K. Tester (eds), *Bauman's Challenge* (London: Palgrave, 2010).

Beilharz, P., 'Australia', in *Yearbook on International Communist Affairs* (Stanford, CA: Hoover, 1976).

Beilharz, P., 'The Australian Left: Beyond Labourism', *Socialist Register*, 1985/86 (1986).

Beilharz, P., 'Bauman', in G. Ritzer (ed.), *Encyclopedia of Social Theory*, vol. 1 (Thousand Oaks, CA: Sage, 2005).

Beilharz, P., 'Bauman and Heller: Two Views of Modernity and Culture', *Comparative Literature: East and West*, 1:1 (2017).

Beilharz, P. (ed.), *The Bauman Reader* (Oxford: Blackwell, 2001).

Beilharz, P., 'Bauman's Coat', in M. Jacobsen, S. Marshman and K. Tester (eds), *Bauman beyond Postmodernity: Critical Appraisals, Conversations and Annotated Bibliography 1989–2005* (Aalborg: Aalborg University Press, 2007).

Beilharz, P., 'Bernard, Wordsmith', in J. Anderson (ed.), *The Legacies of Bernard Smith* (Sydney: Power Institute, 2017).

Beilharz, P. (ed.), *Circling Marx: Essays 1980–2020* (Leiden: Brill, 2020).

Beilharz, P., 'Critical Theory and the New University', in M. Thornton (ed.), *Through a Glass Darkly: The Social Sciences look at the Neoliberal University* (Canberra: ANU Press, 2014).

Beilharz, P., 'Counting Memories? Revisiting Bauman, Reading Wright', *Political Theory Newsletter*, 9 (1997) [reprinted in Beilharz (ed.), *Zygmunt Bauman*, 2002, vol. 4].

Beilharz, P., 'The Decline of the West?', *Thesis Eleven*, 149 (2018).

Beilharz, P., 'George Seddon and Karl Marx: Nature and Second Nature', *Thesis Eleven*, 74 (2003).

Bibliography

Beilharz, P., 'How Did Pierre Chaulieu Become Cornelius Castoriadis?', *Thesis Eleven* (2020).

Beilharz, P., *Imagining the Antipodes: Culture, Theory and the Visual in the Work of Bernard Smith* (Melbourne: Cambridge University Press, 1997).

Beilharz, P., *Labour's Utopias: Bolshevism, Fabianism, Social Democracy* (London: Routledge, 1992).

Beilharz, P., 'Labour's Utopias Revisited', *Thesis Eleven*, 110 (2013).

Beilharz, P., 'The Legacy of Zygmunt Bauman', *Journal of Sociology*, 54:3 (2018).

Beilharz, P., 'Liquid Sociology', in M Davis (ed.), *Liquid Sociology: Metaphor in Zygmunt Bauman's Analysis of Modernity* (London: Ashgate, 2013).

Beilharz, P., 'Lobby and Me', *Thesis Eleven*, 91 (2007).

Beilharz, P., 'To Love and Be Loved: Janina Bauman's Ordinary Life' [with S. Supski], *Thesis Eleven*, 107 (2011).

Beilharz, P., 'Lunch with Bauman', *Thesis Eleven*, 149 (2018).

Beilharz, P., 'McFascism? Reading Ritzer, Bauman and the Holocaust', in B. Smart (ed.), *Resisting McDonaldization* (London: Sage, 1999).

Beilharz, P., 'Modernity and Communism: Zygmunt Bauman and the Other Totalitarianism', *Thesis Eleven*, 57 (2002).

Beilharz, P., *Postmodern Socialism: Romanticism, City and State* (Melbourne: Melbourne University Press, 1994).

Beilharz, P. (ed.), *Postwar American Critical Thought*, 4 vols (London: Sage, 2006).

Beilharz, P., 'The Power of Culture, and Response to Critics', *Prace Kulturoznawcze*, 20 (2017).

Beilharz, P., 'On the Rationality of Evil: An Interview with Zygmunt Bauman', *Thesis Eleven*, 70 (1999) [reprinted in Beilharz (ed.), *Zygmunt Bauman*, 2002, vol. 2].

Beilharz, P., 'Reading Zygmunt Bauman: Looking for Clues', *Thesis Eleven*, 55 (1998) [reprinted in Beilharz (ed.), *Zygmunt Bauman*, 2002, vol. 1].

Beilharz, P., 'Recovering Marx', in B. Ali and M. Musto (eds), *Karl Marx's Life, Ideas and Influences* (London: Palgrave, 2020).

Beilharz, P., 'Remembering Castoriadis', *Thesis Eleven* (2020).

Beilharz, P., 'Review of Bauman, *Legislators and Interpreters*', *Australian and New Zealand Journal of Sociology* 24:3 (1988).

Beilharz, P., 'Robert Hughes and the Provincialism Problem,' in P. Beilharz and R. Manne (eds), *Reflected Light: Latrobe Essays* (Melbourne: Black Ink, 2004).

Beilharz, P., 'Rock Lobster: Lobby Loyde and the History of Rock Music in Australia', *Thesis Eleven*, 109 (2012).

Beilharz, P. (ed.) *Social Theory: A Guide to Central Thinkers* (Sydney: Allen & Unwin, 1992).

Bibliography

Beilharz, P., *Socialism and Modernity* (Minneapolis: Minnesota University Press, 2009).

Beilharz, P., 'Therapy with Bauman', *Anthropological Psychology*, 21 (2009).

Beilharz, P., *Thinking the Antipodes: Australian Essays* (Clayton: Monash University Press, 2014).

Beilharz, P., *Transforming Labor: Labour Tradition and the Labor Decade* (Sydney: Cambridge University Press, 1994).

Beilharz, P., *Trotsky, Trotskyism and the Transition to Socialism* (London: Croom Helm, 1987).

Beilharz, P., 'The Worlds We Make: Fabric, Camp and Polis in Zygmunt Bauman's Critical Theory', in M. Jacobsen and P. Poder (eds), *Om Bauman: Kritiske Essays* [*On Bauman: Critical Essays*] (Copenhagen: Hans Reitzels Forlag, 2006).

Beilharz, P., 'Zygmunt Bauman', in G. Ritzer (ed.), *Major Social Theorists*, vol. 2 (Blackwell: London, 2011).

Beilharz, P., 'Zygmunt Bauman (1925–)', in J. Simons (ed.) *From Agamben to Žižek: Contemporary Critical Theorists* (Edinburgh: Edinburgh University Press, 2010).

Beilharz, P., 'Zygmunt Bauman: To Build Anew', *Thesis Eleven*, 86 (2006).

Beilharz, P., 'Zygmunt Bauman, Culture and Sociology', in J. Edwards (ed.), *Cultural Theory* (London: Sage, 2007).

Beilharz, P., *Zygmunt Bauman: Dialectic of Modernity* (London: Sage, 2000).

Beilharz, P. (ed.), *Zygmunt Bauman*, 4 vols (London: Sage, 2002).

Beilharz, P., M. Considine and R. Watts, *Arguing about the Welfare State: The Australian Experience* (Sydney: Allen & Unwin, 1992).

Beilharz, P., and T. Hogan, 'The State of Social Sciences in Australia', in J. Germov and T. McGee (eds), *Histories of Australian Sociology* (Melbourne: Melbourne University Press, 2005).

Beilharz, P., and T. Hogan (eds), *Sociology: Place, Time and Division* (Melbourne: Oxford University Press, 2006).

Beilharz, P., T. Hogan and S. Shaver, *The Martin Presence: Jean Martin and the Making of the Social Sciences in Australia* (Sydney: New South, 2015).

Beilharz, P., and R. Manne (eds), *Reflected Light: Latrobe Essays* (Melbourne: Black Ink, 2004).

Beilharz, P., and Fu Qilin, 'The Conference on East European Marxist Aesthetics', *Thesis Eleven*, 142 (2017).

Beilharz, P., and J. Qin, 'Bauman in China', *Thesis Eleven* (2020).

Beilharz, P., G. Robinson and J. Rundell (eds), *Between Totalitarianism and Postmodernity* (Cambridge, MA: MIT Press, 1992).

Bibliography

Beilharz, P., and S. Supski, 'Finding Ivan Vladislavić', *Thesis Eleven*, 136 (2016).

Beilharz, P., and S. Supski, 'So Sharp You Could Bleed – Sharpies and Artistic Representation: A Moment in the Seventies History of Melbourne', in A. Michelsen and F. Tygstrup (eds), *Socioaesthetics* (Leiden: Brill, 2015).

Beilharz, P., and S. Supski, 'Tricks with Mirrors: Sharpies and Their Representations', in S. Baker, B. Robards and B. Buttigieg (eds), *Youth Cultures and Subcultures: Australian Perspectives* (London: Ashgate, 2015).

Beilharz, P., S. Supski and G. Macainsh, 'From Sharpies to Skyhooks', *Thesis Eleven*, 144 (2018).

Benhabib, S., *The Reluctant Modernism of Hannah Arendt* (New York: Rowman & Littlefield, 1996).

Berman, M., *All that Is Solid Melts into Air* (London: Penguin, 1982).

Boehme, G., *Invasive Technification: Critical Essays in the Philosophy of Technology* (London: Bloomsbury, 2012).

Bordoni, C., *Interregnum: Beyond Liquid Modernity* (New York: Columbia University Press, 2016).

Britain, I., *Once an Australian* (Melbourne: Oxford University Press, 1997).

Calhoun, C., *Critical Social Theory* (New York: Blackwell, 1995).

Canclini, N. G., *Hybrid Cultures: Strategies for Entering and Leaving Modernity* (Minneapolis: Minnesota, 1995).

Cassirer, E., *Rousseau, Kant, Goethe* (Princeton, NJ: Princeton University Press, 1970).

Castoriadis, C., *The Imaginary Institution of Society: Creativity and Autonomy in the Social-Historical World* (Cambridge: Polity Press, 1975).

Curtis, D. (ed.), *The Castoriadis Reader* (Oxford: Blackwell, 1997).

Davis, M., *City of Quartz* (London: Verso, 1990).

Davis, M. E., *Freedom and Consumerism: A Critique of Zygmunt Bauman's Sociology* (Aldershot: Ashgate, 2008).

Davis, M. E. (ed.), *Liquid Sociology: Metaphor in Zygmunt Bauman's Analysis of Modernity* (London: Ashgate, 2013).

Didion, J., *The Year of Magical Thinking* (New York: Harcourt, 2005).

Dorahy, J., *The Budapest School: Beyond Marxism* (Leiden: Brill, 2019).

Eco, U., *Chronicles of a Liquid Society* (New York: Random House, 2017).

Frisby, D., *Sociological Impressionism: A Reassessment of Georg Simmel's Social Theory* (London: Heinemann, 1981).

Hall, J., 'Liquid Bauman', *Socio*, 8 (2017).

Hall, S., and B. Schwartz, *Familiar Stranger: A Life between Two Islands* (London: Allen Lane, 2017).

Heller, A., *A Theory of History* (London: Routledge, 1982).

Bibliography

Hogan, T., 'Modernity as Revolution: Thomas Carlyle' (doctoral dissertation, La Trobe University, 1995).

Illouz, E., *Why Love Hurts* (Cambridge: Polity Press, 2012).

Jacobsen, M., S. Marshman and K. Tester (eds), *Bauman beyond Postmodernity: Critical Appraisals, Conversations and Annotated Bibliography 1989–2005* (Aalborg: Aalborg University Press, 2007).

Kania, A., 'The Fluidity of Love and Hate. Zygmunt Bauman on Death, Love and Hatred', *Revue Internationale de Philosophie*, 3:70 (2016).

Kilminster, R., and I. Varcoe, *Culture, Modernity and Revolution: Essays in Honour of Zygmunt Bauman* (London: Routledge, 1996).

Kołakowski, L., *Main Currents of Marxism*, 3 vols (Oxford: Oxford University Press, 1978).

Lasch, C., *The Culture of Narcissism: American Life in an Age of Diminishing Expectations* (New York: Norton, 1979).

Lepenies, W., *Between Science and Literature: The Rise of Sociology* (New York: Cambridge, 1988).

Lowenthal, D., *The Past Is a Foreign Country* (Cambridge: Cambridge University Press, 1985).

Manuel, F., and F. Manuel, *Utopian Thought in the Western World* (Oxford: Blackwell, 1979).

Marcuse, H., *One-Dimensional Man* (London: Abacus, 1964).

Nickel, P., *North American Critical Theory after Postmodernism* (London: Macmillan, 2012).

Offe, C., *Reflections on America: Tocqueville, Weber and Adorno in the United States* (Cambridge: Polity Press, 2005).

Rattansi, A., *Bauman and Contemporary Sociology: A Critical Analysis* (Manchester: Manchester University Press, 2017).

Rosa, H., *Social Acceleration: A New Theory of Modernity* (New York: Columbia University Press, 2013).

Sauer, P., *The Story of the Beilharz Family* (Sydney: Beilharz, 1988).

Steinmetz, G., 'Thirty Years of Thesis Eleven', *Thesis Eleven*, 100 (2001).

Smith, B., *Place, Taste and Tradition: A Study of Australian Art since 1788* (Sydney: Ure Smith, 1945).

Smith, B., *European Vision and the South Pacific* (Oxford: Oxford University Press, 1960).

Tester, K., 'Intellectual Immigration and the English Idiom', *Polish Sociological Review*, 17 (2006).

Tester, K., 'On Repetition in the Work of Zygmunt Bauman', *Thesis Eleven*, 149 (2018).

Bibliography

Tester, K., 'Sociology: The Active Catastrophe', *Revue Internationale de Philosophie*, 3:70 (2016).

Tester, K., and M. Jacobsen, *Bauman before Postmodernity: Invitation, Conversations and Annotated Bibliography 1953–1989* (Aalborg: Aalborg University Press, 2005).

Theory, Culture and Society, 15:1 [Bauman issue], (1998).

Wolff, J., 'The Question of a Sociological Poetics', in M. E. Davis (ed.), *Liquid Sociology: Metaphor in Zygmunt Bauman's Analysis of Modernity* (London: Ashgate, 2013).

Index

Index

Bauman, Janina 24, 32, 43, 55–6, 58, 60, 68, 85, 94, 107, 127, 150, 161, 163, 199
  death and absence 79, 81, 164, 173, 175–7, 192
  Dream of Belonging, A 83, 107, 132, 165
  Winter in the Morning 82, 107, 165, 199
Bauman, Lydia 59, 64, 83–4, 104, 149, 173
Bauman, Zygmunt
  44 Letters from the Liquid Modern World 173–4, 182, 200
  before Bauman 6, 9, 16, 60, 156, 161, 172, 201
  brand name 167
  bricoleur 147
  in Canberra 150
  curiosities 142
  daredevil 59
  earlier work (Poland, austerity to consumerism) 173, 198
  generosity, generous 6, 37, 39, 55, 156, 197
  hospitality 9, 55–6, 89, 201
  influences 121, 188
  and Janina 55, 60, 68, 84, 87, 107, 176
  Jewish Polish 123, 127, 179, 189, 198
  kindness 156
  Legislators and Interpreters: On Modernity, Post-modernity and Intellectuals 32, 37, 68, 92, 101–2, 117, 180, 184, 201
  Liquid Modernity 62, 94, 100, 156, 167, 173, 193, 199–200
  Memories of Class: The Pre-History and After-life of Class 9, 31–2, 117, 120, 129, 131
  Modernity and Ambivalence 116, 148, 199

  Modernity and the Holocaust 9, 28, 101, 107, 116, 123, 160, 199
  Mortality, Immortality and Other Life Strategies 61
  photographer 67
  rebirth/second wife 91, 103
  Retrotopia 103–4, 174, 185–6, 188, 200–1
  sociological impressionist 68, 99
  teacher and friend 26, 63
  unwilling celebrity 58, 197
  versus careerism/man on the make 39, 149, 156
  work schedule 61
Beilharz, Dor 47, 59, 77
Beilharz, Peter
  archives 27
  before Bauman 16
  Bauman Reader, The 48, 59, 74, 146–7, 156, 158, 191, 201
  collaborator alongside Bauman 191
  Imagining the Antipodes: Culture, Theory and the Visual in the work of Bernard Smith 9, 136–8, 142, 145
  interpreter 1, 26, 33, 54–5, 116, 135, 163
  Labour's Utopias: Bolshevism, Fabianism, Social Democracy 9, 17, 29, 30–1, 56, 117
  Postmodern Socialism: Romanticism, City and State 19, 26, 117–19, 131–2
  reviews about Beilharz' books 56–8, 137–42
  Sociology: Place, Time and Division 23, 88, 166
  Transforming Labor: Labor Tradition and the Labor Decade 26, 31, 120, 131

Index

Holocaust, the 10, 43, 50, 73, 101, 107,
    116, 145, 147, 160, 199
humanism 72, 180

imaging and imagining 138–9
importance of smell 71, 109, 129
intellectual laziness 10, 21, 72, 98, 100,
    125, 199
intellectuals 32–6, 38, 50, 134, 147, 160,
    185, 199, 202
interregnum 169, 175, 177–9, 180, 192

Jasinska-Kania, Aleksandra 92, 103,
    182, 186, 193

Kilminster, Richard 67, 101, 148, 189
Kolakowski, Leszek 120, 126, 128, 160,
    171–2, 178–9, 198
Kurasawa, Fuyuki 47, 73, 143

Labor 131
    government 44, 130
    New 19, 59, 64, 129
labour 42, 54, 108, 111, 126, 130–1
    ASA 76
    market 35, 45
    movement(s) 17, 31, 120, 132, 190
    New Labour 64, 129
    shared labours 158, 162, 172, 198
    utopias 56, 131
language 5, 17, 84, 92, 96, 125–6, 130,
    167, 171, 176, 198
    of love 110, 162, 204
Lawnswood Gardens 9, 11, 26, 32, 37,
    39, 40, 43, 53–5, 58, 61, 63–4, 68,
    71, 74, 77, 79, 88–9, 92, 102, 107,
    149, 156, 158, 162, 167, 191, 201
library 8, 16, 19, 21, 55, 94, 179
    copy of *Liquid Modernity* 100

personal 23, 102
    dispersing 23–4, 102
    see also collection
libraries
    British 18
    Brotherton 68
    Green 42
    Houghton 17, 65
        see also universities, Harvard
    London School of Economics 31
    National Library of Australia 24, 43
    Stellenbosch University 92, 100
    Widener 47

Macintyre, Stuart 18, 29, 98, 145
manuscripts and proofs 39, 59, 62, 67,
    103, 117, 145, 167
map (noun) 16, 53, 57, 62, 75, 128, 146,
    148, 190, 194, 202
mapping 9, 37, 128, 135, 148, 190,
    195, 200
Markus, George 6, 10, 103, 110
Marx, Karl 5, 11, 16–18, 21, 28, 30, 53,
    56, 64, 71, 74, 82, 86, 94–5, 108,
    111, 121, 123, 125–6, 129, 131–2, 135,
    162, 175, 184, 191–2, 201–2
Marxism (East European) 6, 129
Marxism (Weberian) 148, 194
Marxism (Western)
    as a source/influence 7, 28, 33,
        115, 121
    and *Thesis Eleven* 38
mentors 110–11
    Alastair Davidson 77, 110
modernity 8, 10, 32–5, 38, 45, 54, 56,
    69, 74–5, 78, 85, 92, 94–5, 99, 101,
    110, 115, 120, 122–3, 125, 142, 145,
    159, 160, 163, 165, 177–8, 194, 196,
    199, 201

Index